PHOTOWORKS

ISSUE 25

A New Europe

Editors' Note

Photoworks Annual Issue 25 takes as its theme A New Europe – the same focus as the eighth Brighton Photo Biennial – examining the ongoing state of flux as the UK redefines its role in Europe. The title A New Europe is purposely ambiguous, and will inevitably mean different things to different people. It has been used in the past to describe various unrelated situations, including by Nazi Germany propaganda to convey its ideas for the continent. By contrast, in the early 1990s, it was associated with the opening up of Eastern Europe following the fall of the Iron Curtain, and signified a new, expanded Europe. Now, in the context of the continental shift triggered by the Brexit referendum of 2016, the phrase A New Europe can be seen to embody both regression and hope.

Comprehensive discussion of the present and speculation about the future hinges on an understanding of the past – or at the very least an attempt to understand how we arrived at this point. For this reason, Issue 25 is divided into two sections, 'Then' and 'Now', and structured as a series of long-read essays.

'Then' looks back to work made between 1986 and 1994, a time of widespread change in Europe. We are honoured to include a selection of images from Paul Graham's seminal work New Europe, with the original text 'Thoughtful Traveller' and new postscript by Urs Stahel. We also look back at Photoworks' own beginnings as the Cross Channel Photographic Mission (CCPM) through Neal Ascherson's text 'The Undermining of Britain', which was originally published in the photobook Soundings in 1994, to coincide with the opening of the Channel Tunnel. Soundings brought together eleven projects commissioned by the CCPM between 1987 and 1994. The mission of CCPM and its French counterpart, La Mission Photographique Transmanche, was to document the social, cultural and environmental changes surrounding the construction of the Channel Tunnel in Kent and Calais. Born out of the rich tradition of British documentary practice, the accompanying work by Anna Fox, Huw Davies, and Janine Wiedel is representative of its time.

'Now' provides an opportunity to reflect on the current moment and a space to contemplate the future. We invited contemporary writers to contribute and curate a section of images to accompany their text. Jamila Prowse writes about the transcendent nature of dance and movement, with images by Bernice Mulenga and Ronan Mckenzie. Eliel Jones talks of the possible home-comings and reunited families prompted by Brexit, with images by Joanna Piotrowska. Shoair Mavlian gives an overview of the recent Brighton Photo Biennial with images by Harley Weir and Tereza Červeňová. The issue concludes with two portfolios – Robin Maddock and Aikaterini Gegisian with accompanying text by Allison K. Young.

A New Europe reflects on the past but also embraces the possibilities of the future. Although the UK's status in the EU might be changing, geo-graphically it will remain part of Europe, with a shared history and an intertwined future – whatever that may be.

Contents

Untitled, Belfast, 1988
(woman smoking cigarette)

From the series *New Europe,*
1988–92. Paul Graham

Then

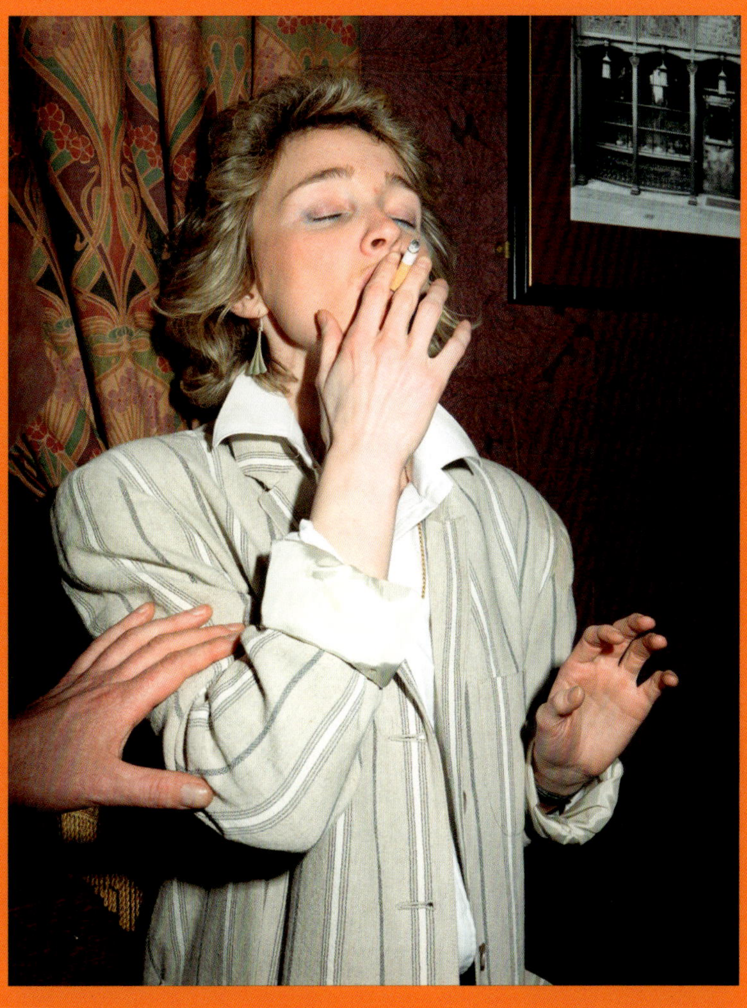

TEXT
THOUGHTFUL TRAVELLER
Urs Stahel, 1993

IMAGES
Paul Graham

The photographic discourse in this book is entitled
New Europe. A bold assertion. Not one made by
Paul Graham, but one that enjoys currency in his
time, our time – as it has for the people of this
continent at various stages in their history. New
Europe. Unfamiliar as a prospect, though familiar
as an aspiration. Only words, but at times loaded
with such distinctly different implications. Yesterday,
with very ambitious and morbidly egotistical
intentions, Hitler brought into the world the most
horrific attempt at implementation of the ideal.
Today and for the future it is a concept to be flirted
with rather than embraced by the European
Community, as much as these times of broken
illusions permit.

Hitler combined the idea of a 'New Europe'
with his plan for a 'Nation Europa' under his rule
– this being the name of a National Socialist
propaganda magazine in the guise of a respectable
journal, aimed at the elite of every Western European
nation, who were to be defeated and their territories
occupied. This elite was to be 'enlightened' and
enlisted as privileged auxiliary troops of the Reich,
subordinate, and yet still assigned a higher position
than the Slavs, Poles and Russians, condemned in
turn to a life of slavery. Hitler's crazed idea failed in
the end because he disregarded the fact that the
nations of Europe were formed from a number of
smaller constituent parts. Each was not in fact
comprised of only one territory, one culture and
one language, but they still emerged into the 20th
century, formed steadily from their individual
cultural groups (while other regional groups were
gradually suppressed) and they were not to be
destroyed overnight in a single conflict, to be
swallowed up by an all encompassing Grand
European Nation. The incomprehensible horror
of Hitler's effort is anticipated in the lines written
by Rabbi Jacob Schullmann, before he died in
1944 in the gas chambers of Chelmno:

'Horror, horror, man shed thy clothes,
Cover thy head in ashes,
Run in the streets and dance in thy madness…
I am so weary that my pen can no longer write,
Creator of the universe, help us.'
(from *Shoah*, the documentary film by Claude Lanzman,
1974–85)

The current impulse towards a 'New Europe' shies
away from using the term earnestly again. It has
become more pragmatic. The notion of a European
spirit is again heralded, but the goal of the present
century, indeed of the millenium, seems to be
'Currency Union' achieved through the 'Single
Market Economy'. The ECU as the anaemic standard
of a world where money takes precedence over
spirit. And because, even for this, strength and
trust seem to be lacking, the way forward and the
speed and rhythm of the execution is submitted
to the logic of computer programs. Everything
happens automatically, at a predetermined time,
even if someone should blast the machine into
the air. Is this the European freedom at the end
of the millenium?

'Everywhere, where the European spirit dominates,
what is apparent is a maximum of needs, a maximum
of work, a maximum of capital, a maximum of relations
and exchange. This ensemble of maxima is what
defines Europe, or the picture of Europe.'
(Paul Valéry, La crise de l'esprit)

Paul Valéry had defined the crisis of the spirit and
the ensemble of European 'idées fixes' a long time
ago. Will this new venture end in horror too? We
are already experiencing unexpected symptoms
and, paradoxically enough, from our individual
retreats, still plead the cause of the great union as
the only possible guarantee against dissipation
and demarcation. Two years ago we were still

unwaveringly convinced that the 'Californian Dream' (George Steiner), the infinite capitalised lightness of being, would be fulfilled in Europe before the end of the millenium, after which Europe would go to the ruin engendered by its own consumption.

Today we are not at the point of a repetition, rather at the point of realisation of a seemingly archaic history, one which we believed to have long overcome, or at least to have got under control on the psychologist's couch, both on the individual and the social level.

Paul Graham's large-scale colour photography work is situated in this context. Ostensibly the journeys of 1988, 1989 and 1990 led him through nine West European countries: through Germany, Switzerland, Italy, Spain, France, Belgium, Holland, England and Northern Ireland. The narrative leads us past various references to historical events: the star of David for example, scratched in and scratched through again; or the Hofbräuhaus in Munich, where the Nazis often met early on; the Photographic memorial display in Holland, from which the Hitler figure has been scratched out; the Pilsner beer, introduced into Italy in the thirties as Italo Pils; the couple reflected in the disco ceiling mirror, reminiscent of Mussolini and his mistress, both hung by their feet; Franco's grave, spat upon and mocked; coins with the Generalissimo's likeness as thoughtlessly discarded as burning cigarettes by video games; the train coupling, taken in Drancy, which, like the toy train reminds us of the deportations from France; the park bench in Belfast, which tells of better times, the word 'religion' written into the grafitti strewn surface of a telephone table in an employment exchange in Belfast; and finally the simple square hole, left behind by a post from the Berlin wall.

These signs are not in themselves a reference to the past, much more they alert our awareness, our memory. They do not look back, but manifest history, show how we deal with it today, how it casts a shadow on daily life, sometimes going almost unrecognised, sometimes violently disputed, occasionally even trivialised, ending up as children's toys. It is history exposed where it is thrust from the depths of time to the surface, whether we stumble over its gravestone, heedlessly walk away or contemptuously spit on it.

In between are placed images of people of today. Pictures of immersion, of escape, into music, into alcohol, into cigarette and drug addiction, the kick of ecstasy. Pictures of universal consumption, the commercialisation of sex and friendship. Pictures of isolation, of the one from the other, pictures of the screamingly colourful, grey daily life of today. Together with the traces of history a portrait of contemporary social reality is formed, unfolding a topography of presence, a social and psychological landscape, the traces of which extend over the lonely indifferent faces, in the nervous gestures, in attitudes altogether defeated, which makes even a park bench seem meaningful, surrounded by the horrible laughter of emptied perspectives.

'I wanted to make images about the bland grey promise of consumption led culture, the rush to the market that dominates everything, whose embrace we must accept or be expelled to the margin.' Even more distant history is commercialised: the 'angel' sits by the till in the department store, 'Maria' is hopelessly isolated and hopelessly thoughtful, the 'Jesus child' has just been overfed with the spoon. The word 'religion', scrawled in doubt or affirmation, reflects the tragedy of the Northern Irish conflict, and the confusions that surround the issues at its core. Symbols of the deregulation of all values. As a rule sacrificed to the possibility of commercialisation. Graham's interest focuses on the point of intersection of the vertical diachronic axis, along which the present becomes comprehensible, and the horizontal, synchronic axis, without which history – inheritance – remains limited or indeed immaterial. He emphasises the permeation of past and present, and shows us the pictures of today's 'state of mind', of the state of our consciousness, of our spirit at the end of the century.

'And I will show you something different.' begins the quotation from T S Eliot's famous poem *The Waste Land*. The war veteran bares his upper body and reveals his wounds, whilst he looks down from the high ground to the edge of a Southern city. Graham shows us a wounded, battered Europe, a spiritual 'wasteland'. History, though often trivialised as in the case of the toy soldiers in the second photograph, marks out the framework, even forms the shadows, from whose darkness the events of the present emerge, and the light in whose glare the present seems small, grey and banal, but in its own shadows finds itself.

'I will show you fear in a handful of dust.' In these pictures Graham stands watch, as the party of the eighties, a period abandoned to laissez faire, continues in full flow. In the dust of Friedrichstrasse station, in the reflection of the flames of German unity, the shadows of the past are watching, as silent as the grave. History, Europe today, in the mirror of its Falangist, Fascist and Nazi past – invokes the image of a cleverly constructed, impasto of history painting. Graham's photographs however are the absolute opposite; no totality, no uniform meaning, but fragments, the series of isolated elements as signs of history, as stations encountered by a thoughtful traveller on a journey through a present loaded with history. Fragments, enlarged to function as a physical experience, images as dominant, but also as simple and as matter-of-fact as a signpost, the colour fields sometimes as expansive and as monochrome as an enamelled trade sign. The hint of the great themes, the hymn, the pathos but nothing more. Not even the tuning up of the orchestra. Then it goes further.

The weightier themes are not to be found on the wider political level, nor in the realm of gestures poignant with history. The secret main themes, which bestow on this work so many surprises as well as density and complexity, are established on a more profound stratum, on a structural and morphological level. Take, for example – in the book one after another, as exhibits in the form of a triptych – the picture of a large-surfaced, orange-coloured, riveted iron girder into which is scratched the aforementioned star of David. To the left is the smaller picture of a man, dressed in late sixties/ early seventies style – orange-brown leather jacket, leather shoulder bag, jeans – awkwardly protecting himself from the natural light. Shading his eyes, does he also shade himself against other influences? To the right, even smaller in format, is a girl of the eighties, who, eyes closed, seems completely mesmerised by the light and sound level. Next photo: the picture of a bolted, almost barricaded door in a poorer London quarter. Following is a triptych, with the display photograph of the rubbed out Hitler and the blood stain remover in the clean bathroom. Both are combined with the dense picture in the Munich Hoibräuhaus. A man in traditional costume is busy drinking beer and smoking at the same time. On his left a man wearing foggy pebble glass spectacles. In the foreground, bottom left, an ash blond 'blind spot'.

Beyond their specific spatio-temporal identification the pictures tell of a general disparity, of light, of glances, of possible insight, if one only wants, if one is only prepared to see, prepared to recognise and to understand. If the will can be summoned to really look at things, even the unpleasant, the painful, to look at people, even others, properly in the face. And with it, the contrasting attitude of looking away, of evading, of disengaging. Dim down the light, dim down everything that could hurt, drown, numb, anaesthetics with beer, addiction, music. Cut off, protect, wipe away, shut out, indulge, get drunk, stupefy. Insight versus stupefication. The here and now versus an elsewhere for anything that is unpleasant.

To go on, a floor strewn with used tissues in a sex video shop, sprays of blood on a white tiled wall, spit on Franco's grave, someone inserting a syringe into his arm, a dark hole left behind by a post from the former Berlin Wall, a doorway coordinated grey on grey. A tunnel of dreadfulness. These pictures, as also the nervous lacing of fingers, the smoking, the injecting, the overeating, the blinking, manifest a condition of heightened critical awareness. Inner tension, individual as well as socio-psychic instability grows. In between, in the middle of the book, the picture of a park bench – built of cement and stone – arresting one's attention. However, one sits there alone, watching, as the square gradually becomes overgrown and wild, without people finding each other there. Lastly this man. who lies on a bed and watches television, surrounded by the wildest colour patterns and tones. A picture suggesting the utmost privacy, the utmost relaxation and satisfaction and at the same time embodying contemporary inertia. Oversatiated with colours, overwhelmed by information, fragments, not knowledge or understanding. A (Western) world at bursting point. As exhibited work, this photograph hangs beside the dark picture of concrete slabs, concrete out of which pieces of straw protrude. A harsher contrast is hardly imaginable. Concrete, society's building material, manufactured from individual pieces of straw. As individuals dedicated to the illusion of great freedom are inexorably woven into the cloth of society.

The pictures and their arrangement are unsettling. False wall? Or real wall with false materials? With wood and brick imitations in plastic. False information? False promises under a blue sky, in full colour and finished in a high gloss?

A picture of the most intimate, fervent passion? Or again only an agitated meeting of two business colleagues? Graham's photographs are also formally unsettling. Often fleeting, precariously balanced, out of array, out of true, out of harmony, even if, in an attempt to avert design artistry, their subject is for once plonked in the middle. There it is! Visible and sufficiently complex! Graham shows what he sees, directly and without nourishes, even sometimes appearing almost banal. Without discernible 'photo-graphics', without that master-photographer style. One always looks at the picture, at its images, and not at the photograph as photography. The picture emerges before our eyes, physically, directly, without glass or frame, interwoven with the other pictures as a visual prose poem.

The historical references set the outer frame, images which break out of the confinement of photography, expanding in the mind of the viewer. The density of his picture world is generated by these morphemes, these single elements, which shatter the calm. Hard edged photography and nothing but. Here and there the legend provides the required topographical information, a story is told, and a single picture becomes a manifestation of history. As when Graham provides the additional information that the war veteran exhibits his wounds in a gay cruising area, when he confirms that it is whores and pimps who intimately embrace, when he reveals that at the easternmost point of West Berlin he had to photograph secretly, hidden, 'from the hip', and that the toy railway cars, in their macabre overlay of form and content, are reminiscent of the children's deportations from France. Children! Lengths the German National Socialists would not have gone to. Make a note of that. It has become a work about seeing, in times of freely chosen short-sightedness. A work about reflection, in times of stupidity. A work about time and history, in times of seemingly timeless youth. It is a work against the peddling (or rubbishing) of all values – without finding fresh ones, without finding a new ideology. Graham's approach is in the best sense modern, which here means thoughtfully enlightening. As in *Beyond Caring*, his book about the English Social Service, as in *Troubled Land*, his landscape photography work in Northern Ireland. Not the attitude, only the form has at times changed slightly, adapting to each particular conception. Be it the seductive beauty of the idyllic landscape pictures, which draw us into the theme of the English-Irish, Protestant-Catholic conflict, or as here the seduction of the large surface colours, a partly mysterious presence combined with clearer, sometimes painful signifiers – all of which promote interest in the picture and its discussion.

'They don't need any perfecting, they're just fine… nothing could be any clearer.' So it is said of the 'miracle glasses' in the Günter Grass quotation. This may also apply to this photowork as far as its approach and conception are concerned. But pictures are and must be more ambivalent, must disturb, worry, without prompting an automatic confirmatory response from the viewer. This Graham understands, and for precisely this reason his multinational journey encourages the thoughtful response.

Paul Graham's *New Europe* depicts a continent in transition. Shot between 1988 and 1992 the seminal photobook was published in 1993 to accompany the inaugural exhibition at the Fotomuseum Winterthur with essay by the founding director Urs Stahel. Graham's fragments of daily life embodied new approaches to documentary practice. Alongside the images sit T S Eliot's *The Waste Land* (1922) and an excerpt from Günter Grass's *Dog Years* (1963).

Paul Graham
New Europe

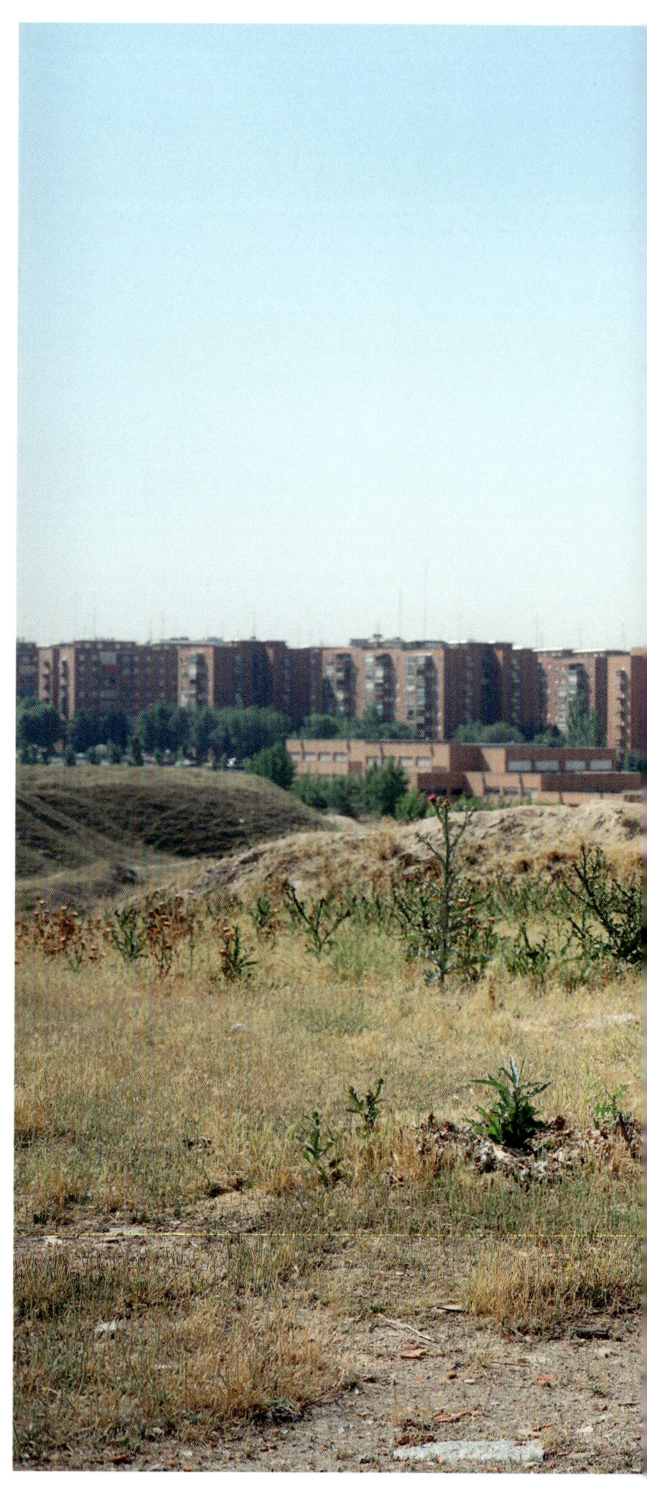

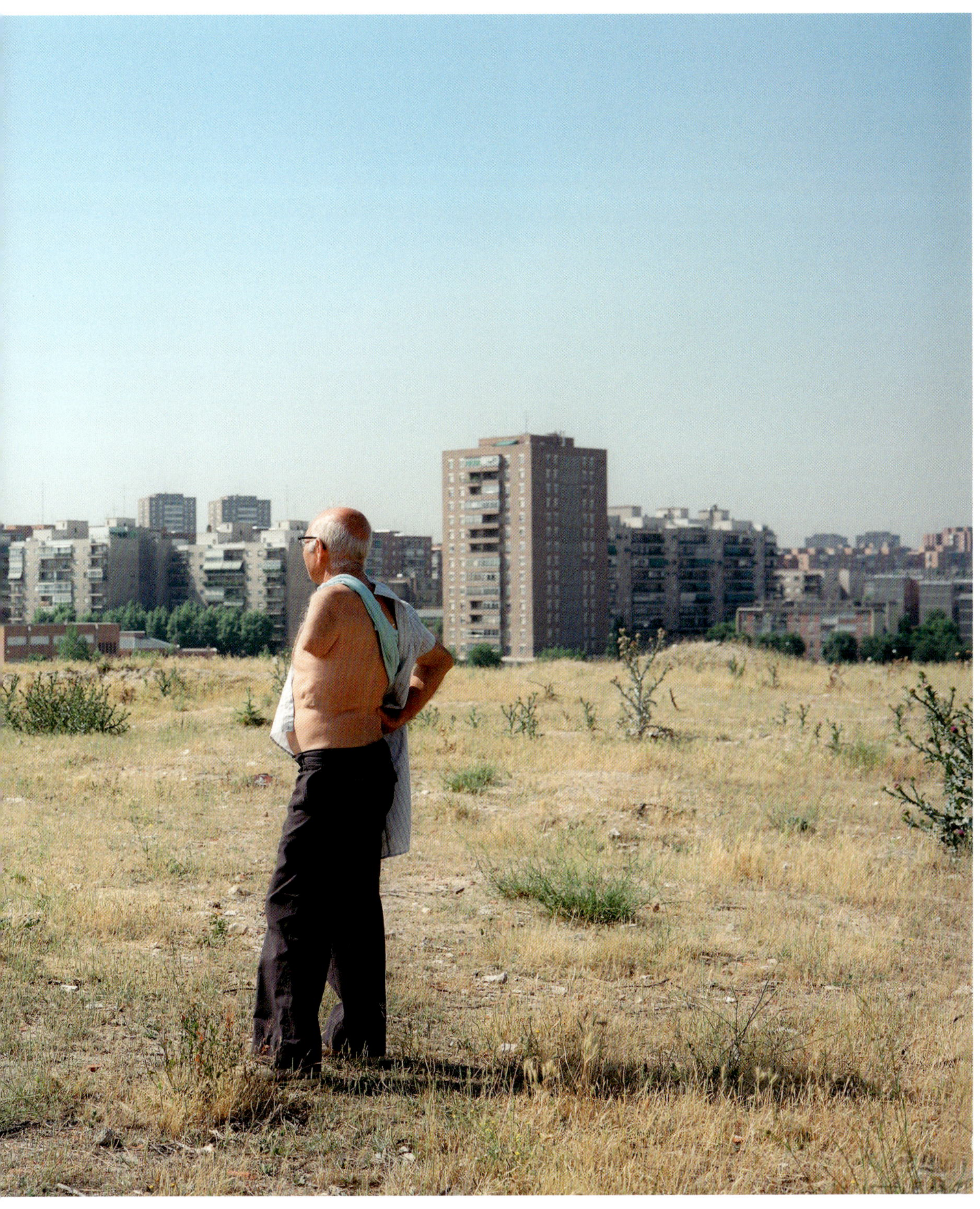

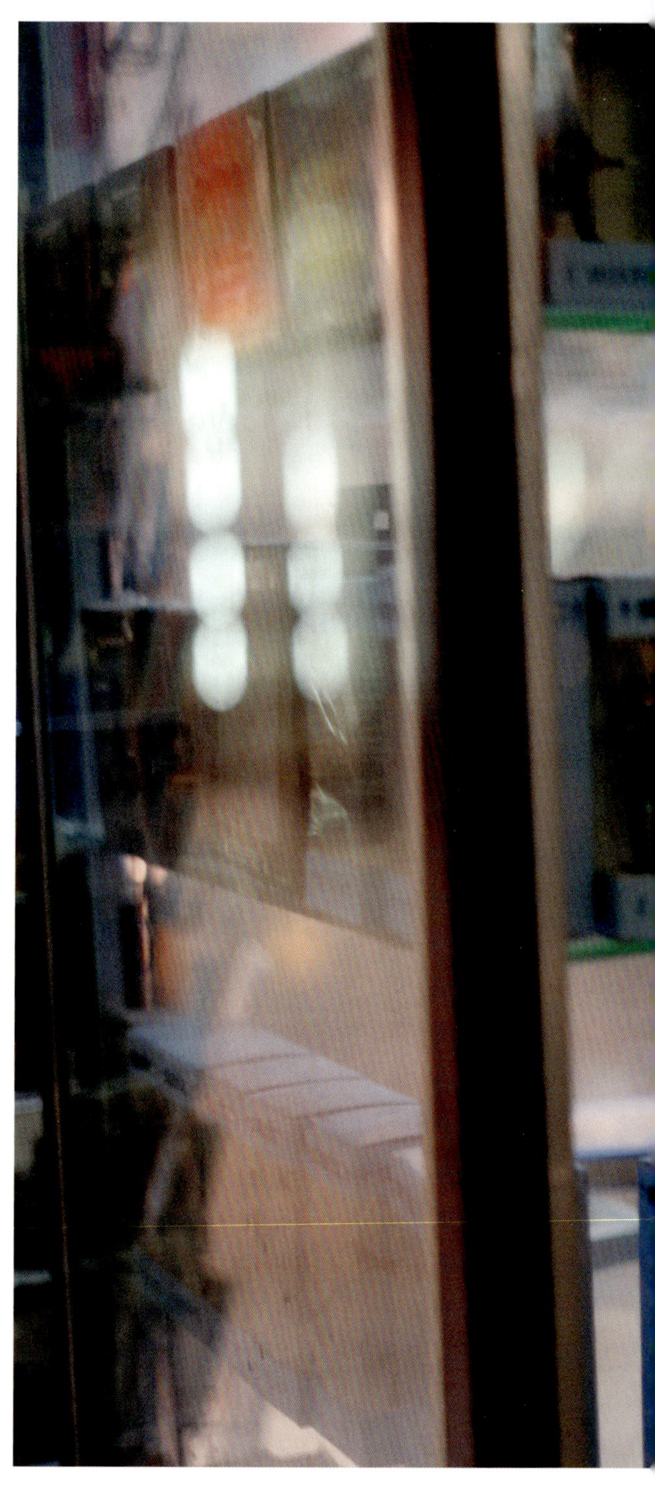

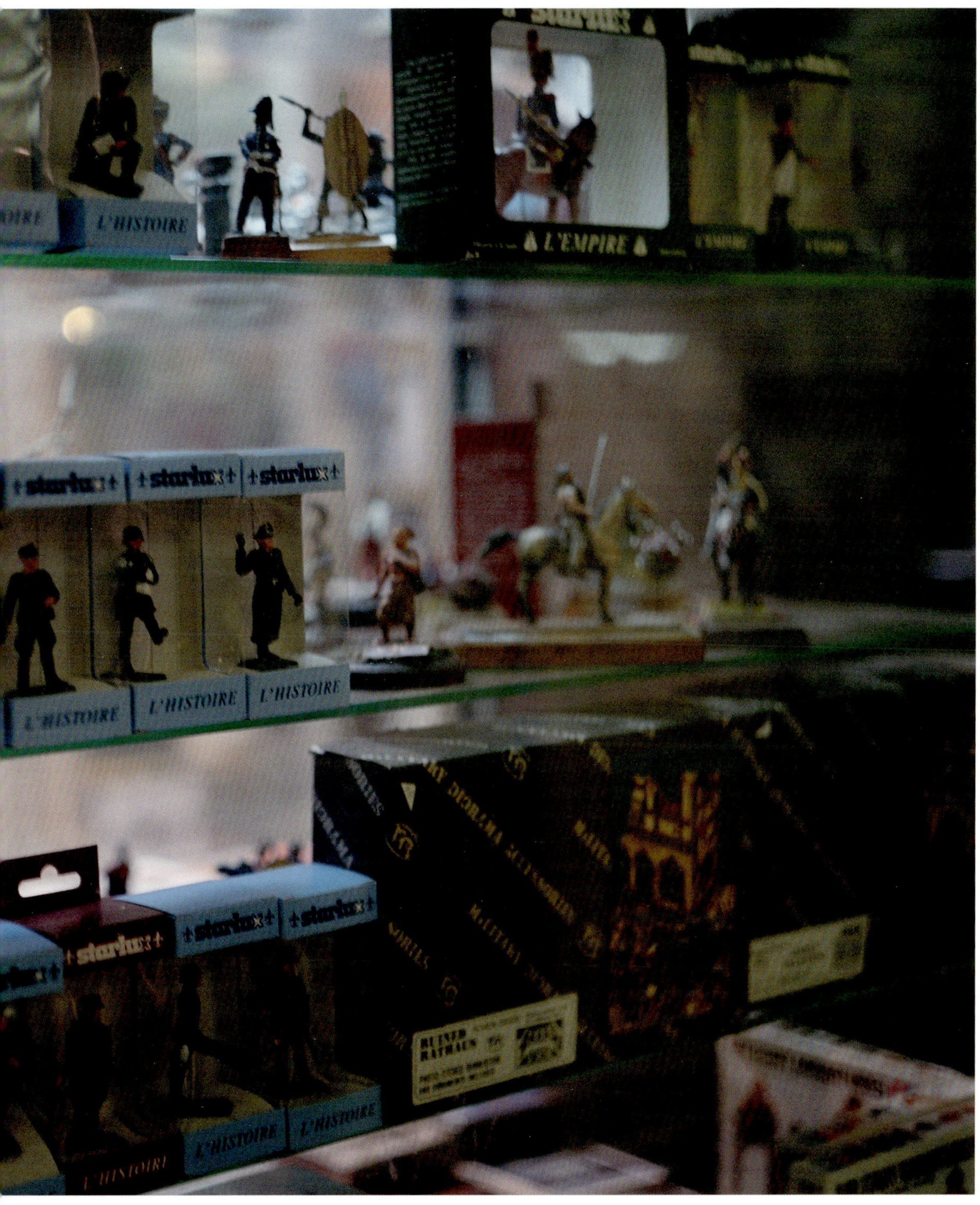
L'HISTOIRE
L'EMPIRE
starlux
L'HISTOIRE
L'HISTOIRE
L'HISTOIRE
starlux
starlux
L'HISTOIRE
L'HISTOIRE
L'HISTOIRE

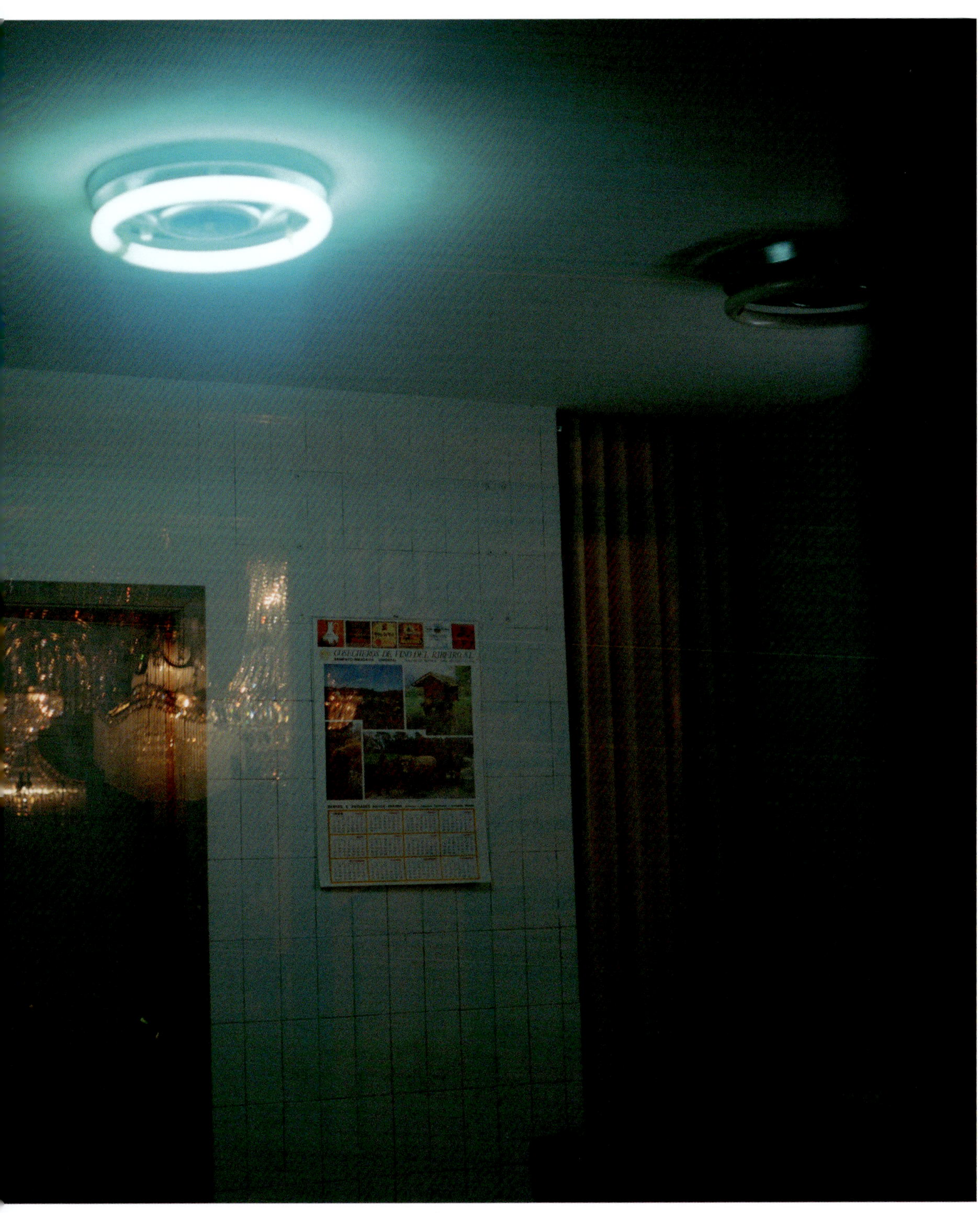

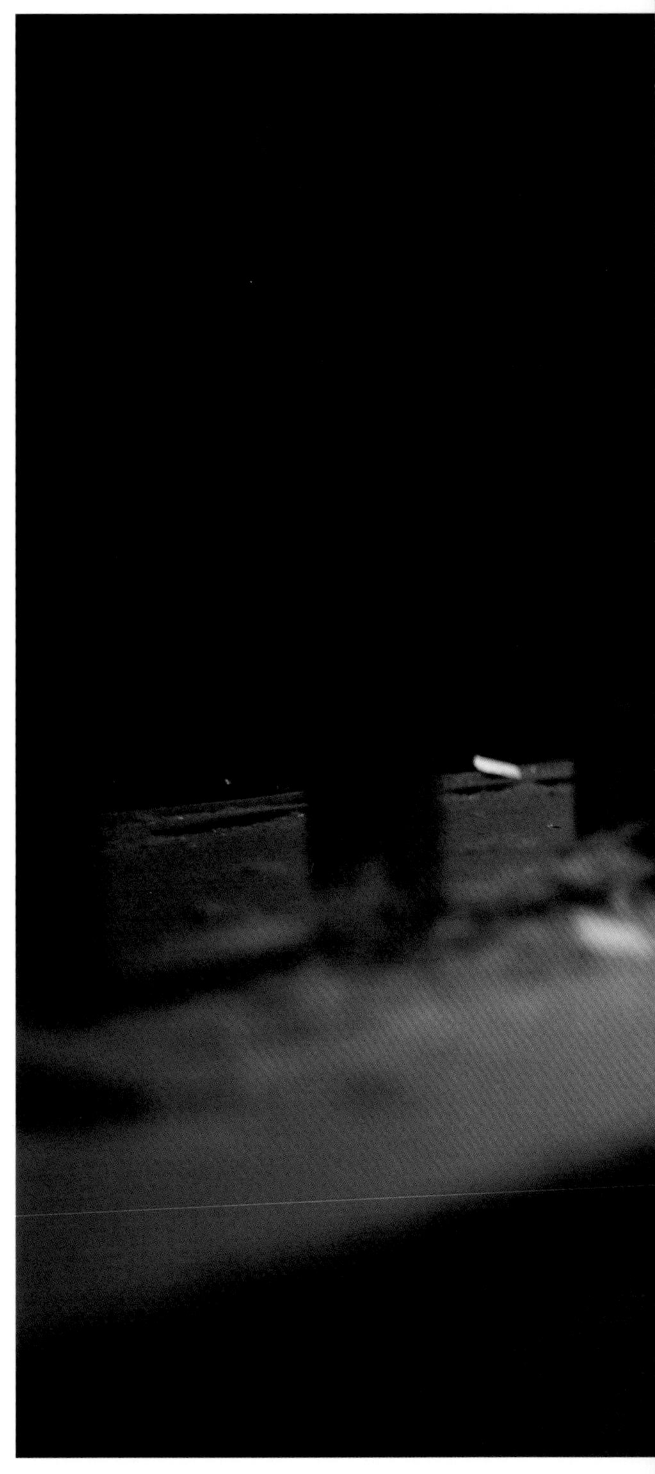

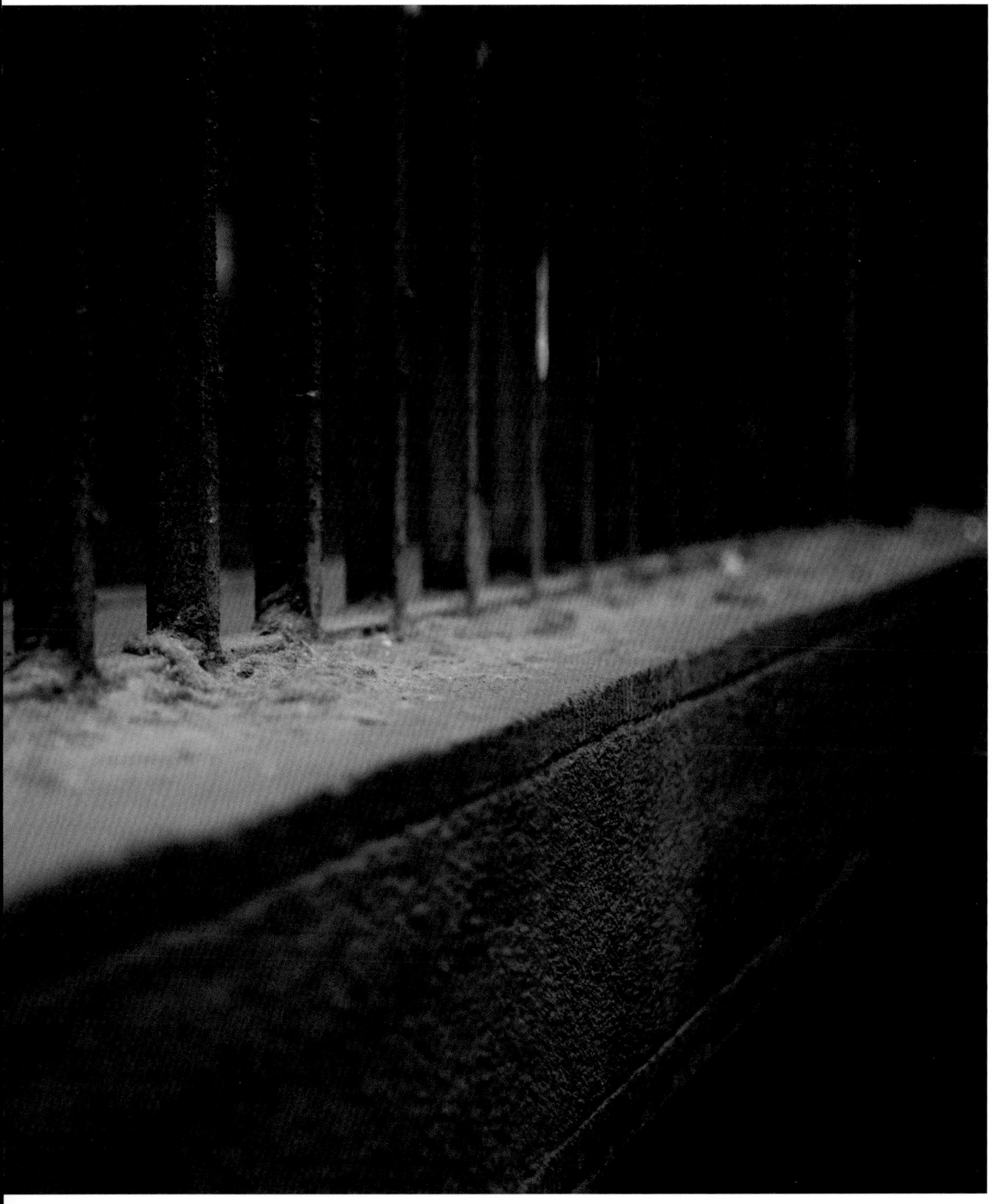

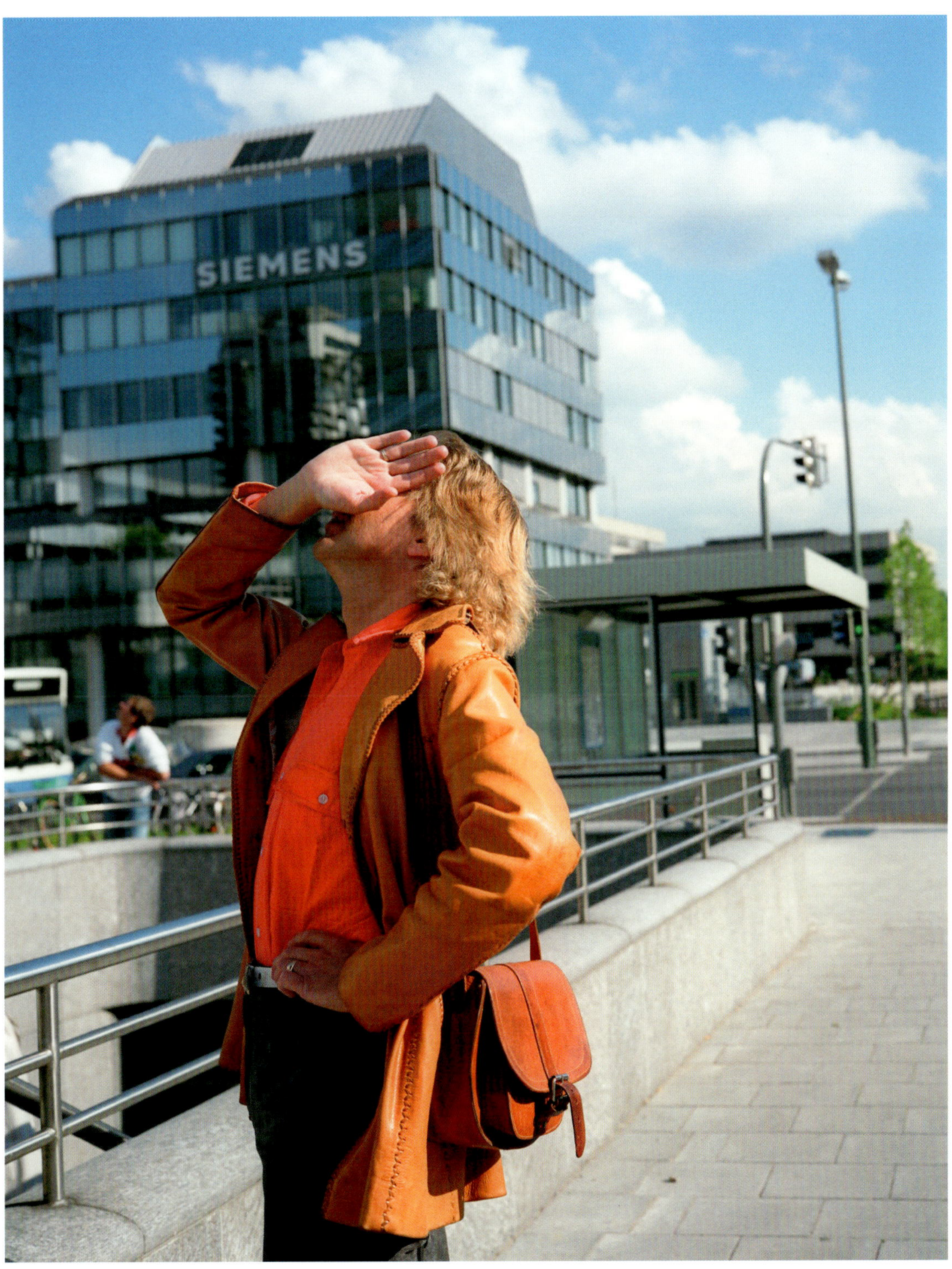
SIEMENS

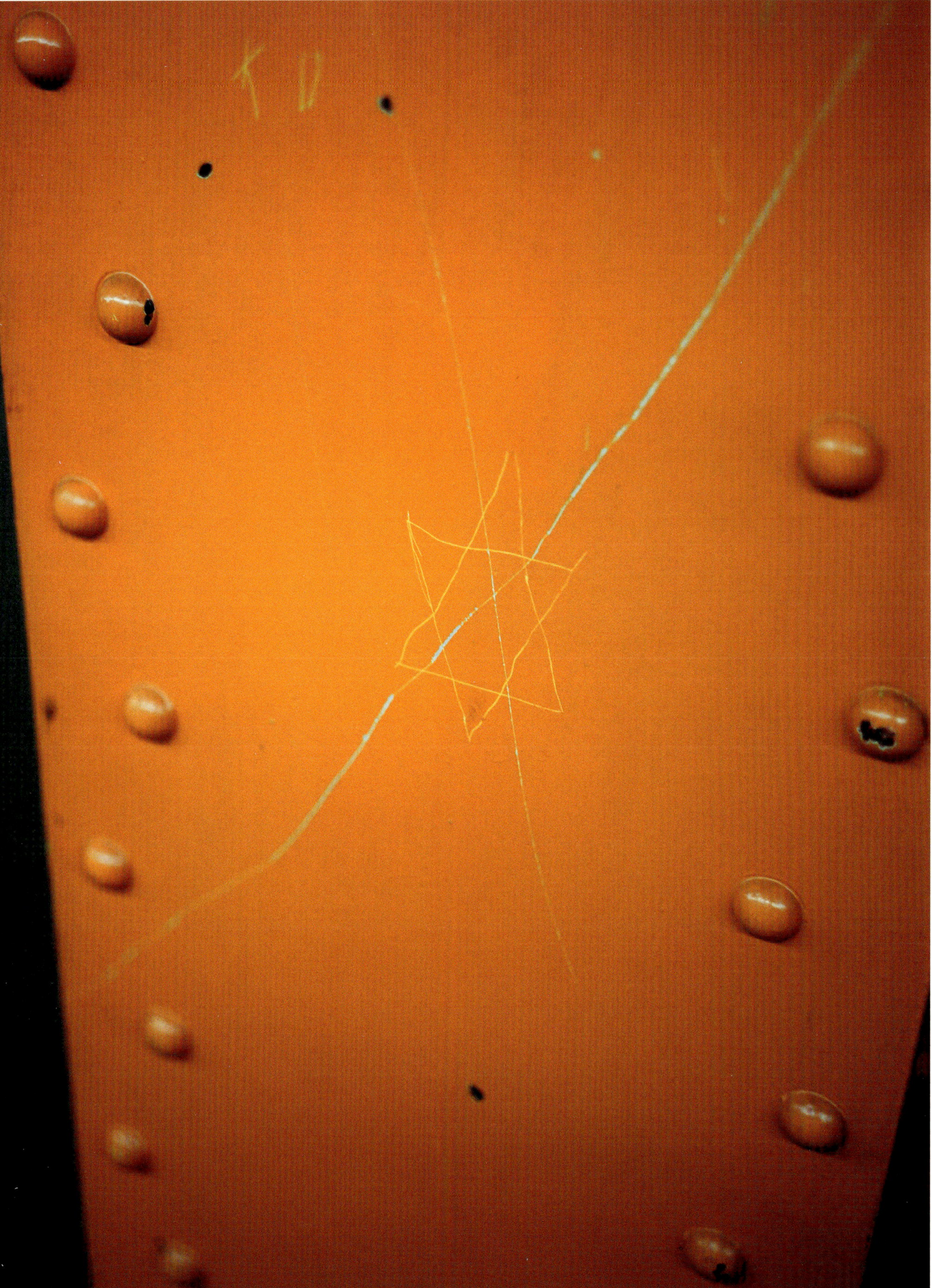

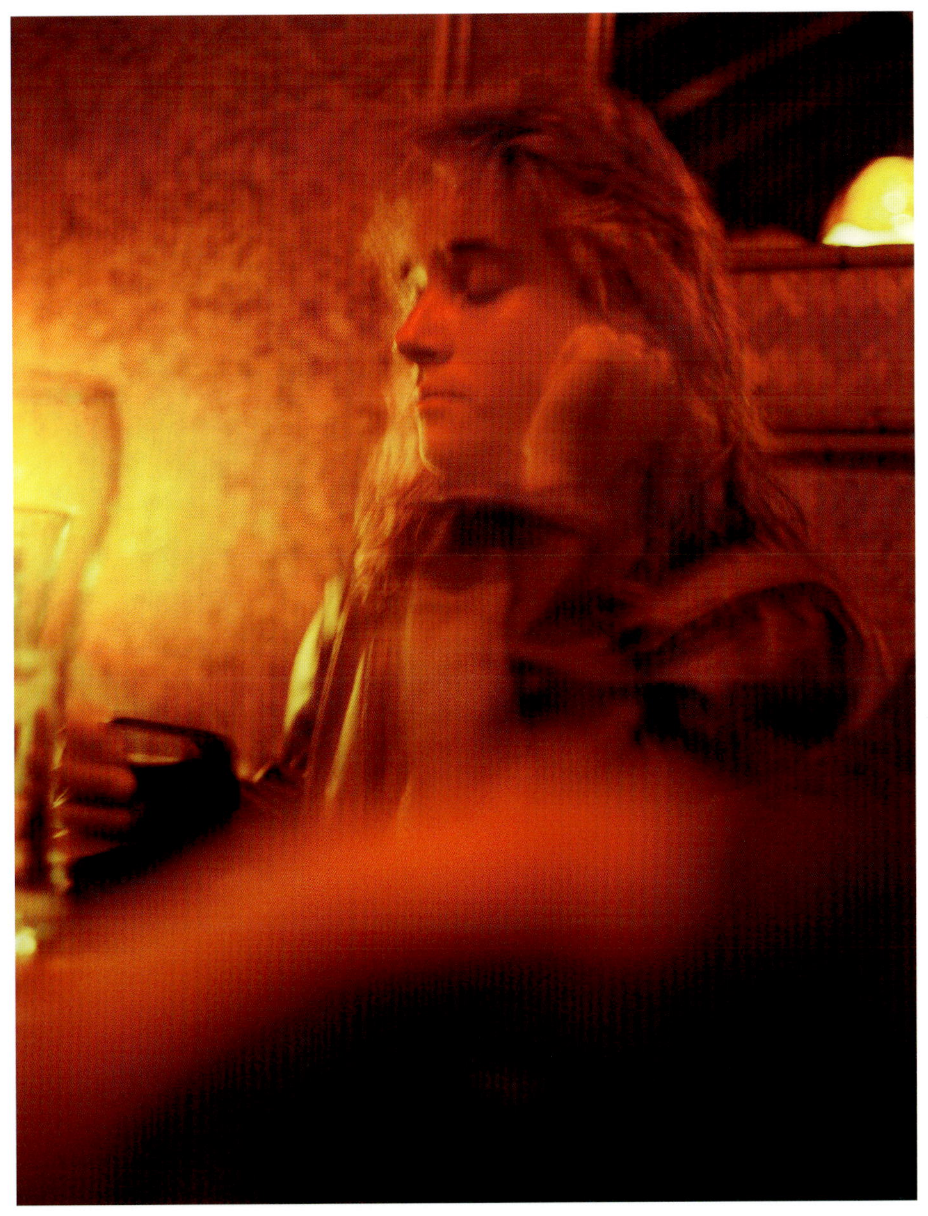

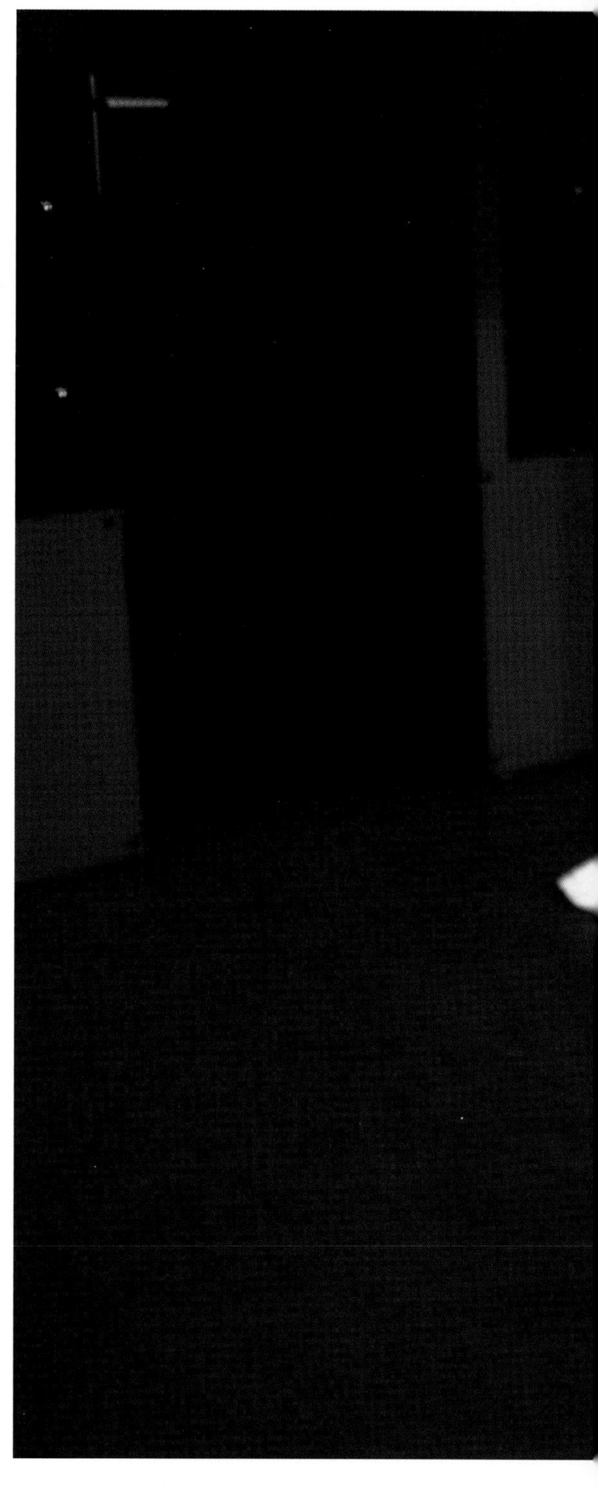

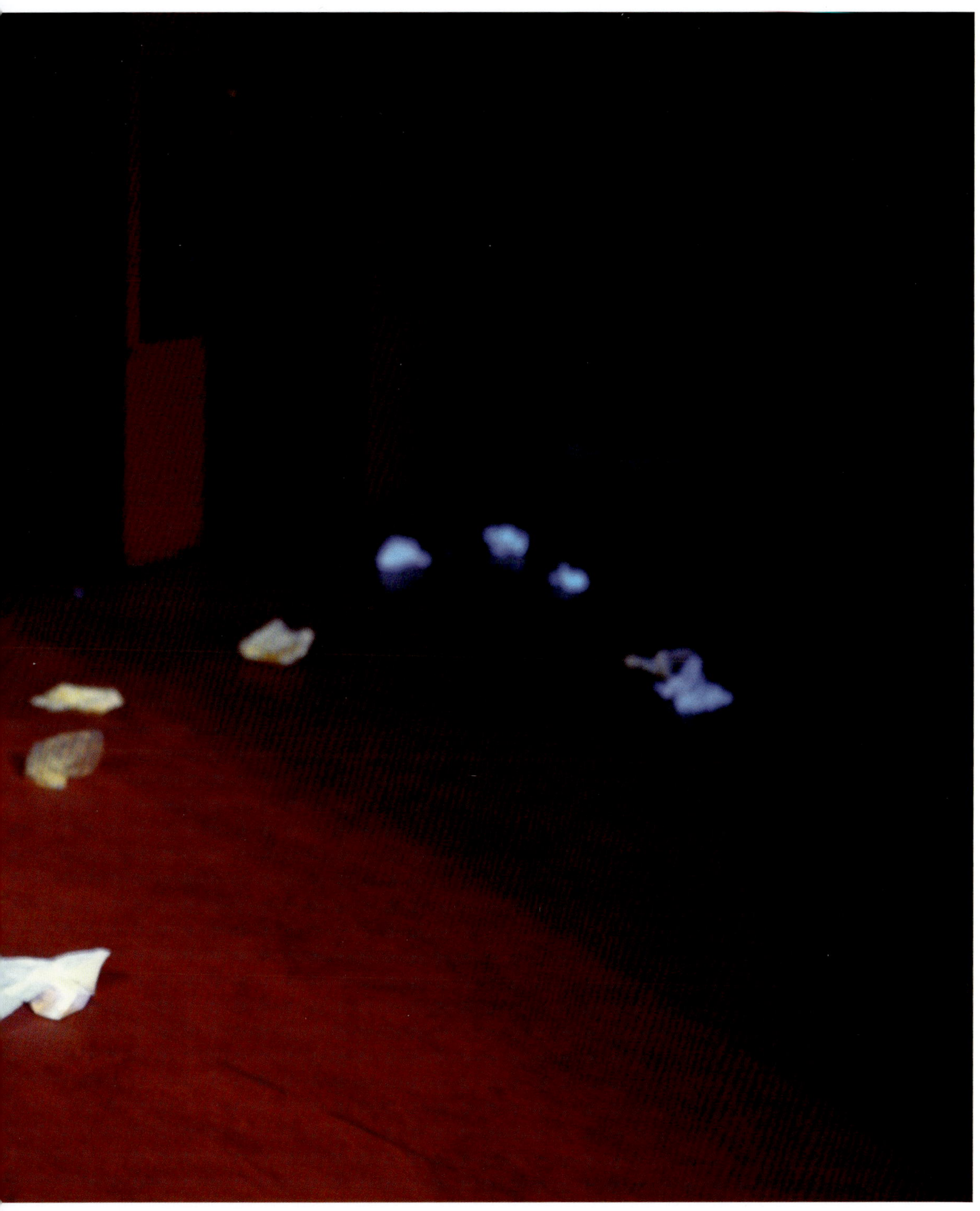

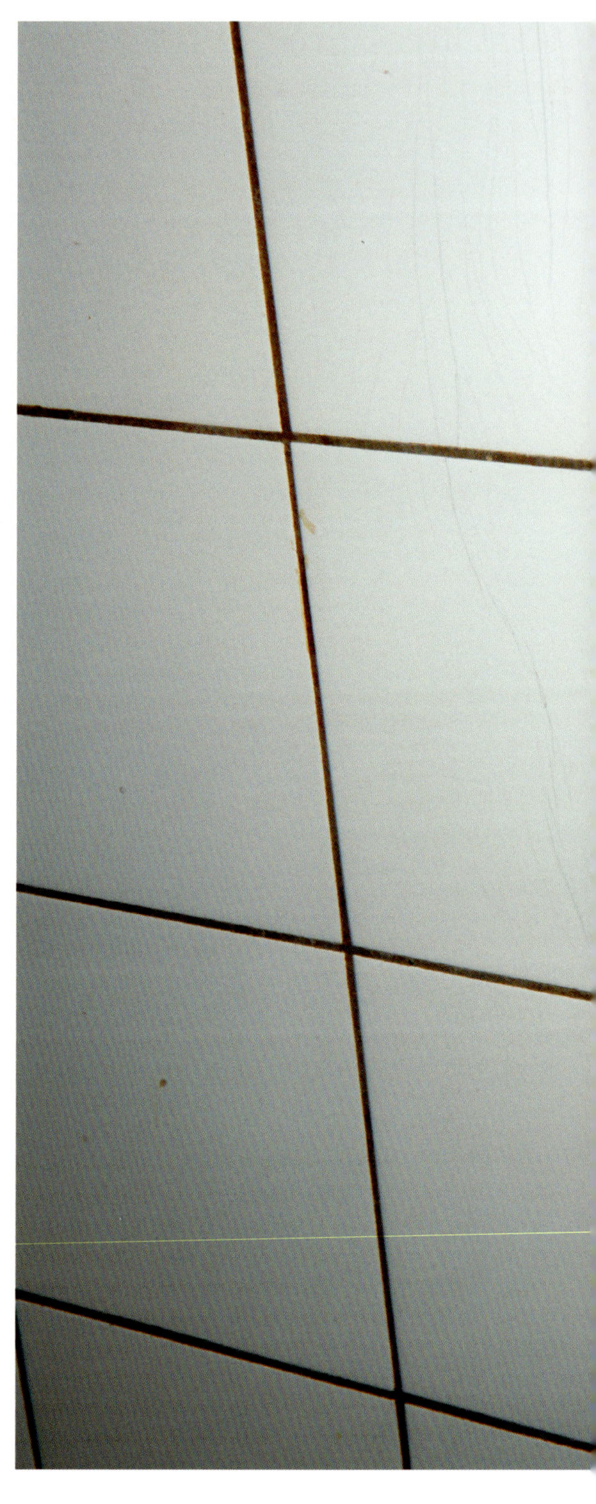

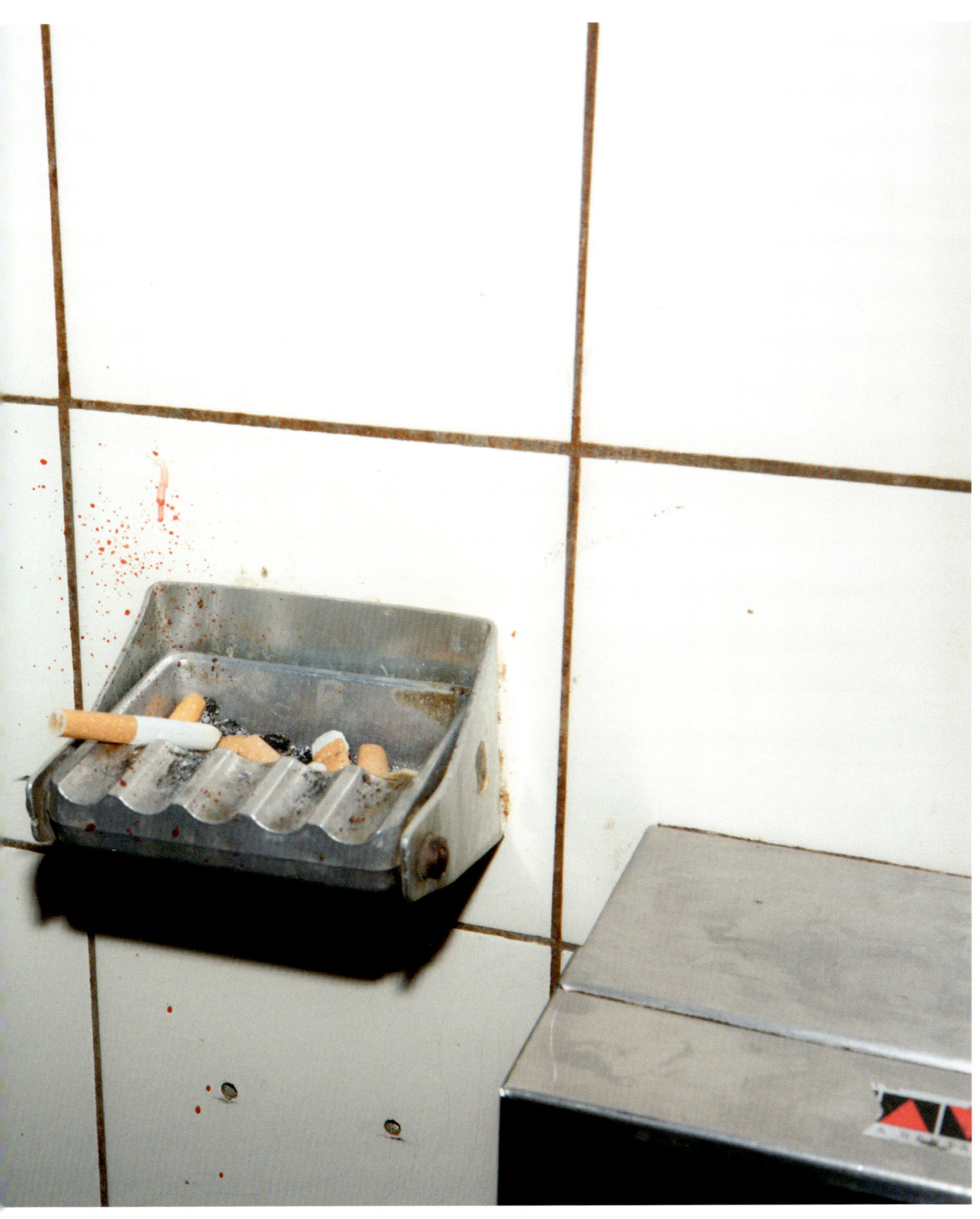

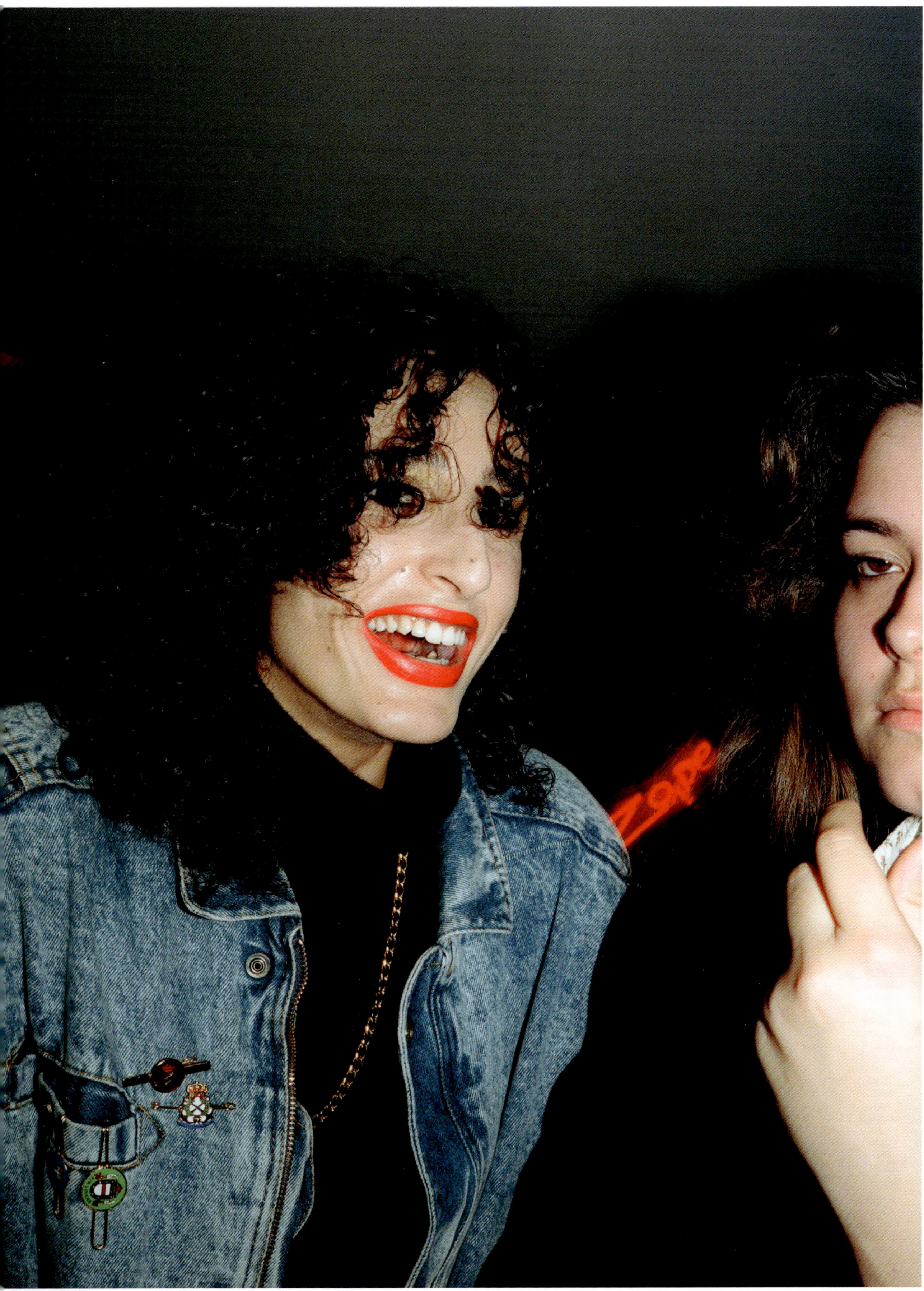

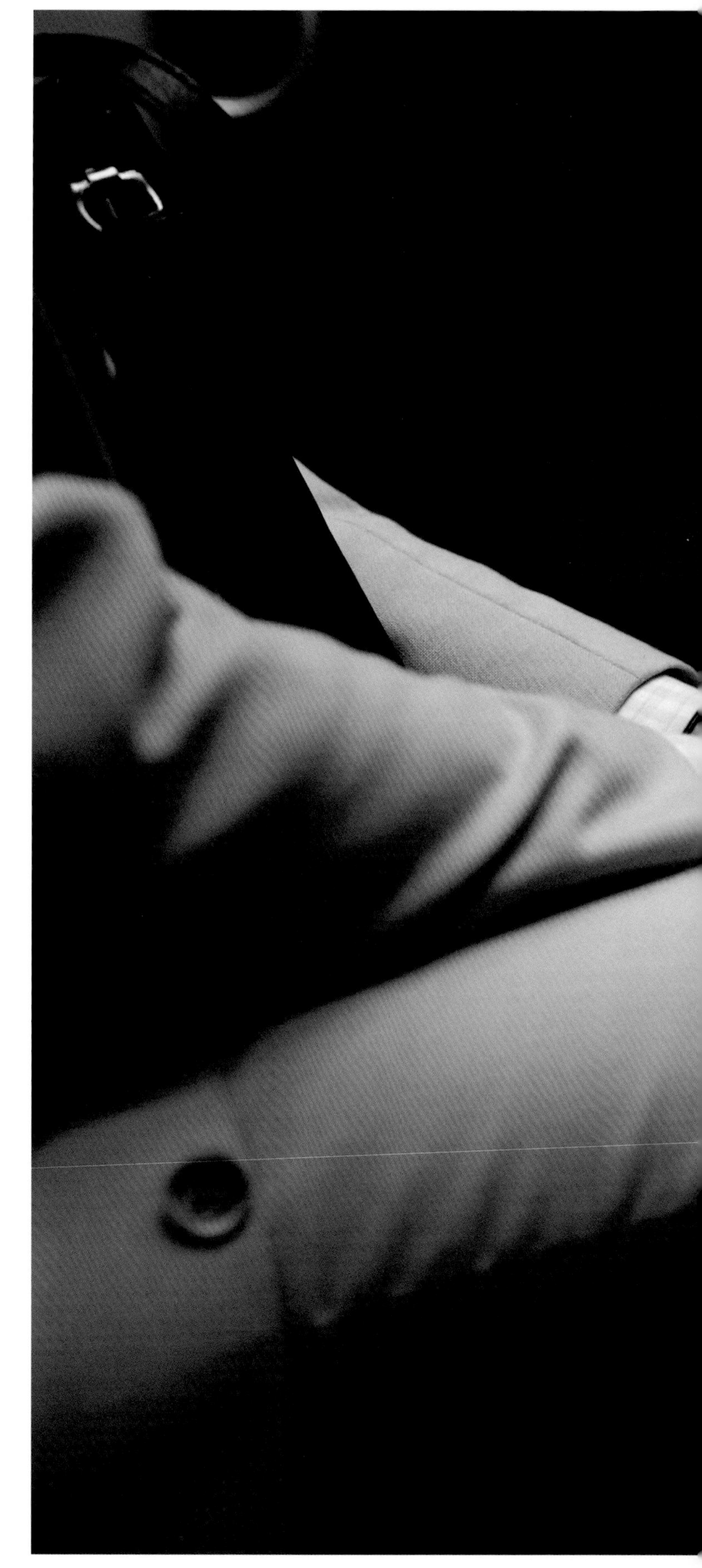

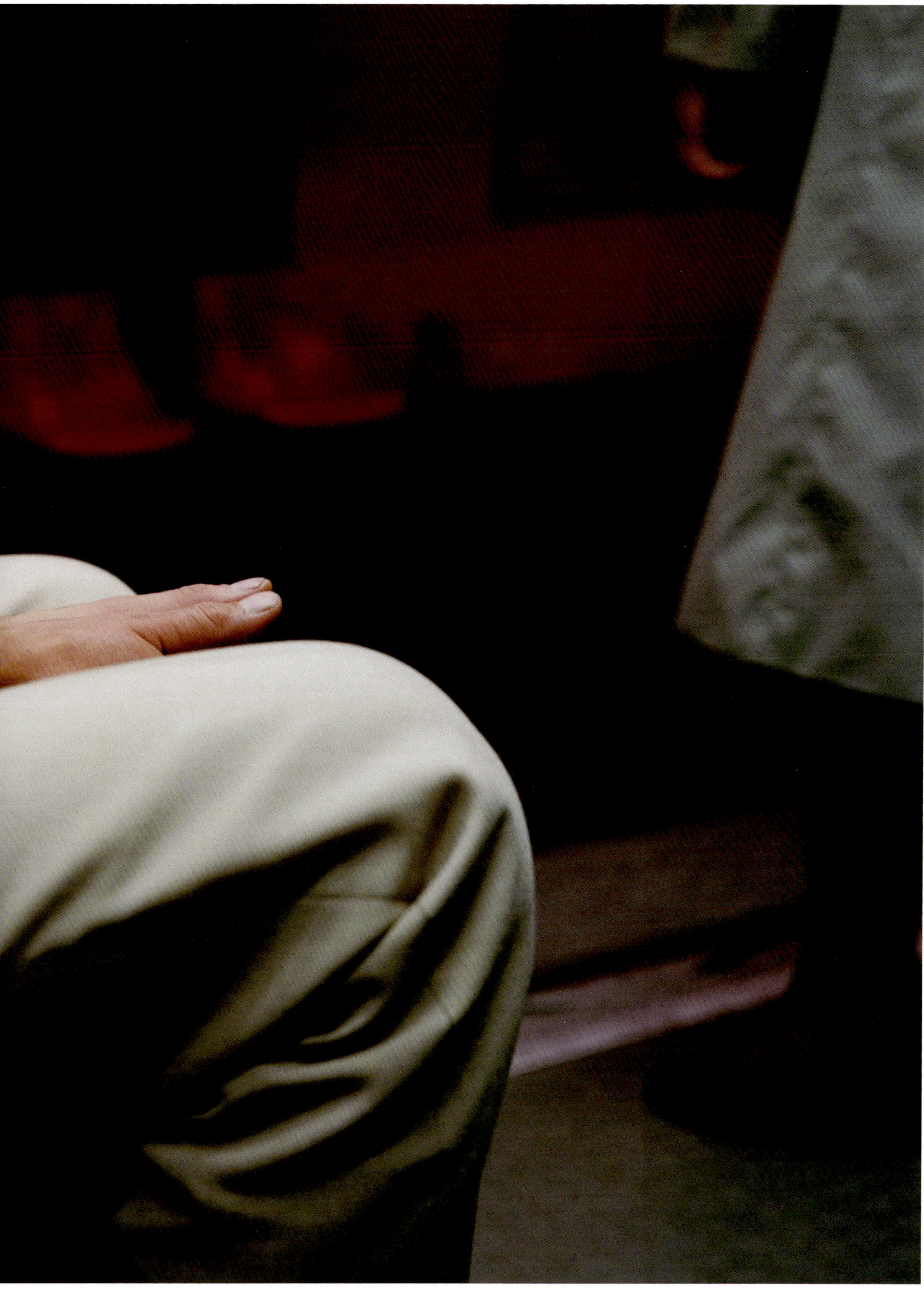

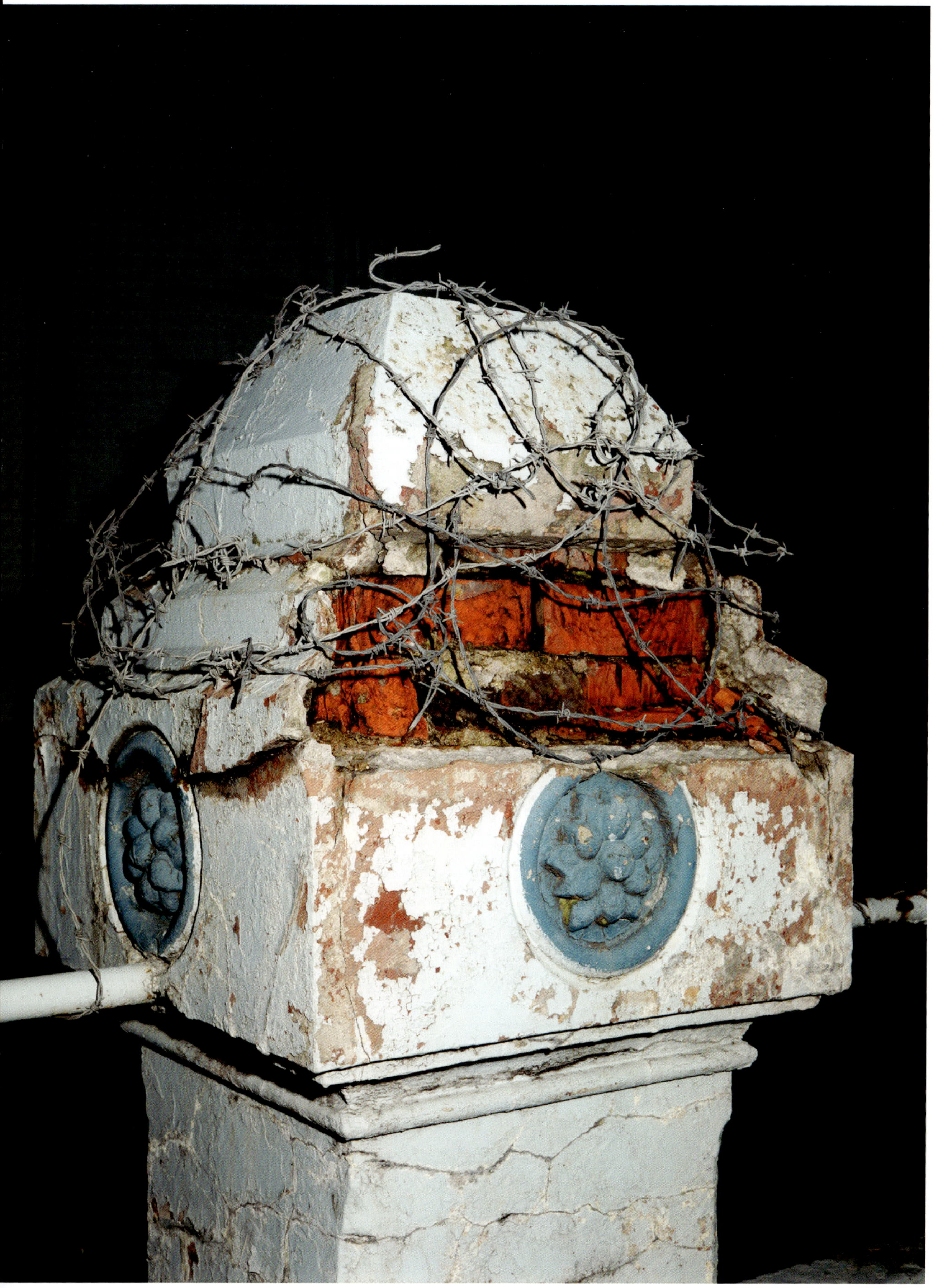

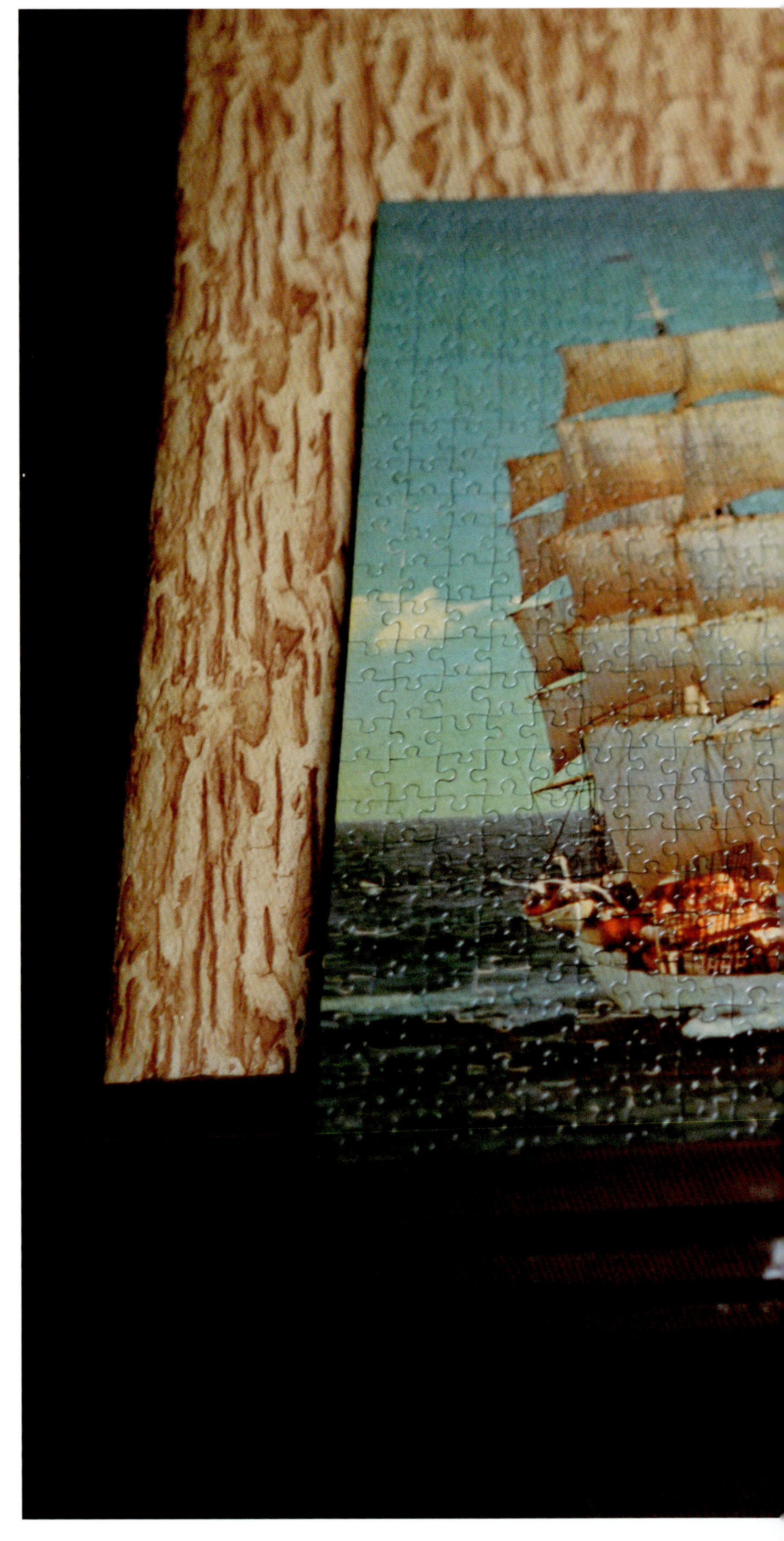

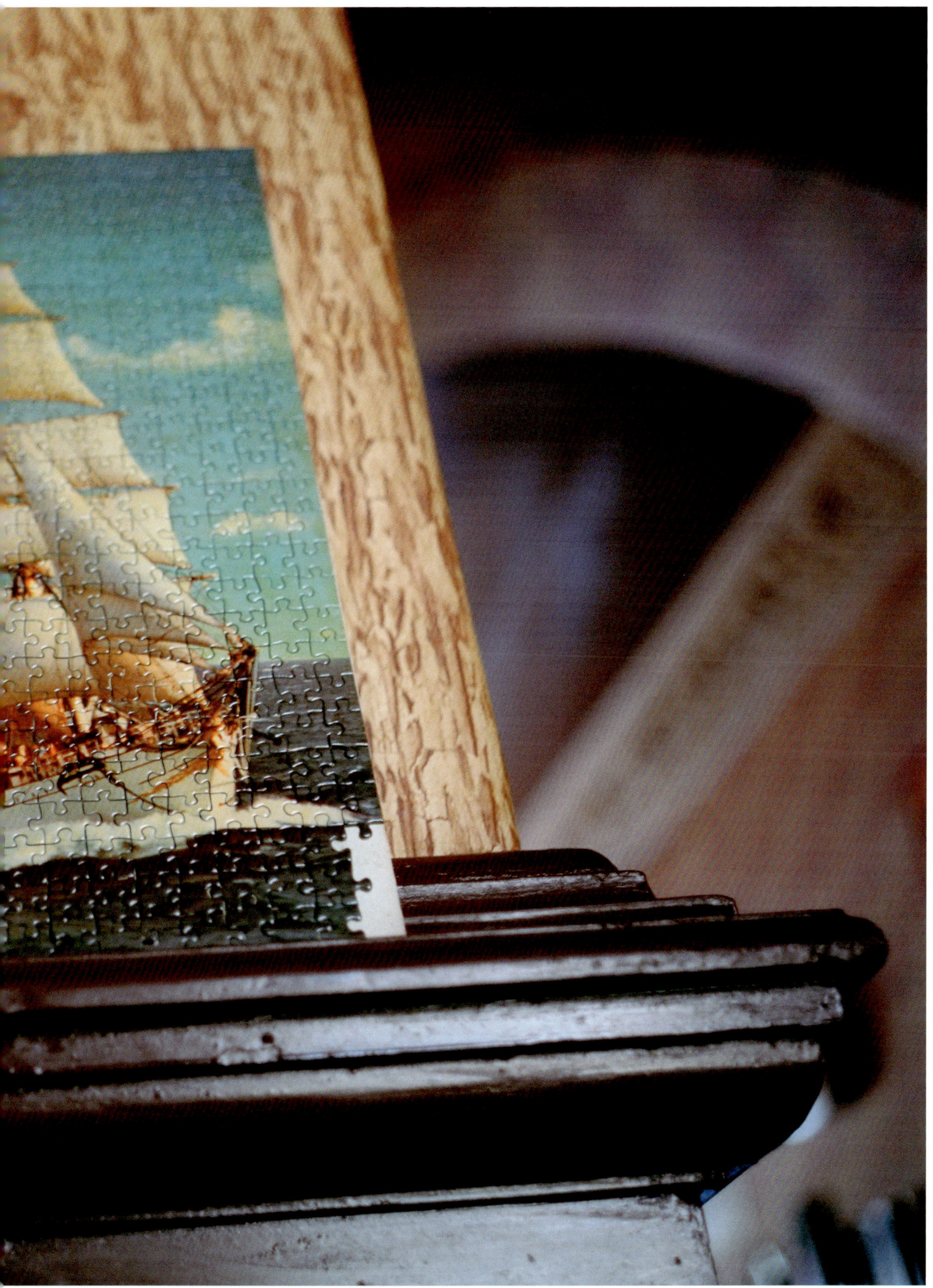

Postscript
Urs Stahel, 2019

In retrospect, I find it difficult not to read the pictures in Paul Graham's visual history *New Europe* as a prophecy. It is almost uncanny. The year 1989 was a hymnic moment for many. The Berlin Wall fell, and the end was in sight for the GDR and the Soviet Union, for ossified, leaden state communism. Europe seemed to unite, and with it the world. The idea of being freed from the history that had determined people's lives in the 1980s seemed to become real – freed from political responsibility on one hand and the social market economy on the other. From this point on, each individual could go their own way without worry, could live out their own identity in all its facets.

Many also heard the first dissonances in this hymnic moment. Some saw a deep, dark shadow behind the bright, promising light. In January, 1993, when the Fotomuseum Winterthur opened with an exhibition of *New Europe*, some already knew how quickly neoliberal capitalism spread, and how it would became sharper while wearing a triumphant, scornful grin. The enemy had broken in, and with it the 'social' in capitalism. Margaret Thatcher had paved the way in the 1980s with the deregulation of the financial sector, privatisation of state-owned enterprises, and deindustrialisation. As for the frivolous notion of freedom from history? In 1991, war broke out in the Balkans at the gates of Western Europe, making it clear that history would catch up to us all sooner or later.

The pictures of *New Europe* are suffused with such ambivalences, premonitions, and shadows. A Spanish diptych pairs the eccentricity and energy of the time in Madrid with a spitting contempt for Franco's tomb. Pictures of exuberant dancers rub up against dark building facades with window crosses that recall gravestones. Real events in history become beer labels in supermarkets. The people seem tense. In all its ebullience, in the transformation of history into images, into products, in the sliding into consumption, sex and drugs, a deep existential loss is felt, a Sartrean nothingness: godless, frameless, meaningless. In the evolution into a world of global consumerism, it becomes apparent step by step that the past clings to our shoes, and that new ways of being bring with them much that is wrong. Graham's book *New Europe* began with a stanza from T S Eliot's *The Waste Land*:

'And I will show you something different from either
Your shadow at morning striding behind you
Or your shadow at evening rising to meet you;
I will show you fear in a handful of dust'.

In 2019, we feel just how much the past and the messiness of politics is catching up to us. New forms of fascism, new forms of radicalisation and ideologisation are making a stir, and we're once again afraid of the next steps in Europe and worldwide, the next great shadow.

Graham photographed the images comprising *New Europe* around 1989, and first published and exhibited them in 1993. In the images, he argues politically, economically, and existentially, linking the fate of the individual with the political and economic structure of Europe. He shows people exuberantly celebrating or introspective, fragile, and tense. Of course, when looking back from today's perspective, the next major field – the idea of the increased presence of the digital – as well as the now far more visible and measurable consequences of industrialisation for the environment are notably absent from the exhibition. Graham was an ideal choice for the inaugural exhibition at the Fotomuseum Winterthur. With him, I was able to showcase not only a highly relevant, multilayered topic, but also the first of a new form of documentary photography, one that oscillates between document and essay, between objective

representation and subjective perspective, one that
asserts itself through variations and size. Importantly,
his photography was in colour right from the start.
We remember how strongly he, Martin Parr, Peter
Fraser, and others in England were attacked for no
longer photographing sociopolitical issues in black
and white, as was expected, but in colour. This move
was hugely contentious, but from the perspective
of many was an important step in the right direction.
Furthermore, this use of colour enabled him to
masterfully explore the tension between image
and likeness, between depiction and design – a
declaration of the searching subjective gaze. Such
tensions were already evident in Graham's previous
works *Beyond Caring* and *Troubled Land*, and
would continue to be explored in later works such
as *End of an Age* and his masterpiece *a shimmer
of possibility*. Thus, from the outset, Fotomuseum
Winterthur helped to lay the groundwork for a
new approach to photography in museums, a
way through which photography can engage with
the world.

From the series
New Europe, 1988–92

Untitled, 1989
(one armed man)

Untitled, 1988
(model soldiers)

Untitled, 1988
(window reflection)

Untitled, 1989 (dust,
Friedrichstrasse, Berlin)

Untitled, Germany, 1989
(man shielding eyes)

Untitled, Germany, 1989
(star of David)

Untitled, Germany, 1989
(woman in discotheque)

Untitled, 1988
(sex video parlour)

Untitled, 1988
(blood spray)

Untitled, Spain, 1988
(laughing woman)

*Untitle*d, Paris, 1988
(man on metro)

Untitled, Belfast, 1988
(wire on post)

Untitled, 1989 (ship jigsaw)

TEXT

THE UNDERMINING OF BRITAIN
Neal Ascherson, 1994

IMAGES

Anna Fox
Janine Wiedel
Huw Davies

To join two countries by a tunnel is a feat of engineering, but also of the imagination. As such, it raises visions and provokes reactions which tell many stories and reveal a great deal about the underlying hopes and fears of those who are to be joined.

Precedents are rare. In the nineteenth century, when the great Alpine tunnels were projected, the Swiss balanced all the commercial advantages against a possible threat to their liberty and independence. They concluded that the risk was worth taking, in contrast to the British who, during the Victorian debates over Channel tunnels took a strictly military view. The film-maker Georg Pabst, in *Kameradschaft* (1931), imagined French and German coal-mines whose galleries connected, and made this theme into a tremendous fable about working-class internationalism and solidarity (in a mine disaster) which transcended all the petty divisions and frontier-fences on the surface a mile above. More recently, the two German states, now one, were connected repeatedly by clandestine tunnels; some dug by desperate fugitives from the East, others constructed by professional *Fluchthelfer* who charged refugees enormous sums in dollars to use their escape-hole, or excavated by intelligence services probing for one another's telephone cables. All these tunnels were associated with optimism in one form or another. It was thought that they would allow a free flow of international understanding, or access to liberty, or simply an increase of information.

An international tunnel, then, is in several senses of the word an undermining. It digs under an obstacle: a mountain range, frontier wall or Channel. But it has also been constantly perceived as the undermining of some established order. Most of the examples I have quoted were founded on the assumption that the existing order was in some way obsolete or undesirable and deserved to be undermined. Progress and commerce had rendered the road passage over the Swiss passes intolerably slow and unreliable. Pabst thought that nation-states deserved to be undermined by the international proletariat. The Berliners burrowed under the Wall as a preliminary to overthrowing it.

This is why the British reaction to the opening of a tunnel under the Channel and its direct rail link between Britain and France is so curious. It is above all a valediction. Something is being undermined here, for good, but the British public imagination is clearly not sure that it wants to lose that something. People visit the route of the rail link across Kent as if to visit a dying relative – to say goodbye to an aspect of England, to see and appreciate it for one last time. Most of these melancholy tourists seem to accept the necessity of the Tunnel, but they are touched by a sense that the loss – that which is to be undermined and overcome – is grievous. England will not be the same again, and they are not certain that England joined directly to France will be a better place.

Many of the artists who contributed to the Cross Channel Photographic Mission have picked up this all-permeating flavour of regret (a flavour almost completely absent in the regions of France affected by the Tunnel). So what is being lost here, and what is being mourned?

The first loss, plainly, is a strip of physical environment, either removed by the Tunnel and the rail route or deformed out of recognition by proximity to them. The damage along this strip, in the context of south-eastern England as a whole, is going to be severe but it would be an exaggeration to call it over-whelming. As far as existing buildings and landscape are concerned, the impact will be heavy on several pretty Kentish villages – parts of which will be rendered barely habitable by construction and permanent train noise – and in spite of the latest proposals for increasing the proportion of track enclosed in tunnels, the North Downs will inevitably suffer scarring. But comparison to what happened in the nineteenth century is instructive. There were two rival railway companies in the 1840s which built lines from the capital to the Channel: the London, Chatham and Dover Railway running out of Blackfriars Station in London and the East Kent Railway which began originally at Rochester. The two companies left a track of ruthless devastation across Kent as their armies of labourers, equipped with little more than picks, shovels and manually-operated tip-trucks, drove straight lines across the county. The route taken by the London, Chatham and Dover teams did the worst damage; it ran parallel to the North Downs across the plain between the Downs and the Thames estuary, across a region which had been densely populated since the Iron Age, ripping through the Saxon and mediaeval centres of one town after another. The loss to history was, in retrospect, horrifying. In between the towns of Kent, the navvies dug their way through Palaeolithic gravel-beds, Roman villas, Iron Age field-patterns and Saxon cemeteries. From time to time, local antiquaries were able to buy back the odd relic from the railway labourers. But all too often, as the early volumes of *Archaeologia Cantiana* record, it was a matter of encouraging them to remember what they had already sold, smashed or thrown away: a 'pipkin' of 'old pennies' i.e. a coin hoard (probably Belgic or Romano-British), or a mysterious cubical 'coffin' of black oak beams supposed to have contained 'clay pots' and ashes (a burial? part of a Bronze Age cargo boat?).

Yet that loss – though resented by the denizens of cathedral closes and by enlightened landowners – was generally held to have been a price well worth paying for railways to the Channel ports. Omelettes required broken eggs, and progress had its cost. Such was the self-confidence of Victorian Britain. In the 1990s, by contrast, a far smaller loss to the appearance, monuments and archaeological potential of Kent is held to be almost intolerable. The corresponding addition to human happiness offered by the Tunnel may just outweigh that loss, in majority opinion, but it is evident that for many it will not.

In any case, that sort of calculus is out of date. We are beginning to realise how deeply Victorian it is to think that decisions – especially vast decisions like the Tunnel and railway project – are made on a simple profit-and-loss matrix, like a village butcher's cashbook. Our fathers and mothers might still have approached choices – a marriage, a purchase, a career option – in this way, by taking a sheet of paper and filling in two ink columns headed 'pro' and 'con'. Until very recently, this has seemed the most rational of procedures. But now, as the whole assessment procedure for the Tunnel and the rail link has shown, responsible people are growing wary of Benthamite arithmetic about pluses and minuses of pleasure or pain. Volume after volume of environmental assessment has been published, estimating in painstaking detail what the Union Railway track will do to this historic woodland, this scheduled ancient monument, this group of seventeenth-century farm buildings or this open prospect over downland. And yet, significantly, nowhere is there a profit-and-loss judgement – not even a page of propaganda hinting that the high-speed Channel crossing is 'worth' the destruction of places of 'low moderate concern'. The judgement will be made elsewhere. And it will not be made by 'pro' versus 'con', but by an almost soldierly appreciation of a battlefield. Here advances the Union Railway, towards (let's say) the River Medway. But there across its path stand an Area of Outstanding Natural Beauty (AONB), several Sites of Special Scientific Interest (SSSI) and squadrons of Special Landscape Areas (SLA). The question for the railway's generals is simply this: are we strong enough to break through them, and what losses (money, time, diversions) might a breakthrough cost?

Decisions now are a calculation about power, not about benefit. Those who wanted the Tunnel thought that it would be good for them, believed that the country could be persuaded that it would be good for Britain too, and then settled down to estimating whether they could overcome the strength of the entrenched lobbies which they knew would oppose them. In the same way, the most dedicated protestors – those who believe that in defending the landscape of Kent they are defending the whole 'natural heritage' of the nation – are not prepared to play the profit-and-loss game.

Damage to this landscape, they would say, is something absolute. They argue that it is irrelevant and meaningless to tot up damage against possible social benefit. Sums like that are utterly subjective, and will be added up differently by different generations. What was an acceptable loss to the Victorians – a Bronze Age barrow dug away, a wood recorded in Domesday Book felled for railway cutting – now appears an unpardonable cultural crime. The loss itself, on the other hand, is not subjective in any way, but all too real. A thousand-year oak which is cut down stays down.

To explore the route of the rail link between Folkestone and the Thames crossing is to begin to understand this strain of 'absolutism' in the opposition. Two things become clear. The first is that the impact of the new rail route on the Kentish landscape will not, after all, be catastrophic (there are a few places in which it will be very serious, but no worse). The second discovery, however, is that the route is littered from the Thames to the sea with evidence of the failure of the 'pro and con' style of argument in the past.

Between the nineteenth and late twentieth century, the impact of railways and then roads along the southward face of the North Downs –

the route of the Channel Tunnel link – has been enormous. The railways broke open what were until then backward and impoverished communities; in the village church at Harrietsham, you can read in the memoirs of a Victorian vicar's wife how violent and isolated the place was, regularly cut off by mud and snow from the outside world until the railway arrived in the 1880s. A 'pro' in terms of social improvement, but at a cost – the railway was laid slap through the ancient village nucleus and it is still there, and just as noisy, while Harrietsham's poverty is not even a memory. And the defilement wrought by railways is nothing compared to the effect of new roads, above all in the last twenty years or so. The 'pro' is presumably faster road journeys between Ashford and Maidstone. But the improved A20 cuts Harrietsham off from its natural hinterland of little fields and orchards on the other side of the road and slices in two the village of Charing, whose companionable main street has become a mortally dangerous traffic torrent.

The ruthless 'landtake' of new roads is a loss which can never be made good. It does not impress the objectors that the additional impact of the Tunnel link will be marginal, but it is nonetheless true. Just north-east of Maidstone, in a once-beautiful lap of country between the Down crest at Blue Bell Hill and the River Medway, the disturbance caused by the new railway will be minor compared to the devastation of the new motorway interchange under construction near Aylesford, or to the ranks of smoking industrial chimneys along the far bank of the river. But those who protest have seen how wrong the calculations of all previous planners went. They are not interested in matching greater environmental damage against lesser. They simply say 'No'. From Blue Bell Hill, it is possible to see what they mean.

At Kit's Coty House and Little Kit's Coty (two majestic 'menhir'-type assemblages of stone slabs which are the remains of Neolithic burial chambers) the alignment of the new railway has been changed several times and eventually buried in a tunnel to avoid disturbing the 'setting' of the monuments and disruption to the old Pilgrim's Way, running along the ridge of the North Downs to Canterbury. This almost obsequious respect to the environment contrasts with the irreparable damage done on the same shoulder of the Downs by road up-grading, especially by the huge new motorway link from Maidstone to Gillingham which dominates the physical landscape with its scarring and has simply eradicated a whole stretch of the Pilgrim's Way. The M20, further east, has transformed a fifteen-mile stretch of Kent countryside under the Downs into a confined traffic corridor between hills and motorway. Here again, the new rail alignment which runs parallel to the motorway is only reinforcing an older intrusion.

So people's sense of loss is not primarily about the physical environment. Rather, it is the feeling that we will no longer be living on an island. This is essentially an English perception; the Scots and the Welsh, understanding themselves as small, peripheral European nationalities, do not worry about it. But English identity, the spirit of the British state, has been built up around the idea of isolation and difference. Obviously, this was not always true. In the late Iron Age, south-eastern England formed some kind of loose cultural whole with Celtic kingdoms in northern France. Then came the incorporation of the Britannia province into the Roman Empire, and much later the cross-channel political links of the Norman kingdom and the Anglo-French mediaeval polity which included south-western France. The 'island identity' was really established in the Tudor period, as England was given an imperial, maritime destiny pointing outwards and westwards. John Dee, the wizard and con-man from Wales, persuaded Elizabeth

that the Tudors, with their Welsh origins, were the rein-carnation of the Ancient British empire of Arthur, which once – supposedly – ruled over all England and Wales before the coming of the Saxons. Elizabeth was therefore the heir to Arthur's mythical overseas empire, an idea confected out of the legends that Prince Madoc had once sailed to America and colonised it, long before the discoveries of Columbus, and the Welsh-inspired theory (which was not finally extinguished until the nineteenth century) that the languages of the indigenous Americans were really a variant of Welsh.

Most nations have to be forged, in both senses of the word. The Arthurian forgery, or myth of origin, served to authenticate the beginnings of the first Anglo-British empire and the turning-away from continental Europe which had begun earlier in the sixteenth century with the Henrician Reformation and the break with Rome. The defence of the Channel barrier, for the next three centuries at least, was understood as the defence of a moral as well as a physical and political frontier: 'across there' were powers, French and Habsburg above all, whose agenda was to impose an alien religion and an absolutist form of government upon England/Britain.

Behind the sea frontier, the British state continued to diverge from European patterns. The first European political revolution – the English Civil War – ended with the 1689 settlement which merely took the doctrine of absolutism away from the monarch and transferred it to Parliament. In consequence, the politics of the Enlightenment and the French and American Revolutions missed Britain almost entirely. The republican project, which means the doctrine of popular sovereignty and the supremacy of a written constitution incorporating individual human rights, did not change the archaic British philosophy of state which has lasted, little modified, from 1689 to today.

Socially, the two sides of the Channel grew steadily further apart. For nearly two centuries, cross-Channel travellers have been intrigued by the visual difference between Kent and the French departments just across the water. The geological structure is much the same: a continuation of the chalk downs which formed a bridge until the sea broke through sometime in the Mesolithic period. But the territory south of Calais or Boulogne is an open, un-hedged country of peasant strips and large villages. Kent, in contrast, is an English patchwork of small hedged-off fields, with a denser population which lived – until recently – mostly in a few large towns or in isolated farms; the villages were generally small. One nation had remained more or less feudal and unimproved agriculturally until the Revolution, when the land was broken up and distributed as the private property of small peasants. Across the water, by contrast, the Enclosure movement and the spread of middle-class wealth had already produced a landscape of hedged fields in which capitalist farmers employed landless labourers.

There was another difference. The Calais region, though agriculturally poor, was close to one of the great industrial basins of Europe: the coal, iron and textile cities which spanned the Franco-Belgian border. Northern France was close to the centre of things, economically. Kent, in contrast, had become a backwater. There were collieries, clustered in the north of the county in a single coalfield, and there were shipyards and dockyards on the Medway. But by the nineteenth century, rural Kent was part of the general backwardness which afflicted most of southern England. The centres of development and prosperity were almost all north of London; the rural south was notorious for ignorance, low living standards, apathy and bad roads. The proximity of London itself meant little to Kent, beyond the arrival of rich businessmen who purchased country estates or the use of East End seasonal labour in the hopfields. Most significantly, the presence of the Channel did little to help Kent. Maritime trade went overwhelmingly through Liverpool, Bristol, Glasgow, Ipswich and the port of London itself; imports and exports through Dover or Folkestone were small stuff, and those towns never grew into great commercial cities or developed an industrial hinterland. The Kent coast had been for centuries the site of fortifications, naval bases and barracks but, with the exception of the great naval dockyard at Chatham, Kent's strategic importance made little impact inland. Even the transit passenger and mail traffic between London and Dover, bound to and from France, did not create any corridor of prosperity until the building of the railways. It was not large, in the sense that little of it was bulk goods, and the overflow of cash from it stayed either with the customs at Dover or with the innkeepers and stable-owners along the Dover road.

Kent's location at the Channel narrows, in short, did little or nothing to help it. Once, in the distant past, this position had drawn Kent strongly into the European mainstream. Later, as the English state developed, it had exactly the opposite effect: to isolate the county as a relatively under-developed peninsula on the periphery, just as if Kent had faced some limitless ocean instead of the visible shores of the European mainland. When some prosperity did reach the area in the nineteenth century, it was largely confined to cash-crop agriculture in West Kent: hops and berries for domestic consumption rather than for export. Ashford became a railway town, Canterbury began to attract mass tourism and the improvement of steamers at last began to multiply cross-Channel passenger traffic through the ports. But even today, at the end of a half-century which has seen the whole base of British wealth-creation shift from the North into the South-East of England, East Kent remains a basically rural place, its population inflated by hundreds of thousands of long-range London commuters but its back still turned to the Channel.

The story of Kent is an example of 'islandism' and its consequences. Looked at in practical terms, a re-connection of this part of England into the Continental economy promises all gain and no loss. But this sense of loss is not about practicalities. Kent is already part of a Euro-region which crosses the Channel, so that it has ties with Flanders which it does not have with – say – Essex. But few people know or care about this. What they mind about is the fear that by 'joining the Continent', England will become less English. Something special, something islanded-off from the harshness of the rest of the world, will leak invisibly away down the Chunnel.

This is worse than superstitious – it is misleading. Englishness, however we define that, is not at risk. The English will not become less English by the physical fact that traffic to the Continent passes under the water rather than over it. Neither is 'Anglitude' menaced by the social-political consequences of European Union, because it is an infinitely flexible description. What is at risk here is not a nation but a state. The Channel Tunnel does mean that England will become less British.

The British state is an artefact, as are all states, but this one was made at the end of the seventeenth century. Its foundations were the principles of authority and modified absolutism. Its orientation was away from Continental Europe and towards the oceans. English in design and spirit, it soon incorporated Scotland by guile and already possessed Ireland through force. This artefact has been repeatedly redecorated and repaired, with all kinds of small modernisations but in outline the old structure is still with us. Yet this state, through a series of decisions over the last thirty-five years, has committed itself to forming part of a united Europe.

The member-states of the European Union, and indeed the central apparatus of the Community or Union itself, belong to the Enlightenment tradition. They have long ago abandoned the old idea of absolute national sovereignty, and adopted the idea that a written supreme law stands above all parliaments, rulers or supranational associations. But this conflicts with British constitutional doctrine which, for example, cannot allow that any decision by any person or body is immune to being overthrown by the House of Commons – by a majority of one or more. It conflicts directly with a state doctrine which holds that official information is a state monopoly: everything is by nature secret, except that ministers may from time to time agree to allow the public access to that information. It declares a 'rights culture', incompatible with the British reliance upon authority tempered by humanity and common sense. It proclaims that state sovereignty can be broken up and distributed, as to the states of a federation whose laws, in certain cases, cannot be overruled by the central government.

This principle, flagrantly denying the absolute and indivisible sovereignty of Parliament, cannot be applied by the British state – which is why Irish Home Rule was rejected by Parliament in 1886, and why blood has been flowing more or less ever since.

This is the special nature of Britishness. As European Union becomes more real and as – year by year – Britain in practice participates in 'federal' institutions at a European level, this artefact will begin to disappear. Obsolete, a relic of history, it is not compatible with the design of modern citizenship which the Union is elaborating. Already, the Court of European Human Rights rejects British legislation and the House of Commons, grumbling, amends it or withdraws it. A written constitution, a Bill of Rights, perhaps even a 'UK Federation', are on their slow way in. The British state, equally slowly, is on the way out.

And the English sense of loss? The Channel Tunnel symbolically undermines the British state, which was created out of English experience and preference so many years ago. It is not England but that old state, in its crusty uniqueness, which is the real island; something which can only remain itself by keeping a moat of water between it and the modern world.

But a tunnel is also a voice-pipe, through which echoing shouts of warning or encouragement can be heard. Up through the big hole near Sandling, all the way from France in the time of Revolution, comes the voice of Thomas Paine. He is, as he always did, asking the question which really matters. Paine asks why the English have to live in the British state? The fact that their leaders constructed it three hundred years ago need not condemn the English nation to inhabit it forever, still less to identify their own qualities with this particular set of rules. States are made by peoples, as shells are made by snails. When they grow confining, they are shucked off and exchanged for a better one.

England can live without Britain. The message of the Channel Tunnel, indeed, is that England will be obliged to do so, because the approach to Europe is beginning to expose the British state to the sort of radiation which will change it out of all recognition. The state has been frankly anti-European. The nation does not have to be so, and in the long ages before the constitutional settlements of the sixteenth and seventeenth centuries, England was no more or less 'European' than Denmark or Catalonia.

The mourning, then, is not for a lost physical England to be ravaged by a tunnel and a railway. It is not for Englishness, either, which will probably be enriched by its recovery of Europe and renewed by the modernisation of life and thought which will accompany it. The grief is for a fallacy: the notion that England and Britain are identical, and that with the decay of the unreformed British state a whole way of life must go into decline. But this is like

saying that a man grows sick when his shirt begins to fray. All we are losing is an outdated set of institutions, an *ancien régime* overdue for replacement. And that loss is necessary, even welcome: the washing-away of waste which every community has to organise if it is to stay healthy. Perhaps, after all, the Channel Tunnel's supreme function is that of a drain.

First published in: *Soundings*, Jane Alison and Brigitte Lardinois (ed.), Cross Channel Photographic Mission, 1994.

Anna Fox
The Village

**Women, Compton, West Sussex
1991–93**

This project focused on the lives of women in the West Sussex village where Fox's grandmother lived. Capturing country life with its imposing history of deep-seated community values and structures against a backdrop of rural change. Conceived as more than a series of still photographs the project was a collaboration with Val Williams and was first exhibited as an installation, a constructed room within the gallery contained a projection and a sound track filled with whispers and mantras. Fox remembers how 'Essentially I wanted to look behind the scenes of this very conservative environment, to consider the particular values that I was brought up with and the roles that women played in this rural community'.

The project questions the popular myth of village life as rural and idyllic, exposed by the sharp flash of the camera and the perceptive viewpoint of the photographer.

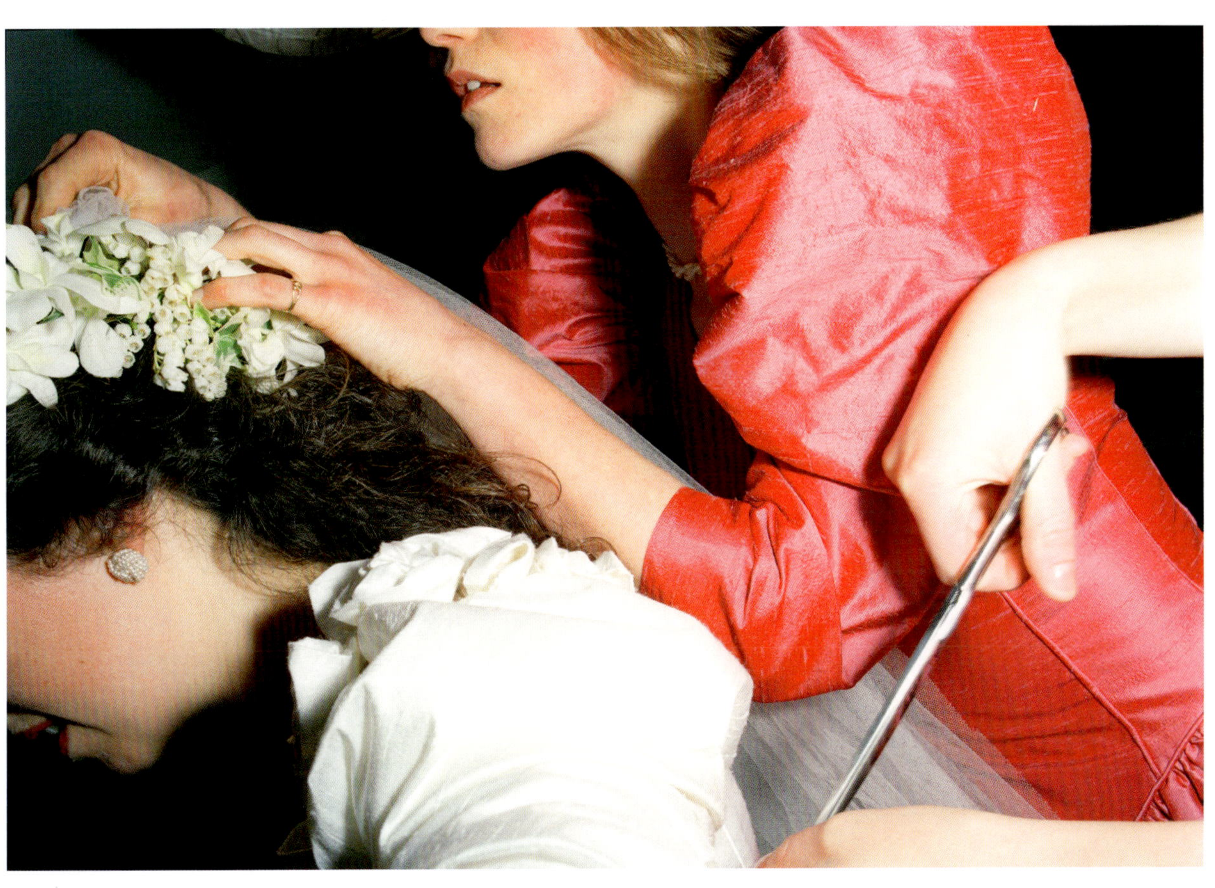

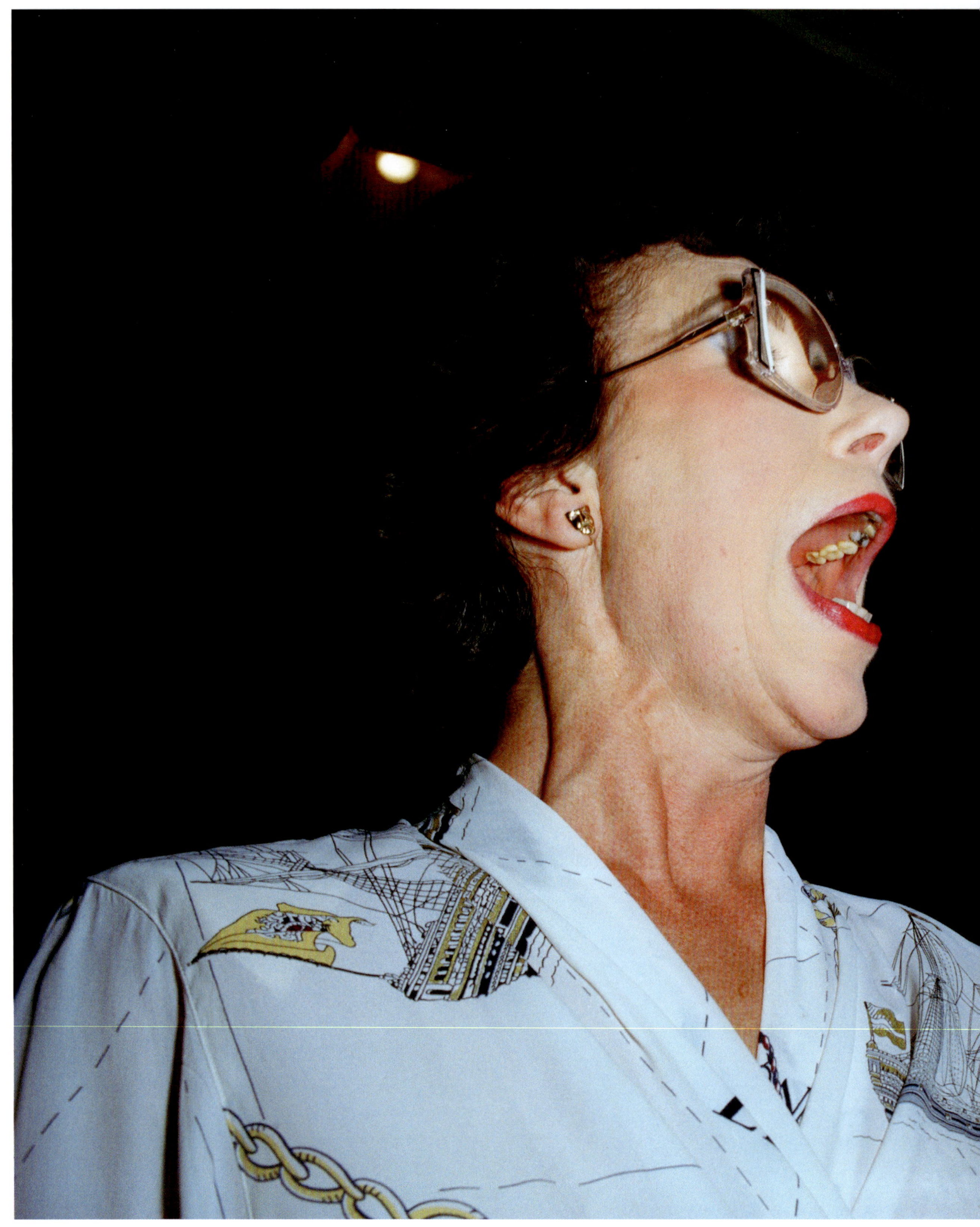

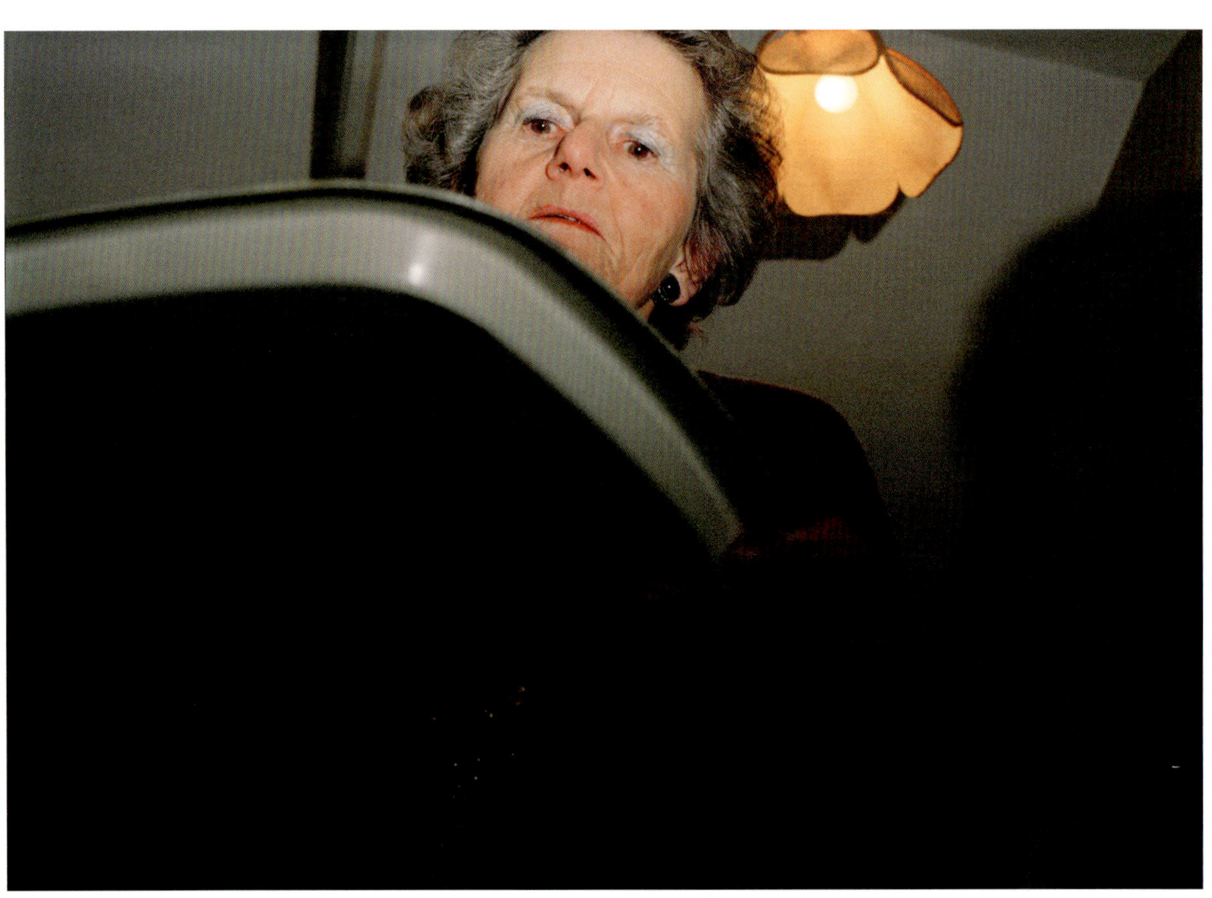

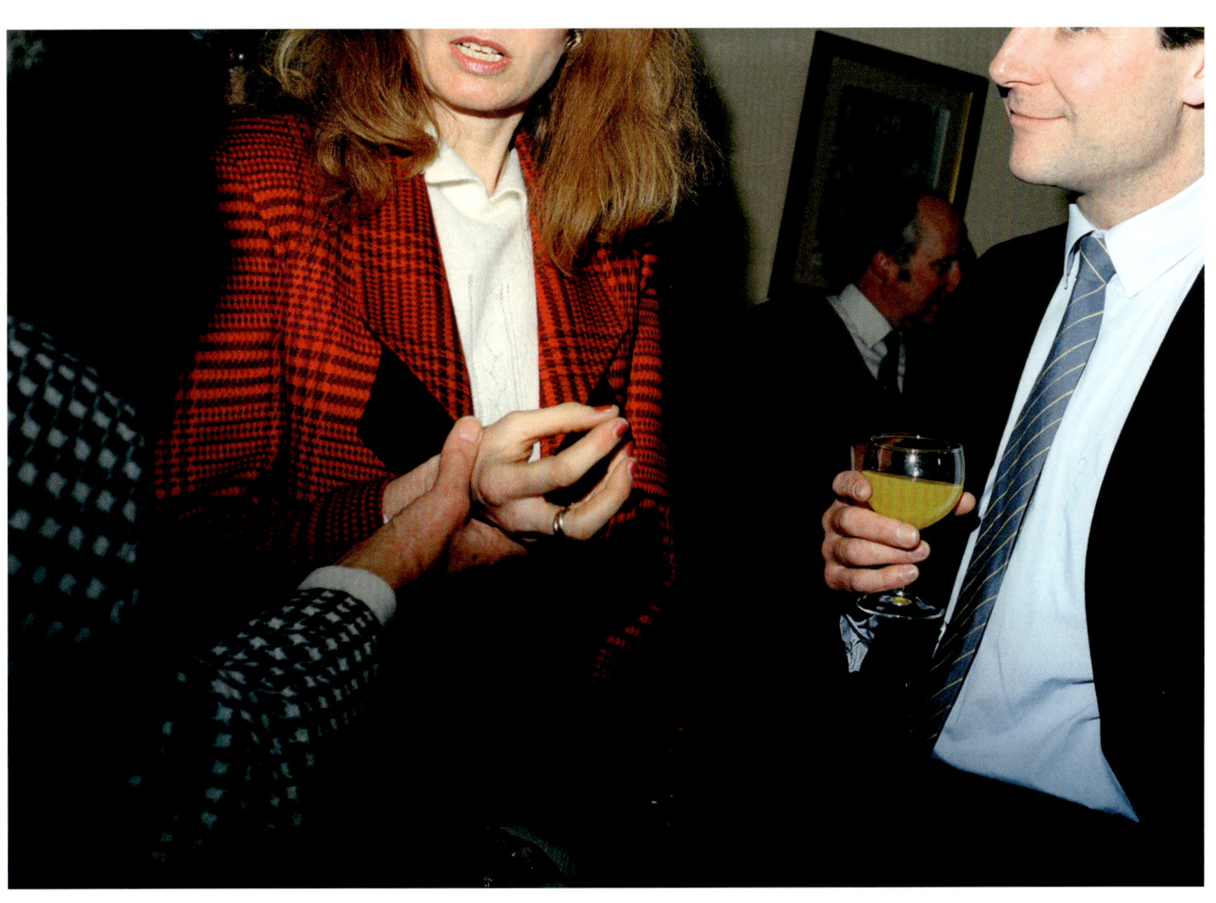

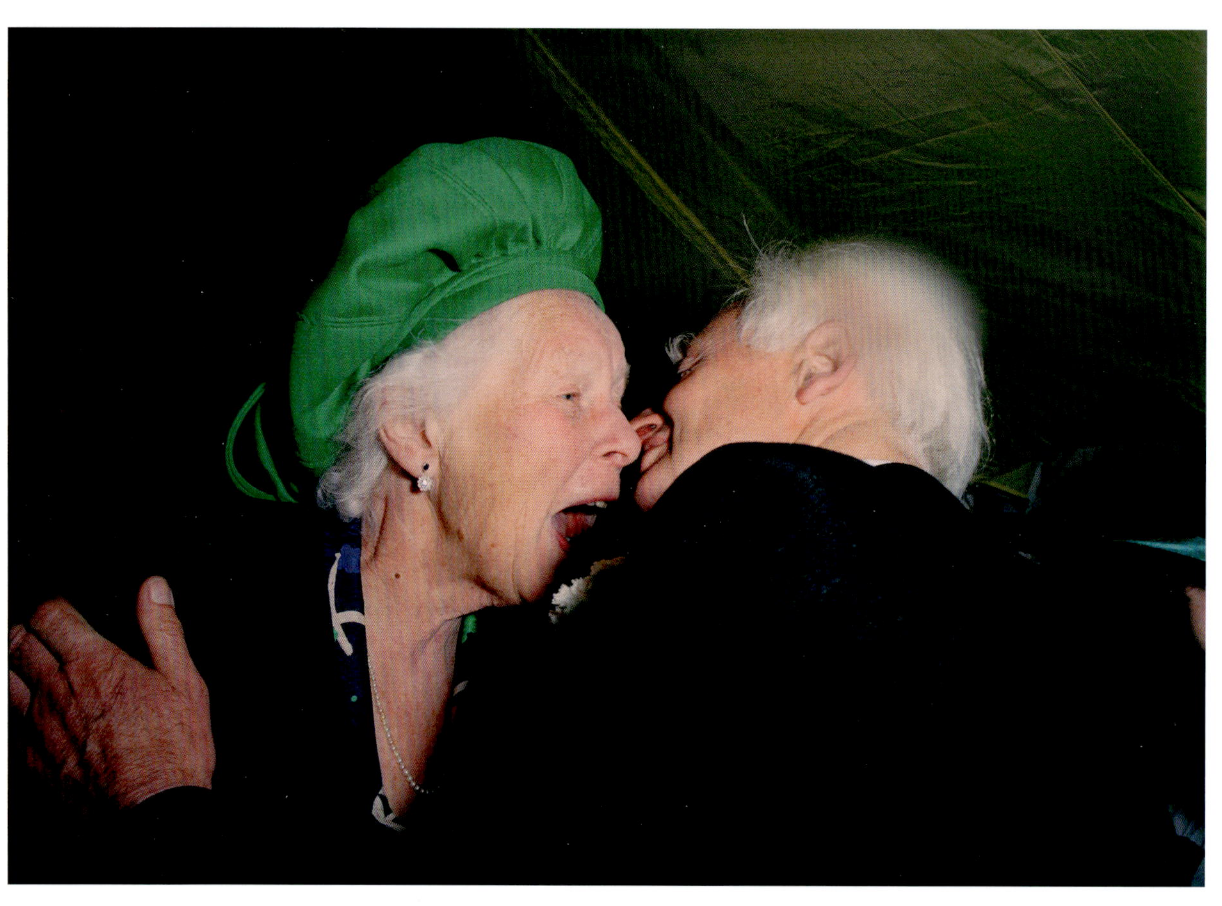

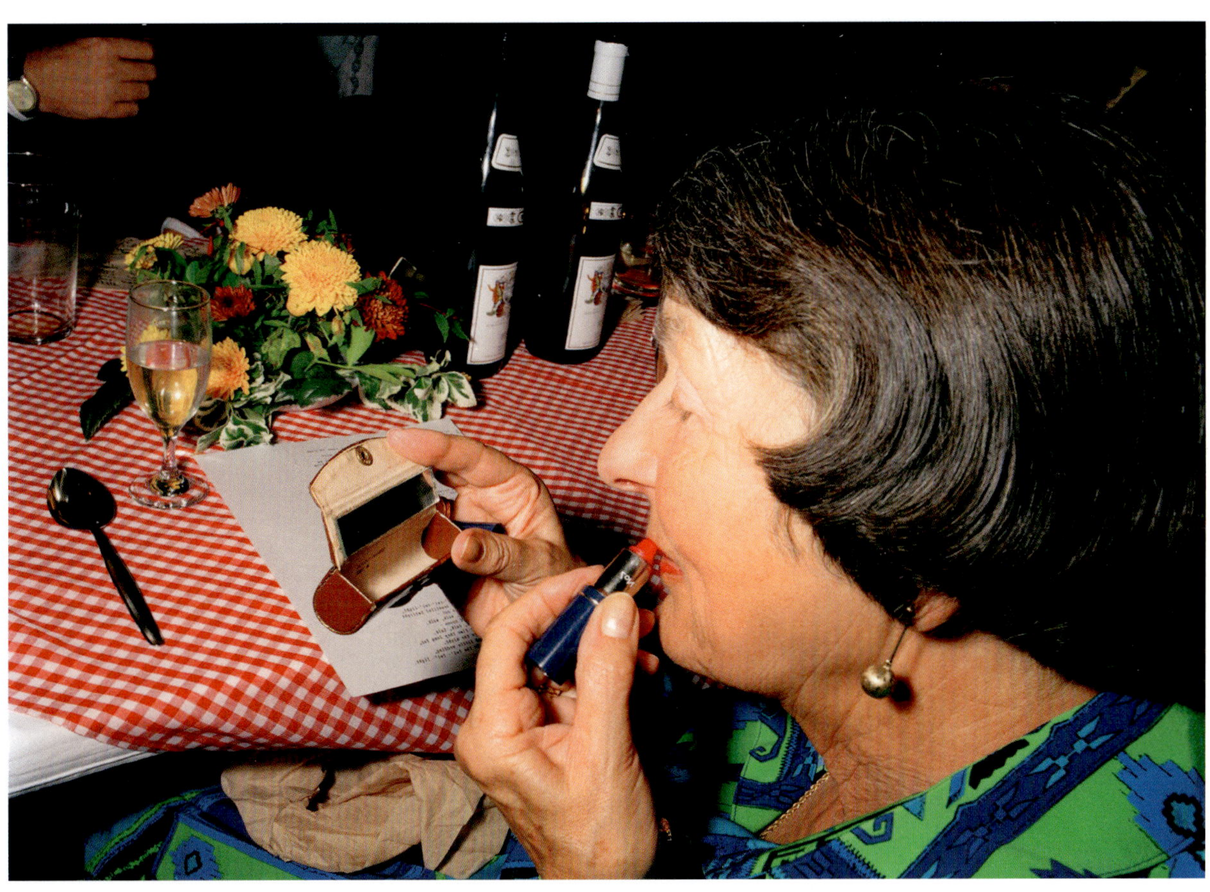

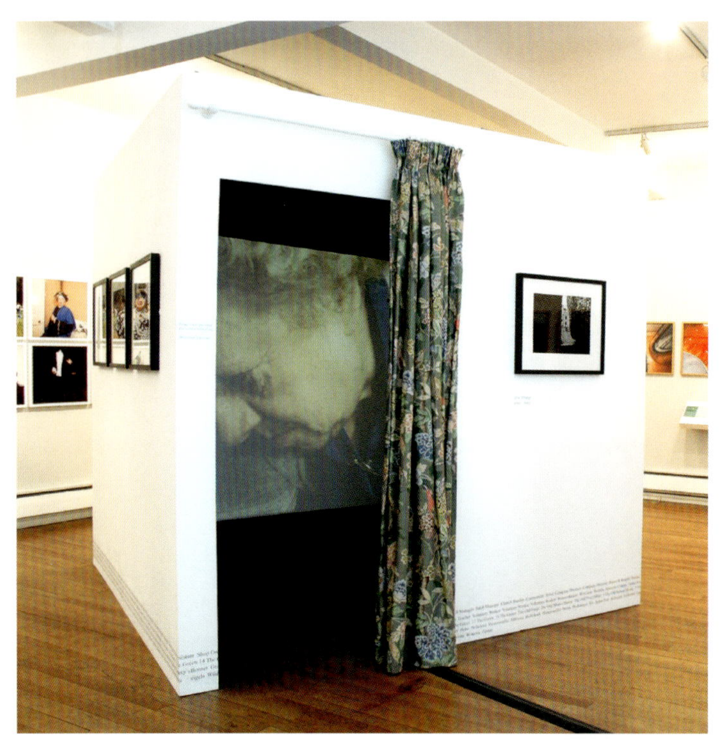

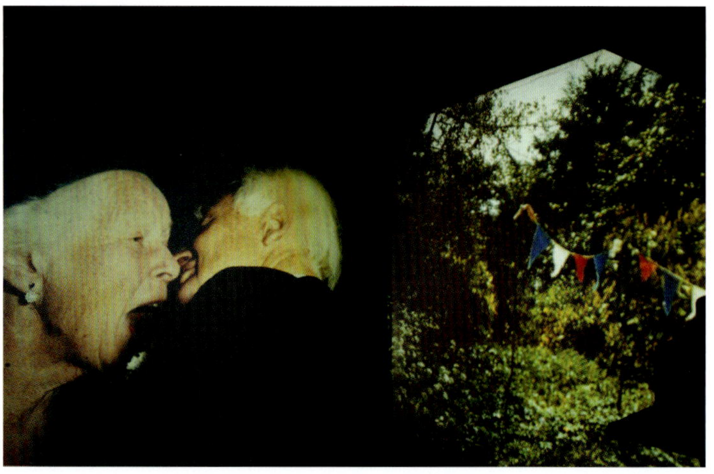

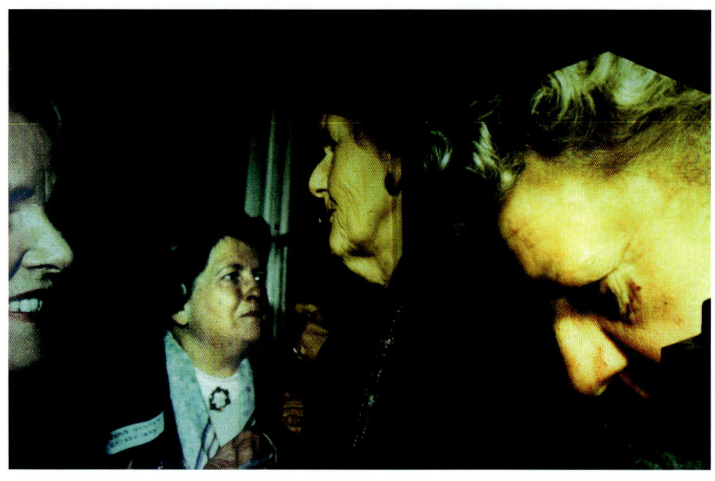

51–58: *Untitled*. From the series, *The Village*, 1991–93

58: Top Left: Installation shot, from the exhibition *Cockroach Diary and Other Stories*. Curated by Anne McNeill, Ffotogallery, Cardiff

Janine Wiedel
The London Fancy Box Company, Dover

From the series, *Dover: A Port in a Storm*, 1989–1990

Wiedel was commissioned by the Cross Channel Photographic Mission (CCPM) to photograph the busy port town of Dover. She explored the hidden and mundane, capturing places of work, commerce, leisure, education and daily life. Wiedel photographed Dover's London Fancy Box Company, a family-run business founded in 1894. It produces boxes for a wide range of luxury products. In 1990, with a workforce of mainly women, it was one of the main employers outside of the port. Looking back, Wiedel's study of the women at work draws reference to projects such as *Women and Work: A Document on the Division of Labour in Industry 1973–1975* by Margaret Harrison, Kay Hunt and Mary Kelly and Helga Paris's images of East German textiles factory *Women at the Treff-Modelle Clothing Factory* from 1984. Wiedel captured a focused perspective of life for women in Dover immediately prior to the arrival of the Channel Tunnel and any change that came with it.

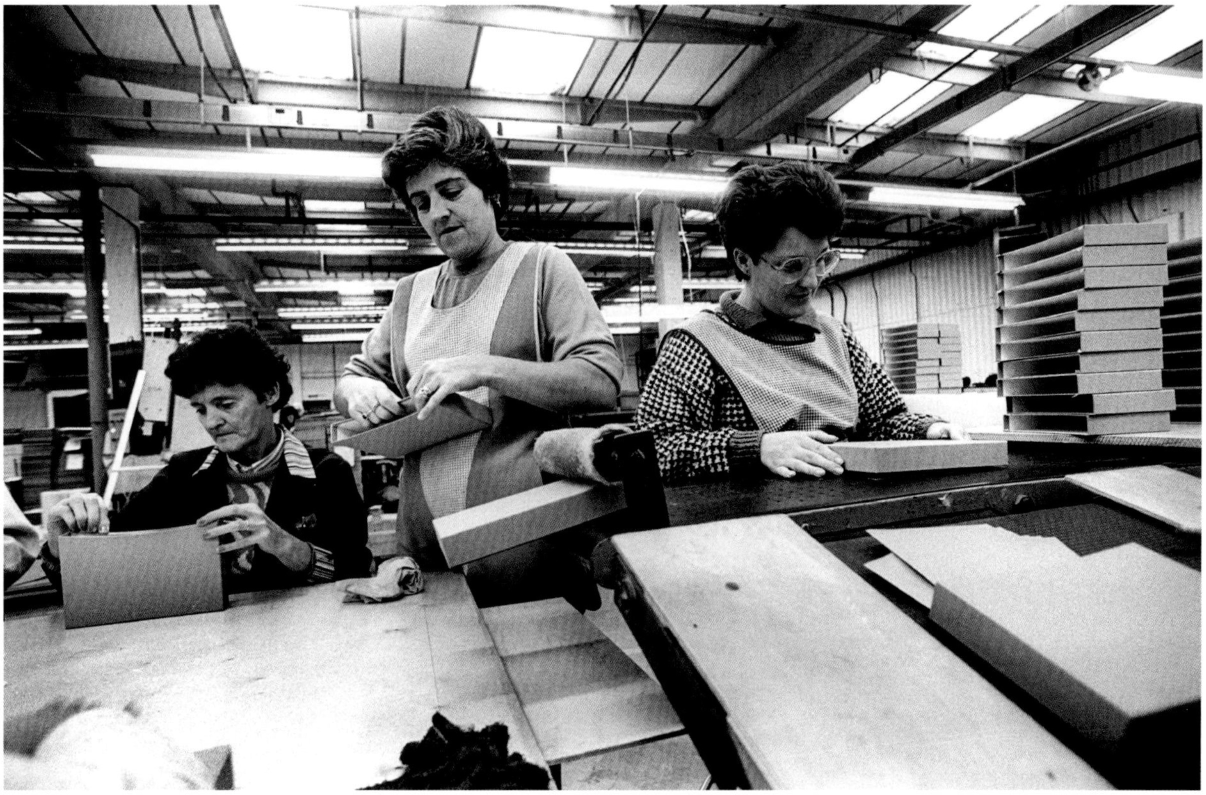

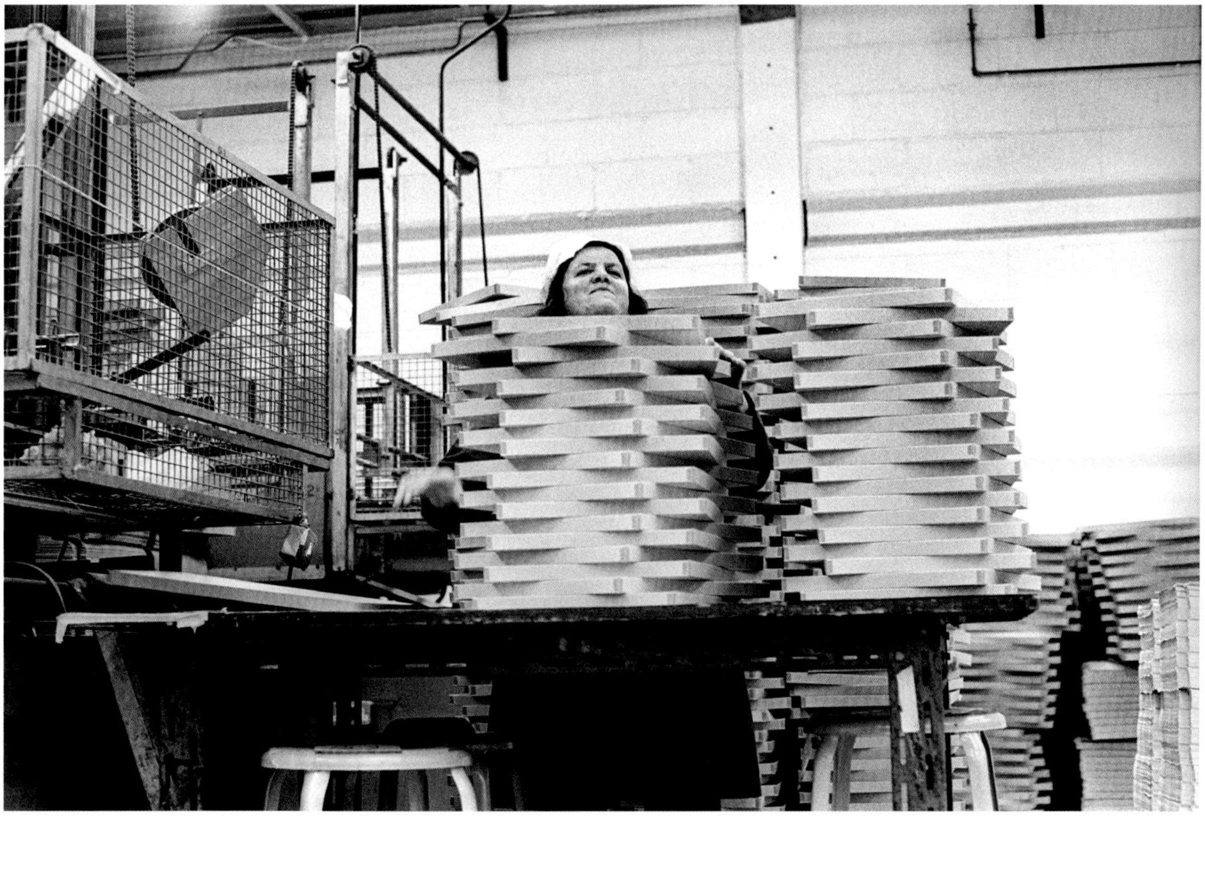

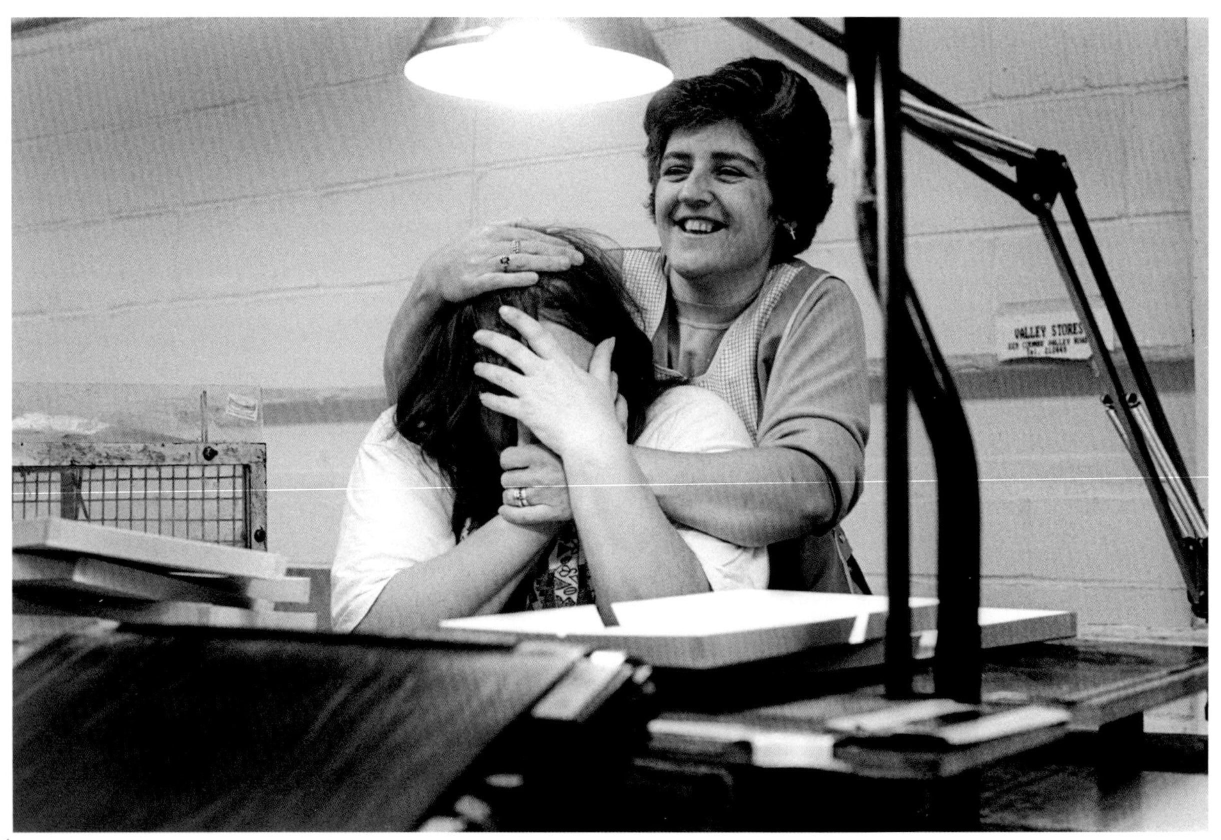

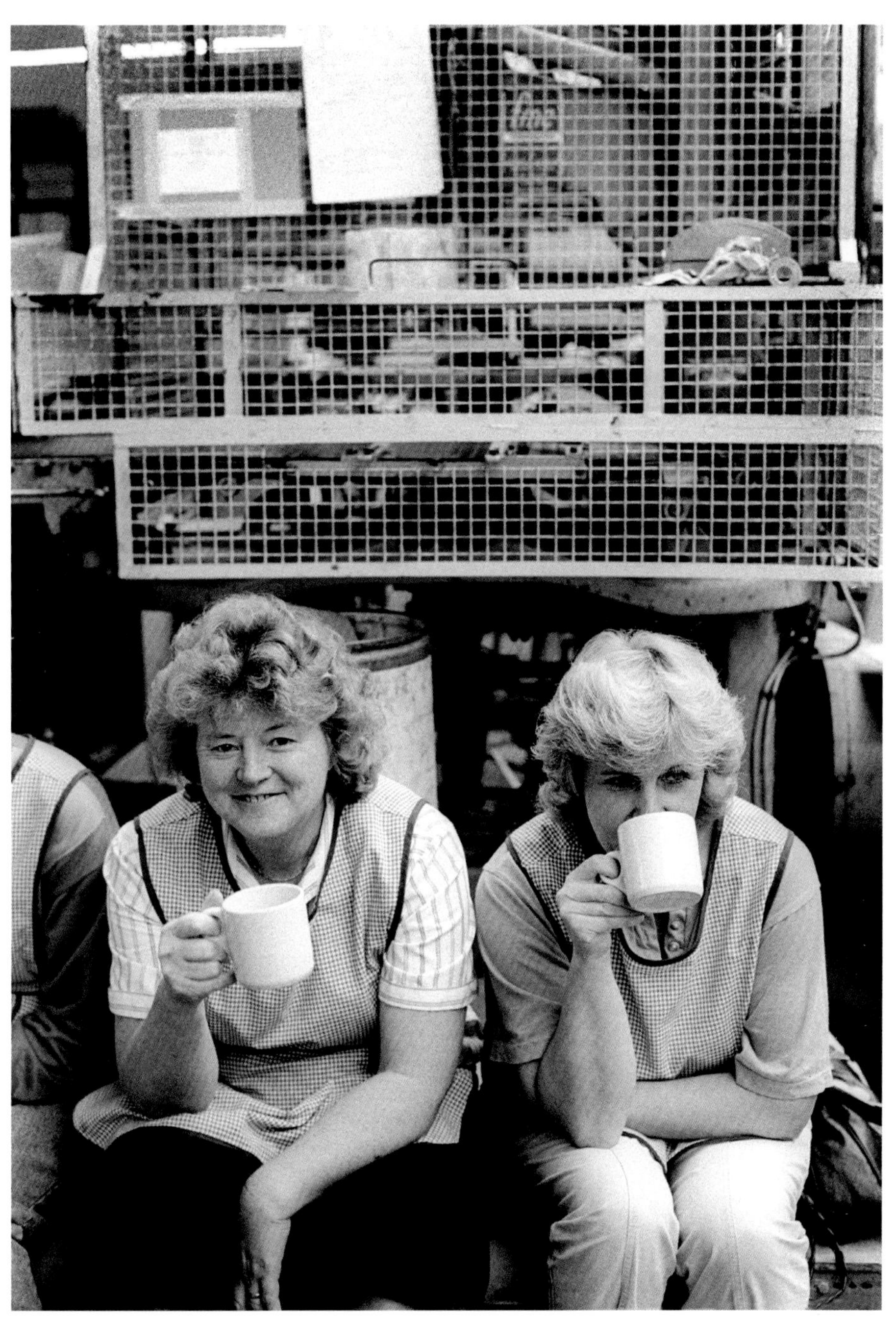

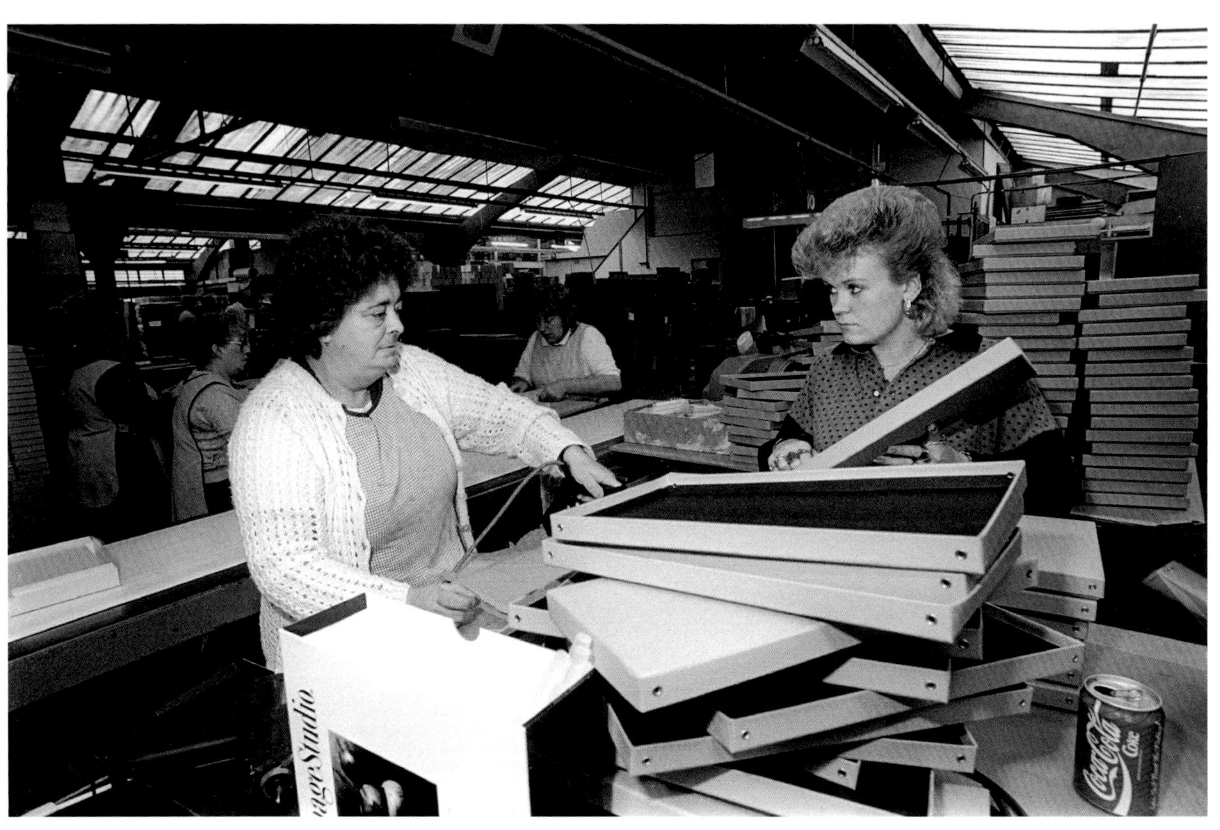

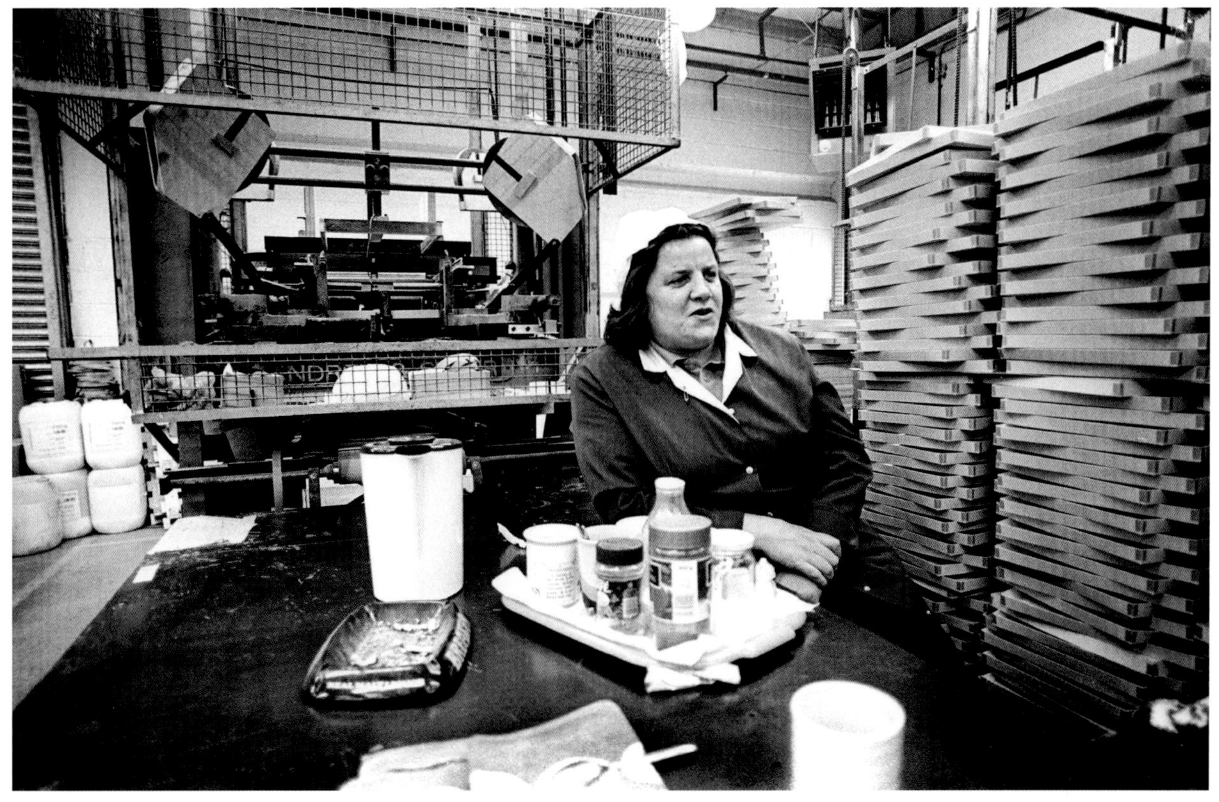

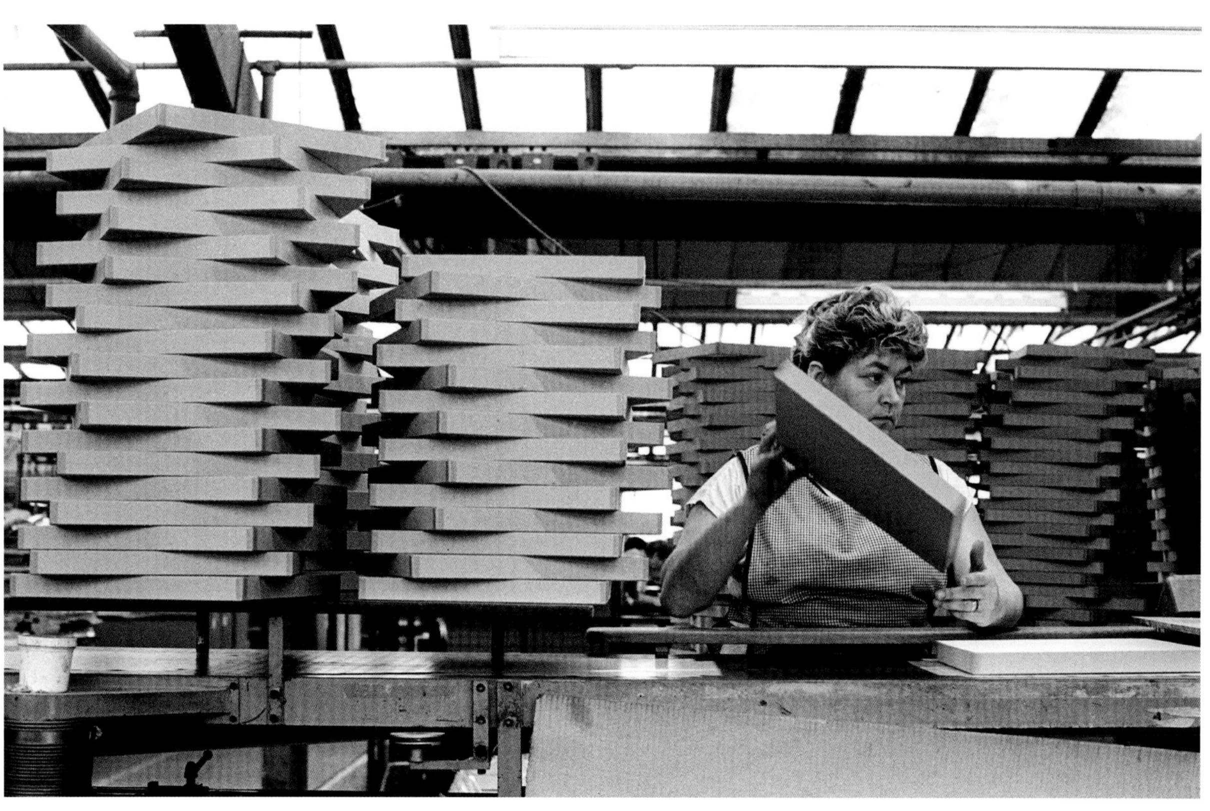

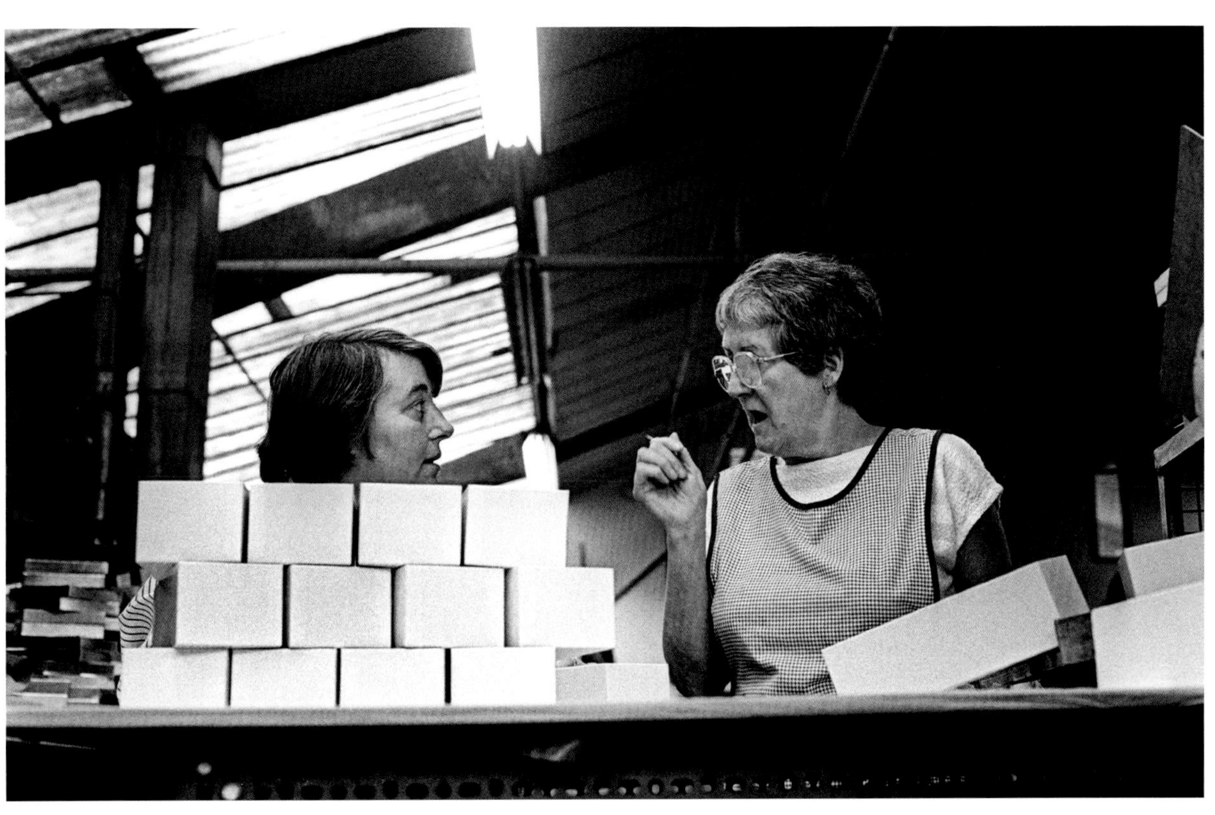

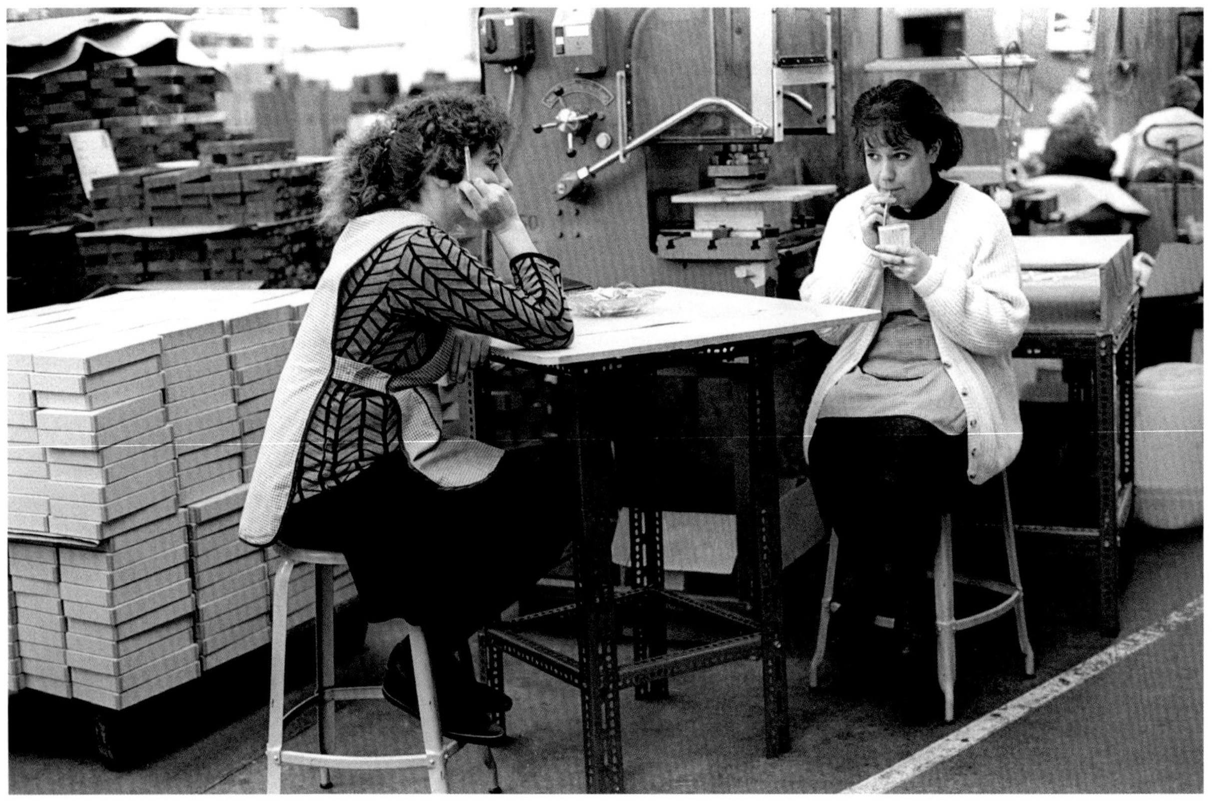

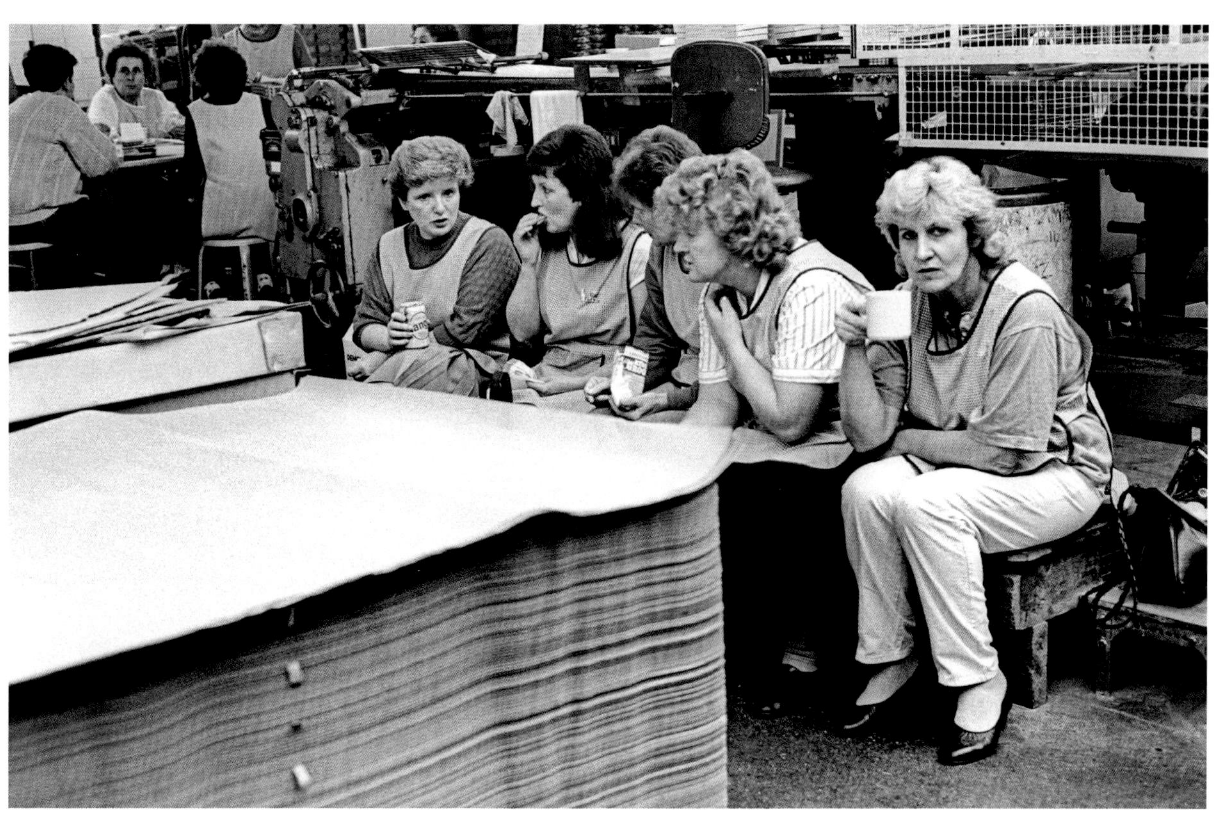

The London Fancy Box
Company, Dover

From the series, *Dover: A
Port in a Storm*, 1989–90

Huw Davies
Home from Home

The British in the Pas-de-Calais, 1992–93

Like the Eighties our evening ended badly.

It seems hard to remember it all now – with unemployment at the three million mark and house repossessions at an all time high – but that's how it was. Back then.

Property prices in particular were going through the roof. Then, over half a million Londoners left the city for the country, forcing up the price of cottages and making them unaffordable for locals. Farmyards became barn conversions. Fields became 'The Paddocks.' Commuters replaced countrymen; Porsches took the place of pigs; leisure of land-work. Already the English countryside was owned by the well-off, but now it became colonised by the mass of the middle class.

And as rural England became occupied, France was the new frontier. In estate agents' lingo it was the 'New England' and Nord Pas-de-Calais was re-christened South Kent.

Between 1992 and 1993 Davies travelled to the Pas-de-Calais and documented the lives of British citizens who had recently relocated to France. The accompanying text is an excerpt from *Toujours Calais* by Nigel Duckers. Both text and images were commissioned by the CCPM.

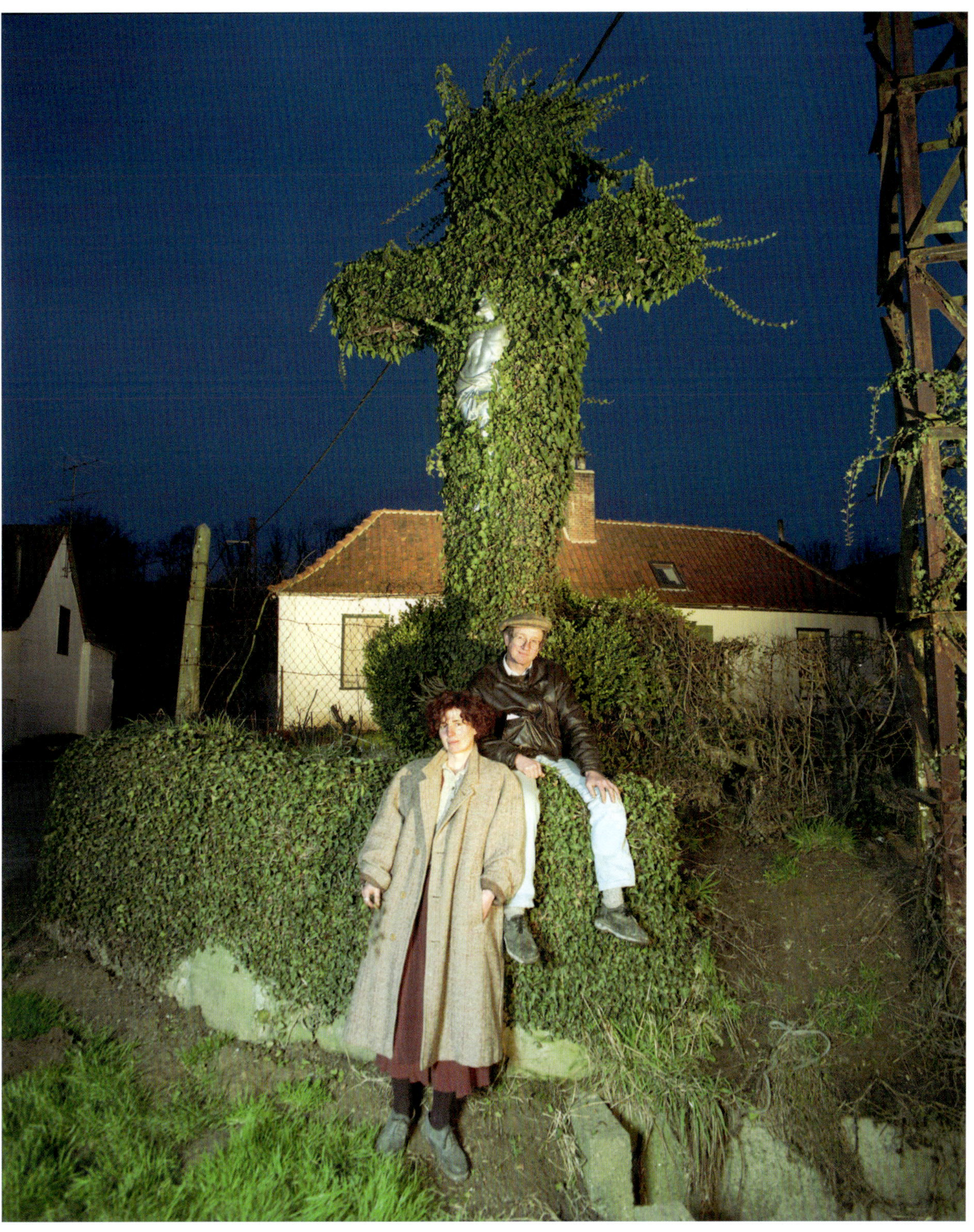

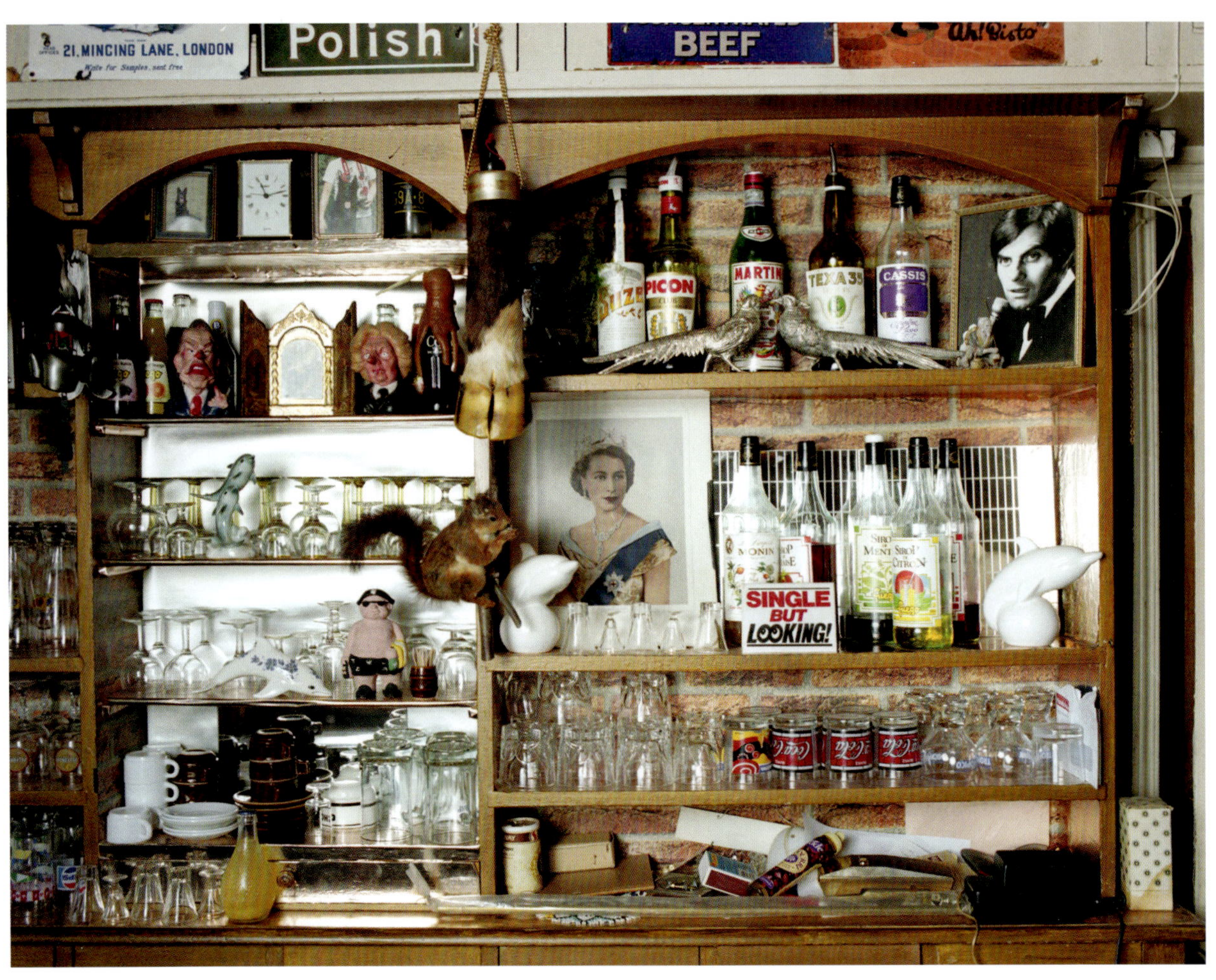

21, MINCING LANE, LONDON
Polish
BEEF
Ah! Bisto
SINGLE
BUT
LOOKING!

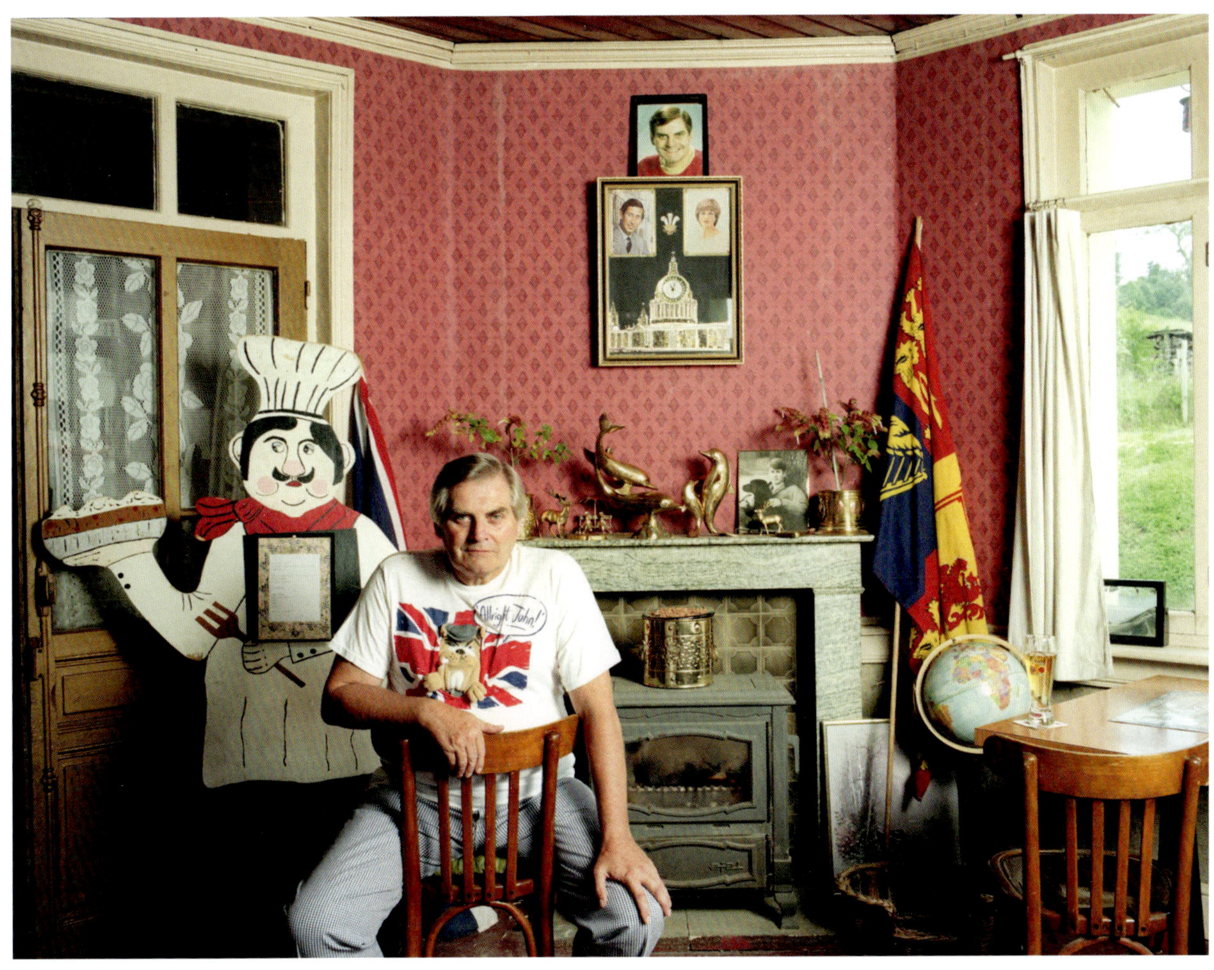

73

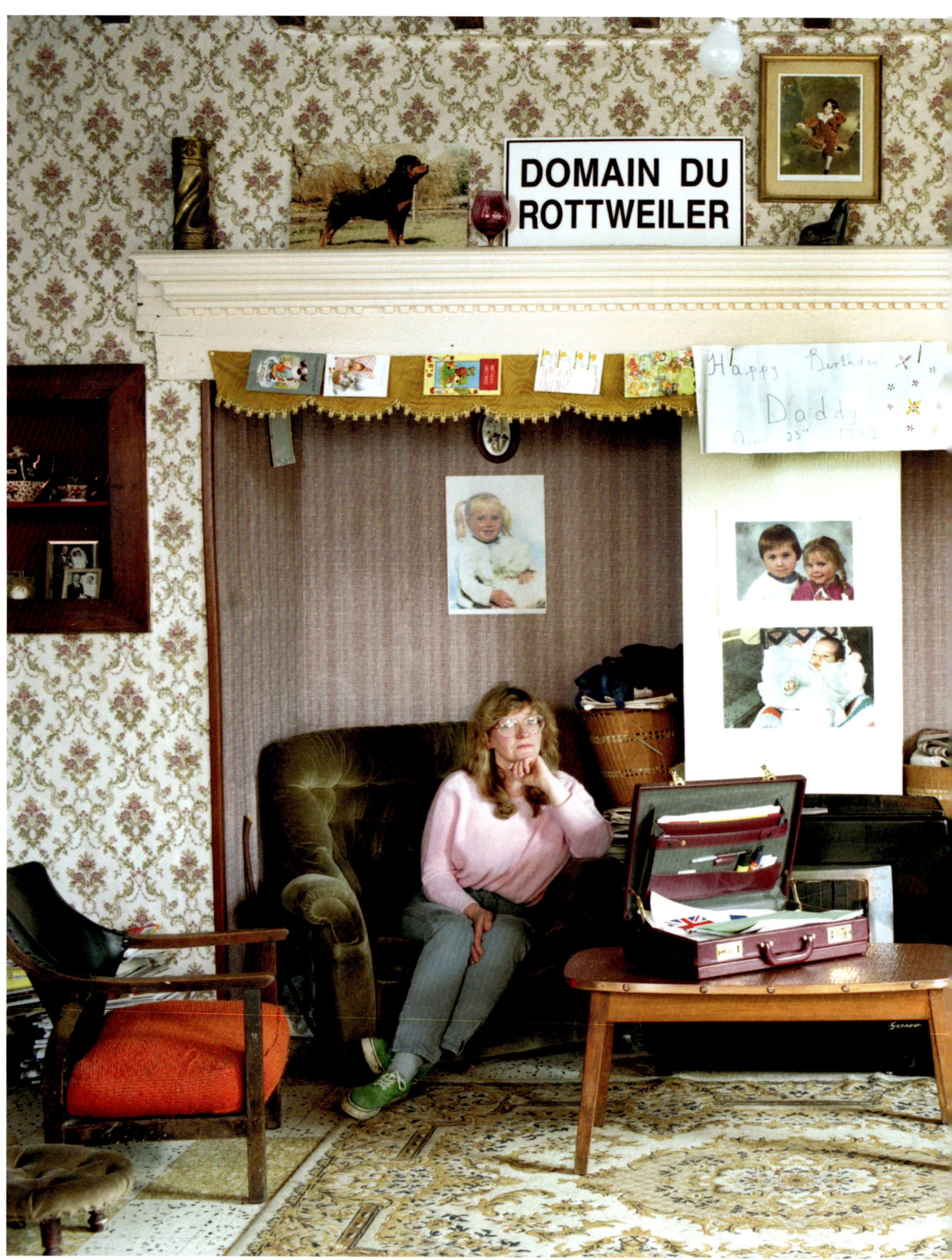
DOMAIN DU
ROTTWEILER
Happy Birthday
Daddy

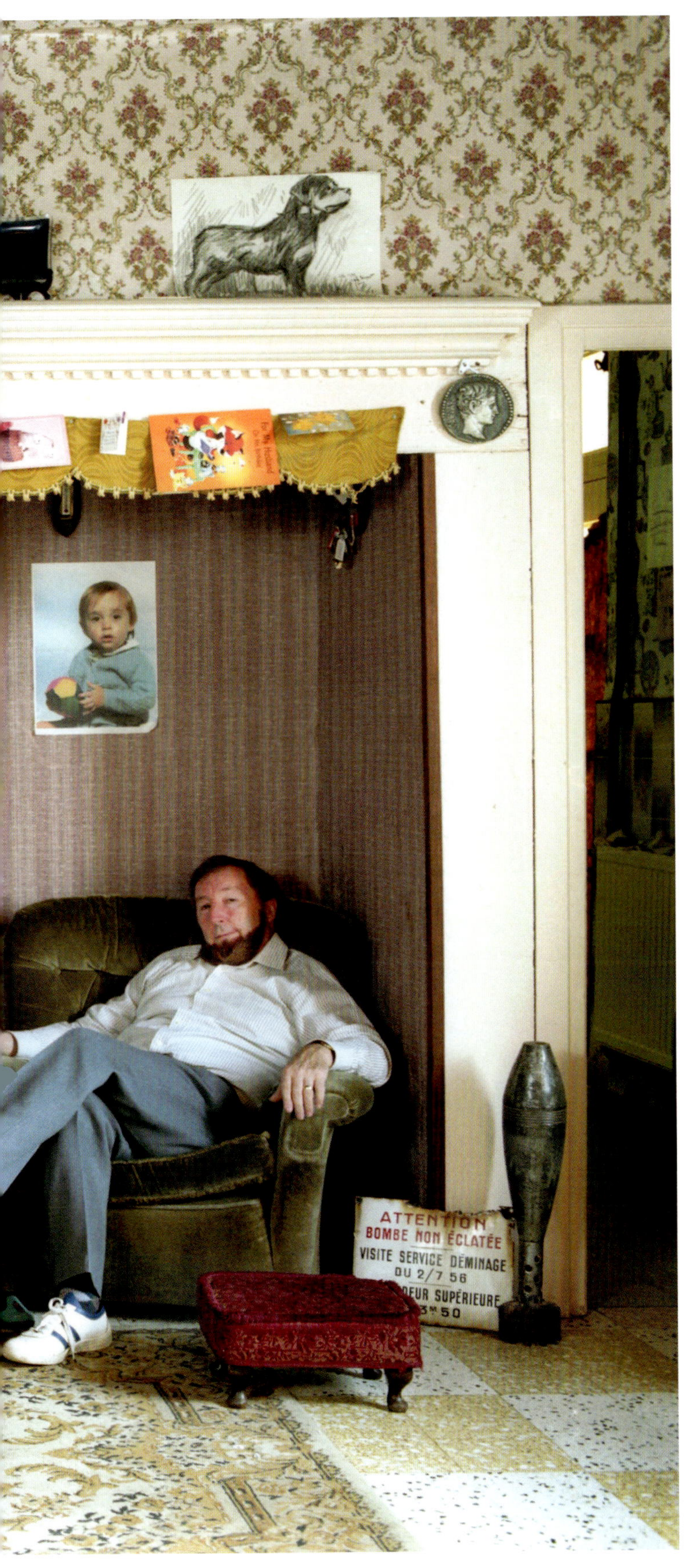
ATTENTION
BOMBE NON ÉCLATÉE
VISITE SERVICE DÉMINAGE
DU 2/7 56
...EUR SUPÉRIEURE
...3M 50

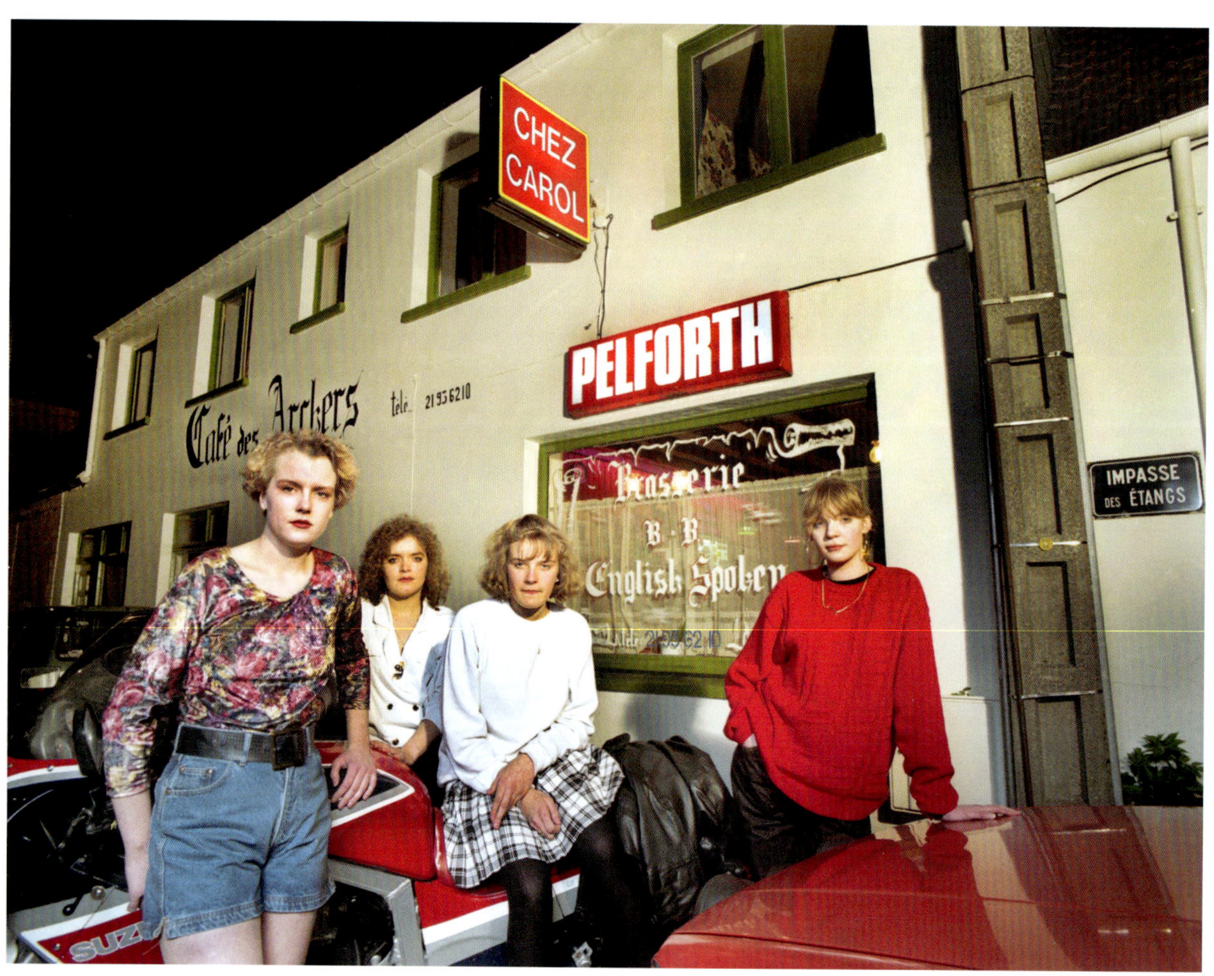

CHEZ
CAROL
PELFORTH
Café des Ateliers
tele. 21 95 62 10
Brasserie
B.B.
English Spoken
IMPASSE
DES ÉTANGS
SUZ

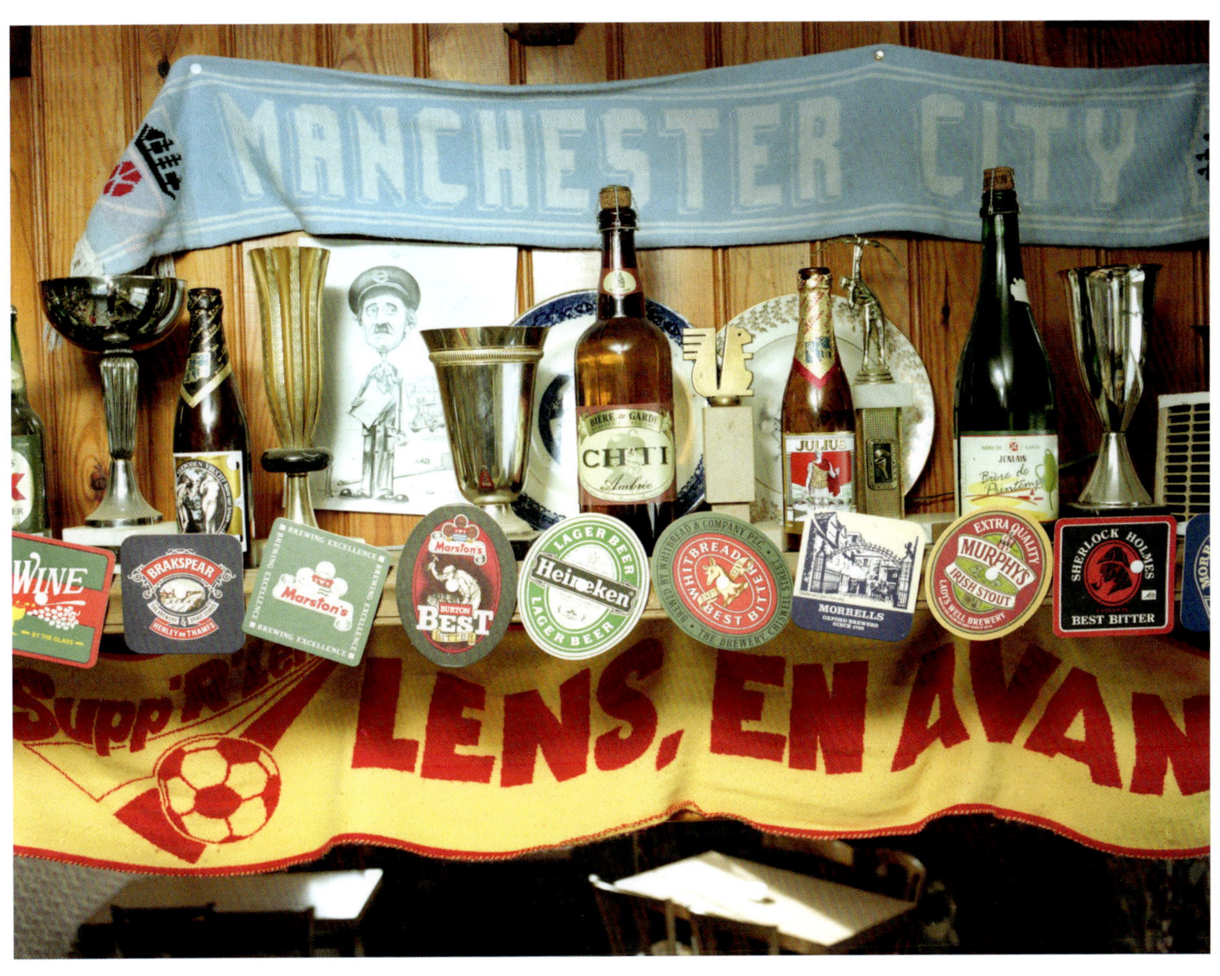
MANCHESTER CITY
WINE
BRAKSPEAR
Marston's
BURTON BEST BITTER
Heineken
LAGER BEER
WHITBREAD BEST BITTER
MORRELLS
MURPHY'S IRISH STOUT
EXTRA QUALITY
SHERLOCK HOLMES
BEST BITTER
BIÈRE de GARDE
CH'TI
Ambrée
JULIUS
Bière de Printemps
Supp'R
LENS, EN AVAN

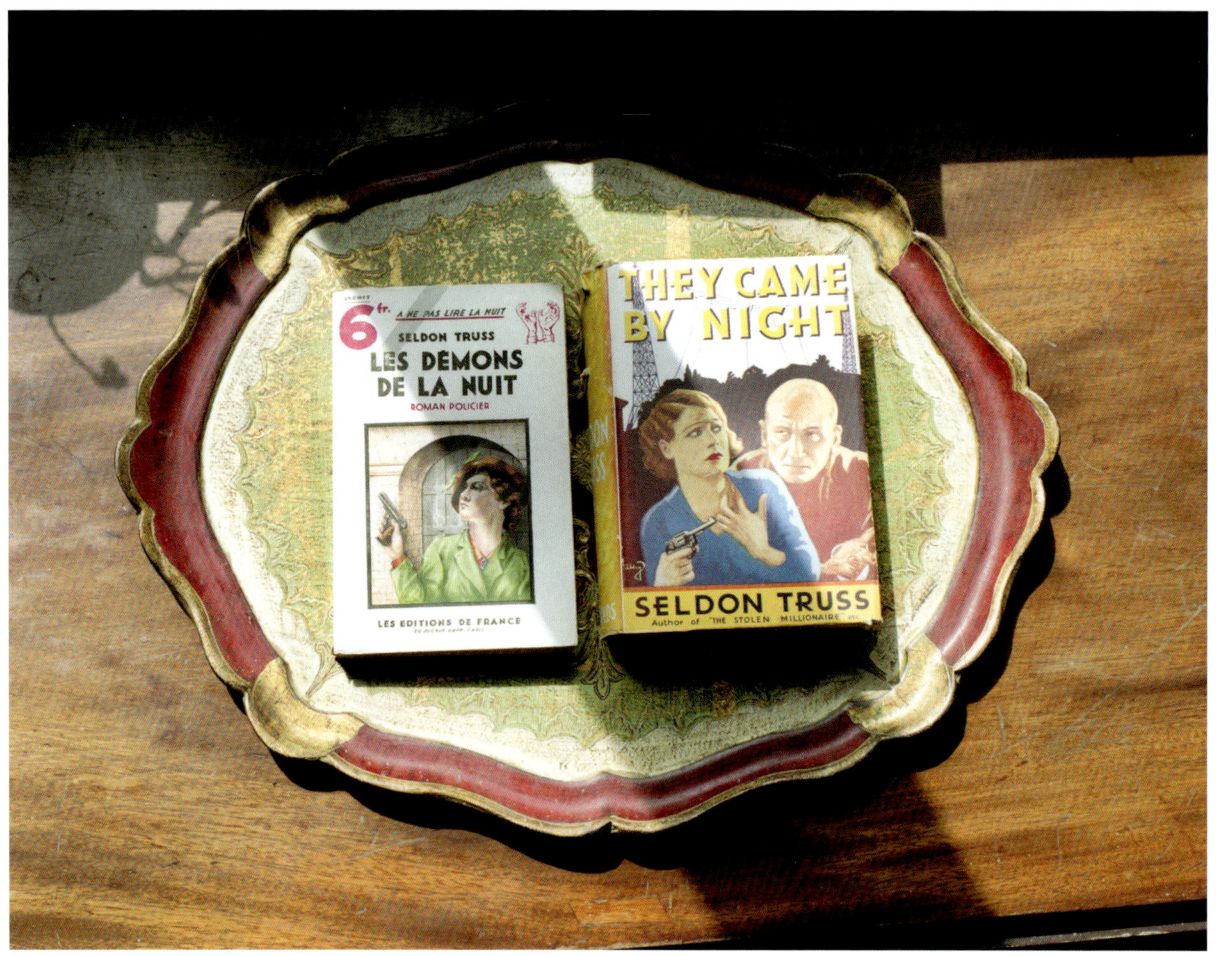

From the series, *Home from Home*, 1992–93

Film-makers Judy Marle & Nick Gifford, St Remy au Bois. 1993

Detail, Bar Dolphin, Enquin-sur-Baillons. 1992

Peter Dolphin, Publican, Enquin-sur-Baillons. 1992

Paul & Janet Jones, Estate Agents & Rottweiler Breeders, Setques. 1992

Sally & Lucy Best with French Friends, Café Archers, Houlle. 1992

Detail in Bar, Houlle. 1992

Detail in House, St Sylvestre. 1992

Postscript
Neal Ascherson, 2018

When the Channel Tunnel opened in 1994, a brilliant new day seemed to be rising over the sparkling water, the green turf of Kent, and the white cliffs of Dover. 25 years on how different the weather has become! At the time of writing, the United Kingdom is mere months from its tragic rupture from the EU. A stormy darkness seems to have closed over England, while the coast of France, veiled by angry squalls, is becoming hard to see.

My hope back then was that the Channel Tunnel would allow England to become more European, and thereby – paradoxically – even more English. This connected-up England would slowly regain its ancient self-confidence and its sense of nationhood, as membership of the EU blurred the outlines of an increasingly unconvincing British statehood. I welcomed the Tunnel as a sort of drain, down which the harmful vestiges of Great British imperialism would slowly flow.

It hasn't happened like that. Instead, the mixture of grievances that is fuelling new populist movements globally took a particular form in England – a wish to 'take back control' from supposedly remote lawmakers in Brussels who, among other offences, subjected the entirety of the United Kingdom to the free movement of people. This was, note well, not a *British* wave of emotion: although Wales also narrowly voted Leave, Northern Ireland and, above all, Scotland strongly demanded to remain in the EU. Thus, the vote for Brexit was essentially an expression of English national feeling. It derived from a well-justified hunger for democracy – a resentment of metropolitan elites and their economic policies – but was skilfully diverted from London to target Brussels, appealing to an 'embers of empire' feeling that the UK was more than merely a medium-sized nation-state like so many others.

I wasn't entirely misguided in my optimism, though. During the past 25 years, the southeast of England, at least, has become much more familiar with northern France. Why fly to reach the Dordogne when you can drive to a resort on the Somme River? Contemporaneously, there was massive French immigration to England. The sight of a French family whose breadwinner commuted between the City of London and a handsome Kentish manor house became common. So did the appearance of young French men and women behind the bars of London's pubs, returning to Paris every other weekend through the Tunnel.

The hope I expressed in the introduction to *Soundings*: 'The Undermining of Britain' – that a new closeness to Europe would gradually dissolve the archaic British state and help its component nations, and England above all, to modernise themselves and enrich their identities – has not dissipated. But now we have to ask how many of the Tunnel's achievements will survive Brexit and the potential restrictions on free travel and trade that it may bring about. I remain a guarded optimist. Even the most rabid Europhobe is not going to put a cork in the Tunnel. The past 25 years have changed Kent profoundly, restoring its ancient intimacy with northwest Europe. Now it is up to young people on either side of the Channel to organise and insist that this intimacy remains and grows.

Now

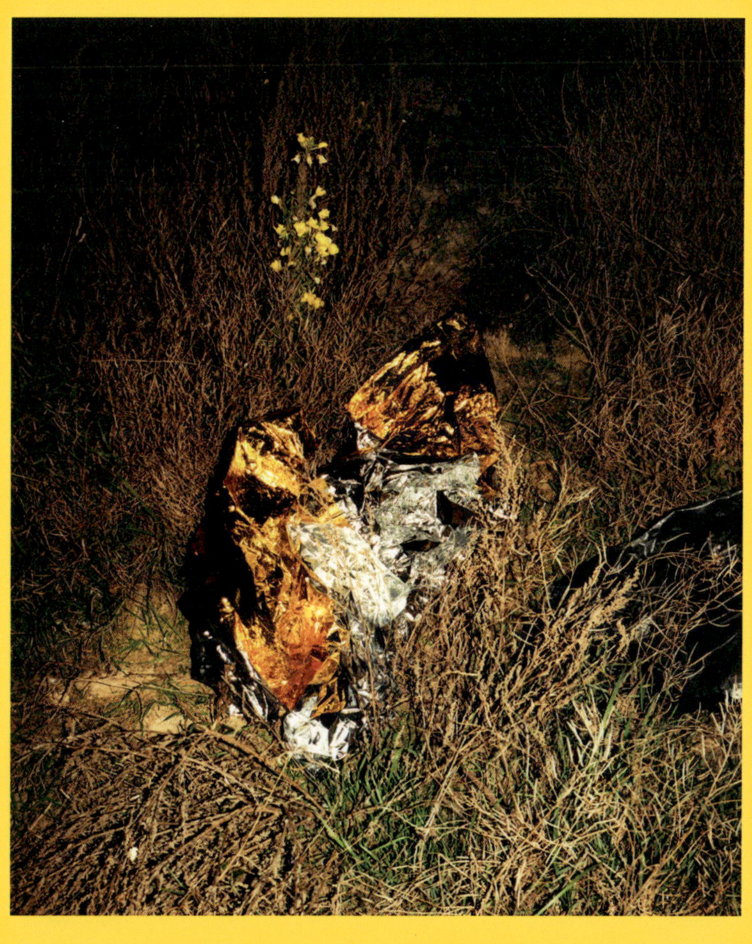

TEXT
A NEW EUROPE
Shoair Mavlian, 2019

IMAGES
Harley Weir
Tereza Červeňová

The eighth Brighton Photo Biennial brought together the work of eighteen international artists, including solo presentations by Heather Agyepong, Bill Brandt, Teresa Červeňová, Aikaterini Gegisian, Uta Kögelsberger, Émeric Lhuisset, Robin Maddock, Hrair Sarkissian, Harley Weir, and Donovan Wylie. With the ambiguous title *A New Europe*, the intention was not to predict the future. Rather, the aim was to acknowledge the present state of flux and to ask broad and open questions in an attempt to understand how we got to this point. How do geographical landscapes shape national identity? How has the geography of Europe, surrounded by sea, been used to convey the refugee crisis? How has photography helped to shape national and supranational identity? The following text gives an overview of various artists' perspective on these questions and our current predicament.

Immediately after the EU referendum in June, 2016, Belfast-based artist Donovan Wylie began to explore ideas of family dynamics and fractured relationships as a way to understand the UK's current situation. Inspired by Virginia Woolf's 1927 novel *To the Lighthouse*, which investigates the complexities of seeing, loss, and the passage of time, Wylie photographs the afterglow of distant lighthouses to process the tensions and complexities of identity and isolation. By photographing a singular lighthouse in France, as seen from the opposing coastline in Dover, Wylie confronts the physical barriers created by the sea. The images simultaneously represent closeness and distance, interrogating how the isolation of the landscape contributes to under-standing British national identity. That Britain is an island is crucial to its history, with the natural barrier created by sea acting both as a protectant but also as an impetus to develop a strong naval tradition, which was integral to Britain's history of colonisation. However, does the isolation of the island landscape also come with limits? From Wylie's vantage, the French coastline – and by extension the European mainland – across the Channel is just 21 miles away, visible as a flicker of light but equally unattainable.

In some ways, the view from England to France is not too dissimilar from the view from Turkey to Greece, or from Morocco to Spain, pairs of nations separated only by small bodies of water. In the latter two examples, however, the gulfs between the two countries are significantly more difficult to bridge. These seas and others around the periphery of Europe have come to symbolically embody the refugee crisis. In an image from the series *L'Autre Rive*, Émeric Lhuisset illustrates in one frame the gap between the EU and non-EU states of Greece and Turkey. Inspired by a story told by his grandmother, who was one of many Europeans who escaped to North Africa during World War II (a small detail of recent history we seem to have forgotten), *L'Autre Rive* documents Lhuisset's migrant friends within the privacy of their daily lives – people who are both part of Europe's future and future Europeans. Interested in the physical properties of the photographic medium, Lhuisset printed the images as cyanotypes, but purposefully left them unfixed – and, therefore, unstable. The work thus evolves over time, with the images eventually transforming into blue monochromes, 'the blue of the sea into which so many vanish, but also the blue of Europe', as Lhuisset explains.

Harley Weir's work *Homes* celebrates the resourceful ingenuity of those living in the migrant and refugee camps of Calais, known informally as the Jungle. Taken immediately before and during the clearing of this provisional settlement by the French authorities in October, 2016, Weir's images emphasise the domestic and familiar against a backdrop of displacement and uncertainty. With

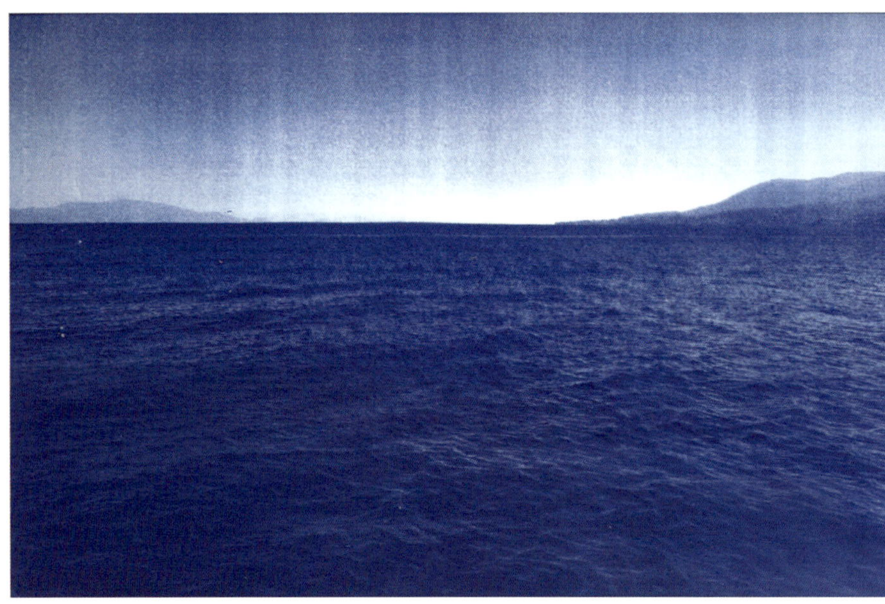

Émeric Lhuisset,
L'Autre Rive, Iraq, Turkey,
Greece, Germany, France,
Denmark, Syria, 2010–18

a background in fashion, Weir's photographs of Calais are sublime, capturing visually striking images amid horrendous conditions – an intentionally different perspective on a dire situation that has been photographed so often in recent years.

Much of the work made around the refugee crisis focuses on movement of people and their physical presence across Europe. Little is seen of where they came from or what is left behind. For *Homesick*, Hrair Sarkissian constructed and then destroyed an architecturally exact scale model of the apartment building in Damascus that his parents still live in (like many of their generation, they have refused to leave Syria). Sarkissian grew up in this building and lived there until he left Syria in 2008. To him, it represents more than just a house. Beyond providing shelter to his family, it's 'the place he belongs, a container for his memories, and a place for his family's collective identity'. *Homesick* confronts the fear of death in times of uncertainty. In an attempt to regain control, Sarkissian addresses his own nightmare and destroys his family home before anyone else has the chance, questioning whether we can fast-forward the present, acknowledge loss, and begin reshaping a collapsed history before the event has actually happened. There is a long and rich history of photographers striving to capture

and present representations of identity, and representations of national identity in particular. Examples include survey projects such as August Sander's *Face of our Time* (1929), which gives an overview of a specific time and place – namely Germany in the 1920s – or Bill Brandt's *The English at Home* (1936), in which he presents a series of stark contrasts between wealth and poverty. Born and raised in Germany, Brandt's images were taken from an outsider's perspective, in an attempt to understand and document his new surroundings. Brandt's photobook is often referred to as one of the first photographic attempts to capture English national identity. Nearly one hundred years on, his work begs the question: is England a fairer society today?

After the EU referendum, many photographers returned to the subject of national identity, embarking on journeys across the UK and Europe or exploring their local communities in an attempt to understand contemporary society. In his project *Nothing We Can't Fix by Running Away*, Robin Maddock attempts to build an egalitarian portrait of English national identity.

Whereas Maddock's project is restricted to England, in her project *June*, Tereza Červeňová takes a much more expansive approach. Born into a generation who has known nothing other than being part of the European project, with the ability to travel, study, work, and fall in love anywhere in Europe, for Červeňová the EU referendum signified something being snatched away. An autobiographhical response to the vote, which roughly coincided with the beginning of her MA at the Royal College of Art, Červeňová spent the following twenty-three months diaristically documenting daily life. Taken in various locations across Britain and Europe, each image is titled simply by location and date, the significance of which becomes apparent when read together. 'St James's Park, London 2nd July 2016': the date of London's first big anti-Brexit march. 'Nice, France, 14th July, Bastille Day, 2016': the date a truck was driven into celebratory crowds. 'Shadwell, London, 27th January, 2017': the date Donald Trump announced the so-called Muslim ban. 'Borough Market, London, 8th June, 2017': the date of the hastily called UK general election, but also five days after the terror attack at Borough Market. When viewed in retrospect, the work emerges as not only a record of daily events, but also a timeline of significant dates that will be, or have already been, etched into history.

The idea of *A New Europe* is as ambiguous as the continent itself. The Europe we know today was born out of the ashes of World War II: part peace project, part economic federation, part social experiment. It is both a geography and a social–ideological construct, fixed and moving. It has constructed a distinct identity from its rich and complicated make-up. It has expanded over the years, but is on the verge of contracting its borders for the first time. A fluid concept, like the sea which surrounds it, Europe will continue to reinvent itself and evolve, and, in the words of Virginia Woolf, 'We must wait for the future to show'.

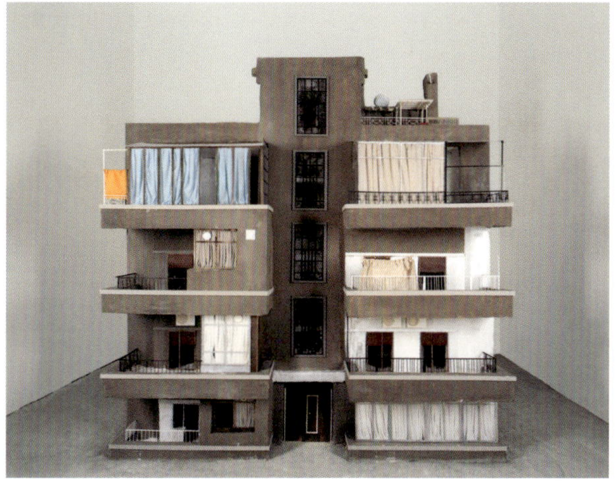
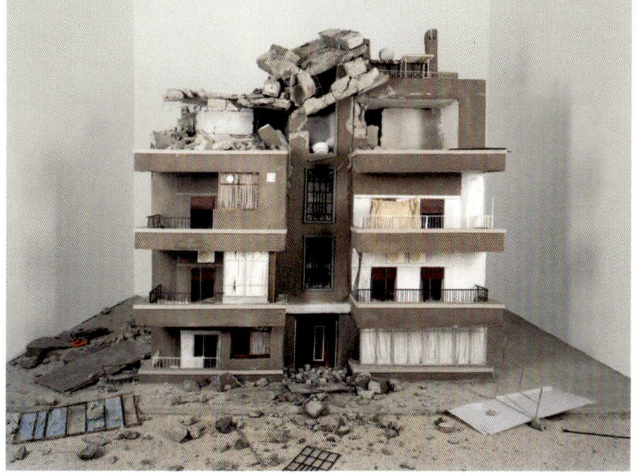

Hrair Sarkissian, *Homesick*, 2014

Harley Weir
Homes

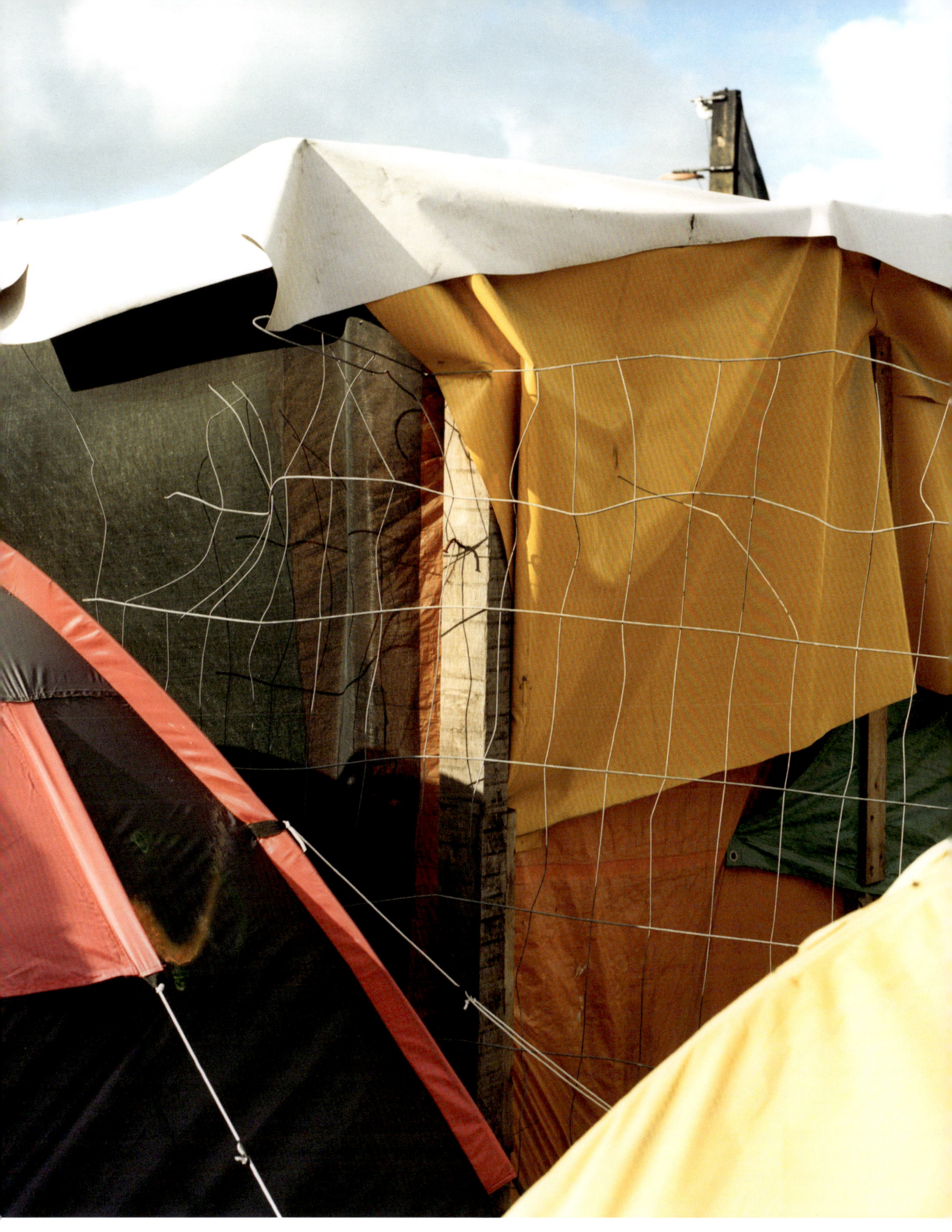

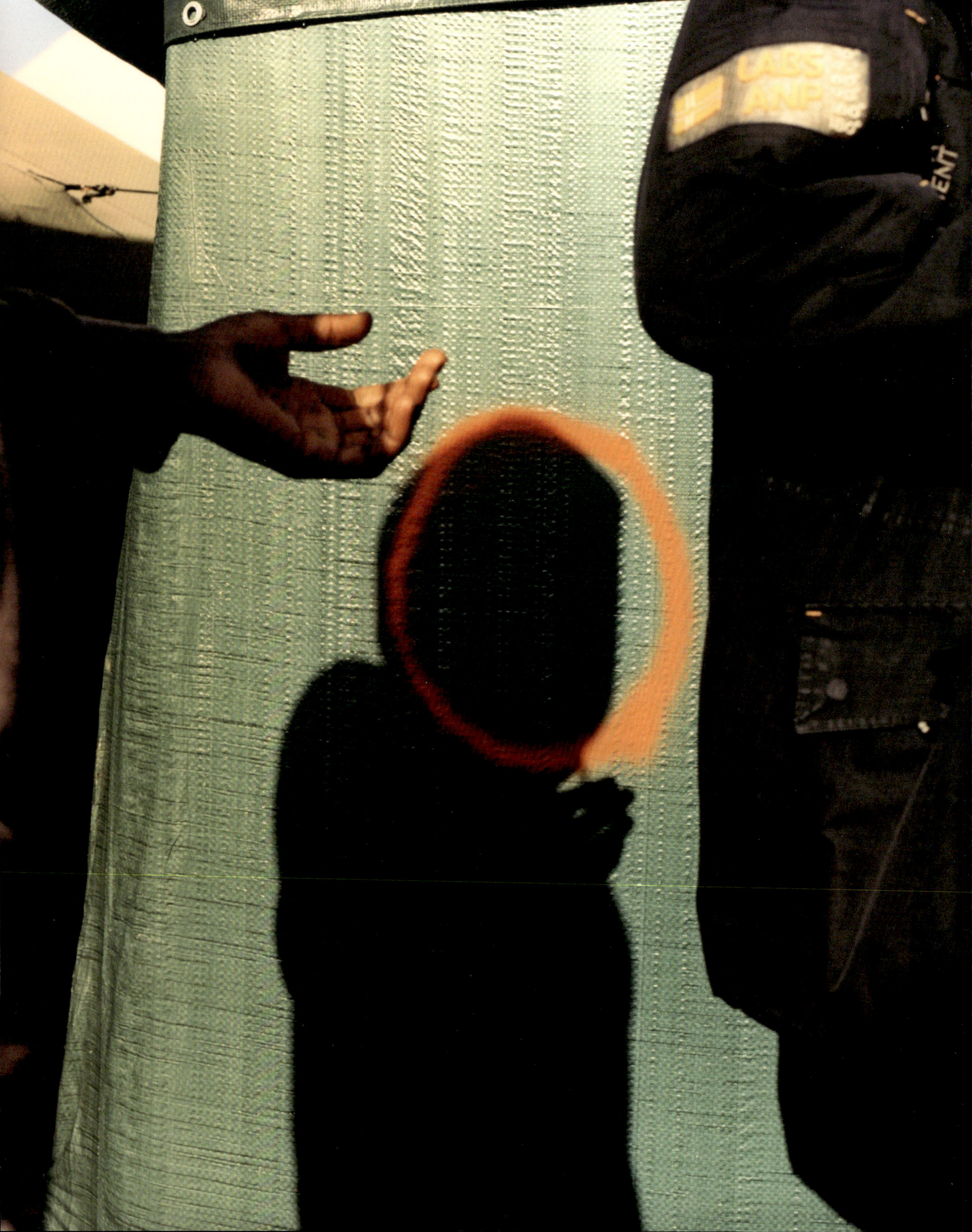

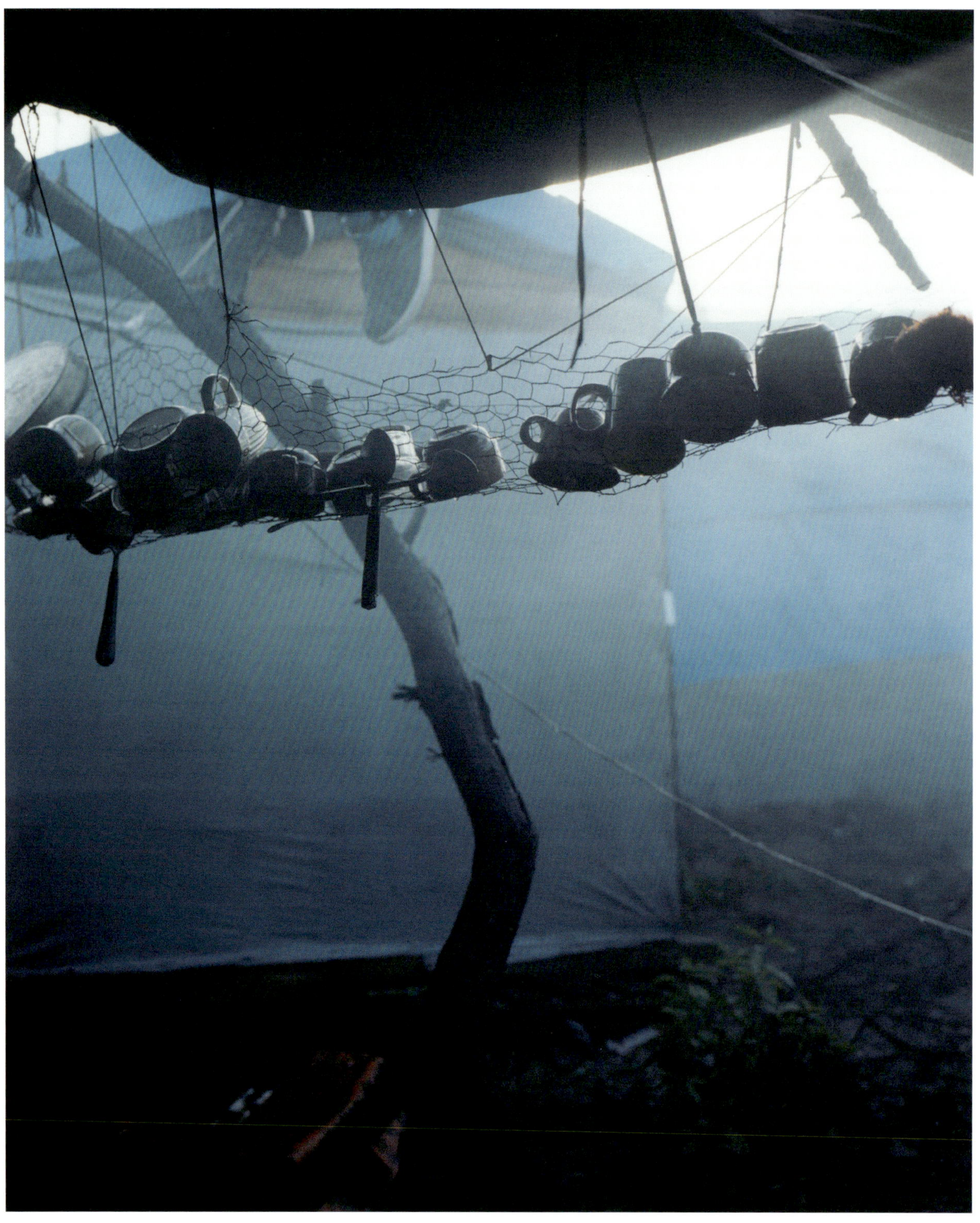

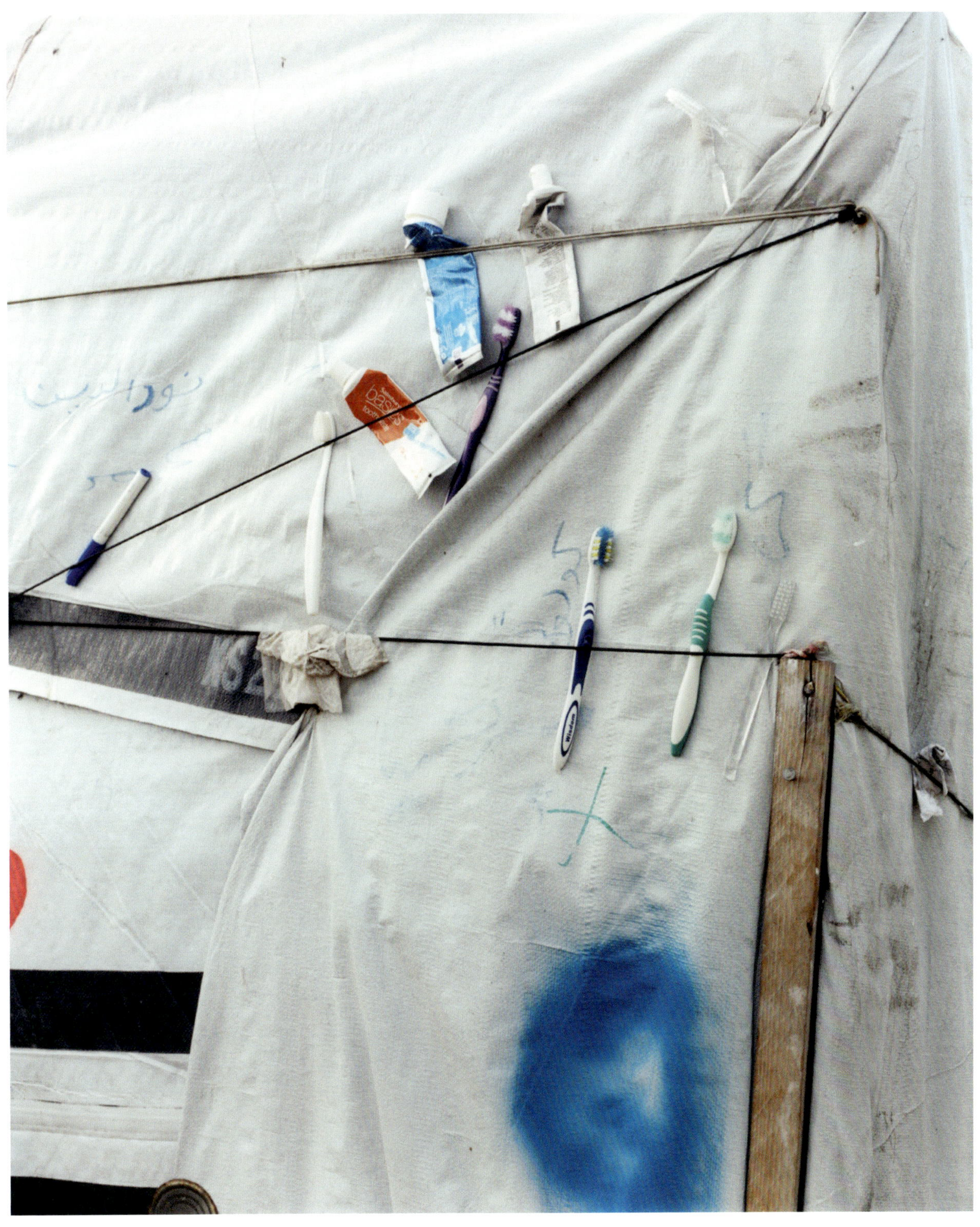

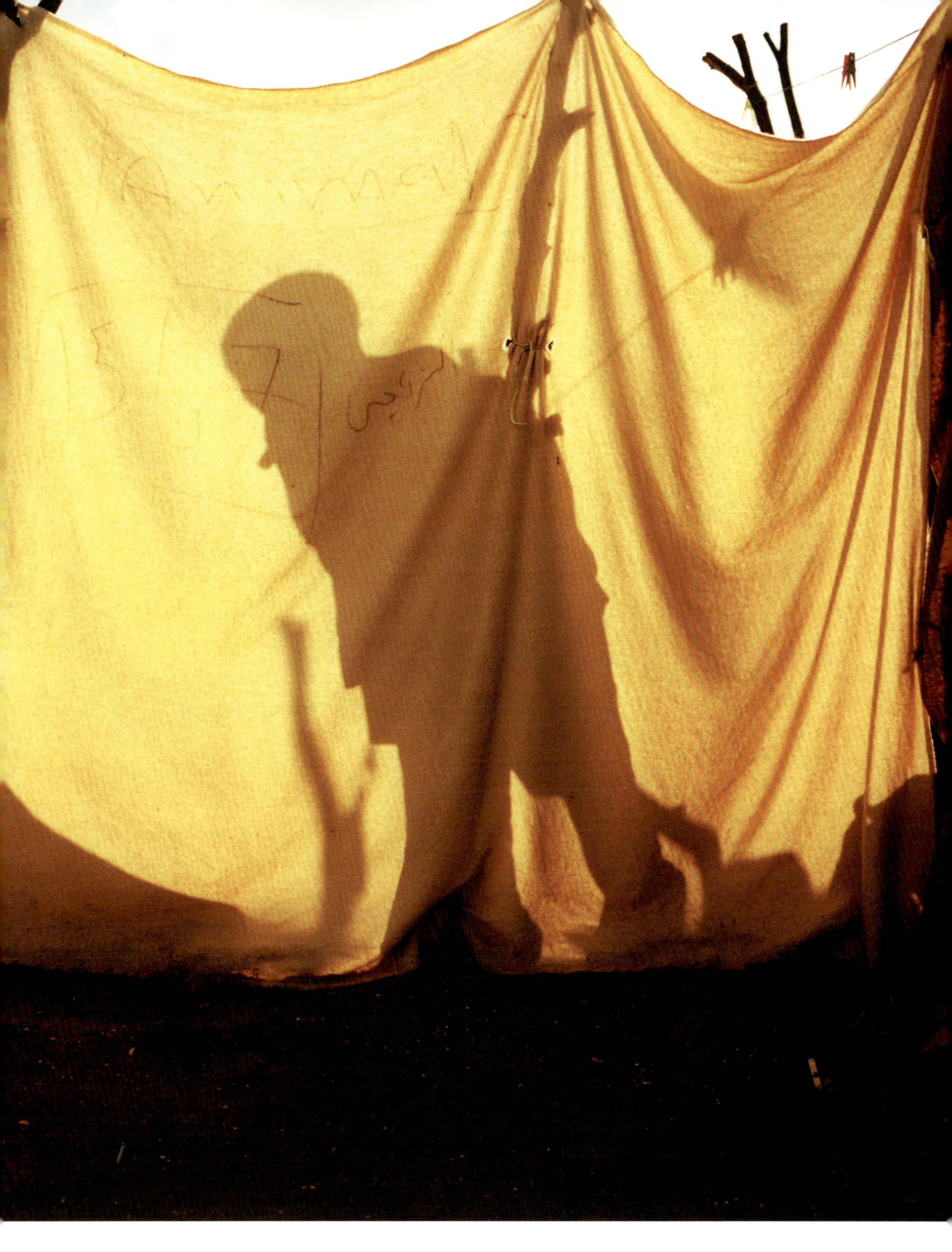

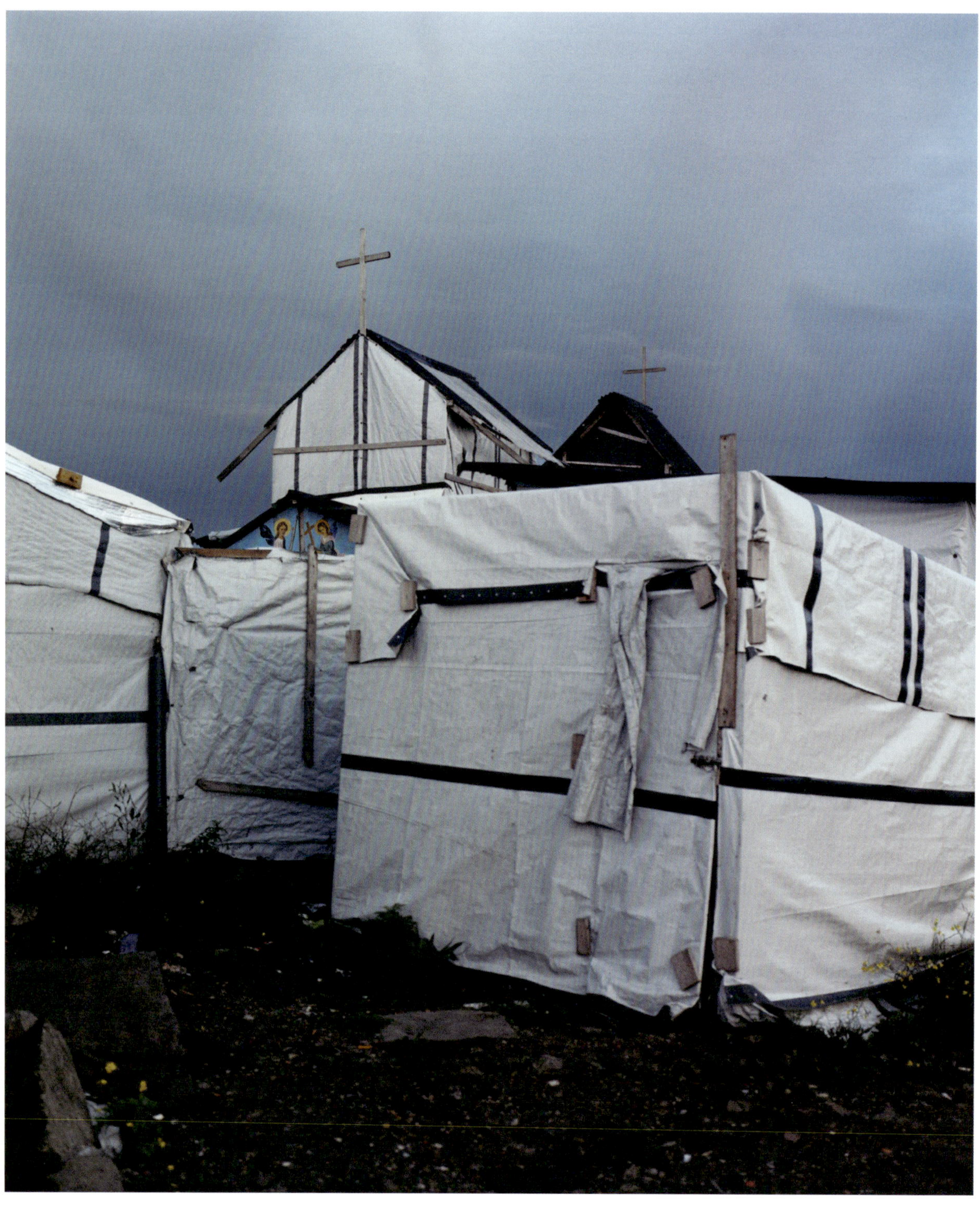

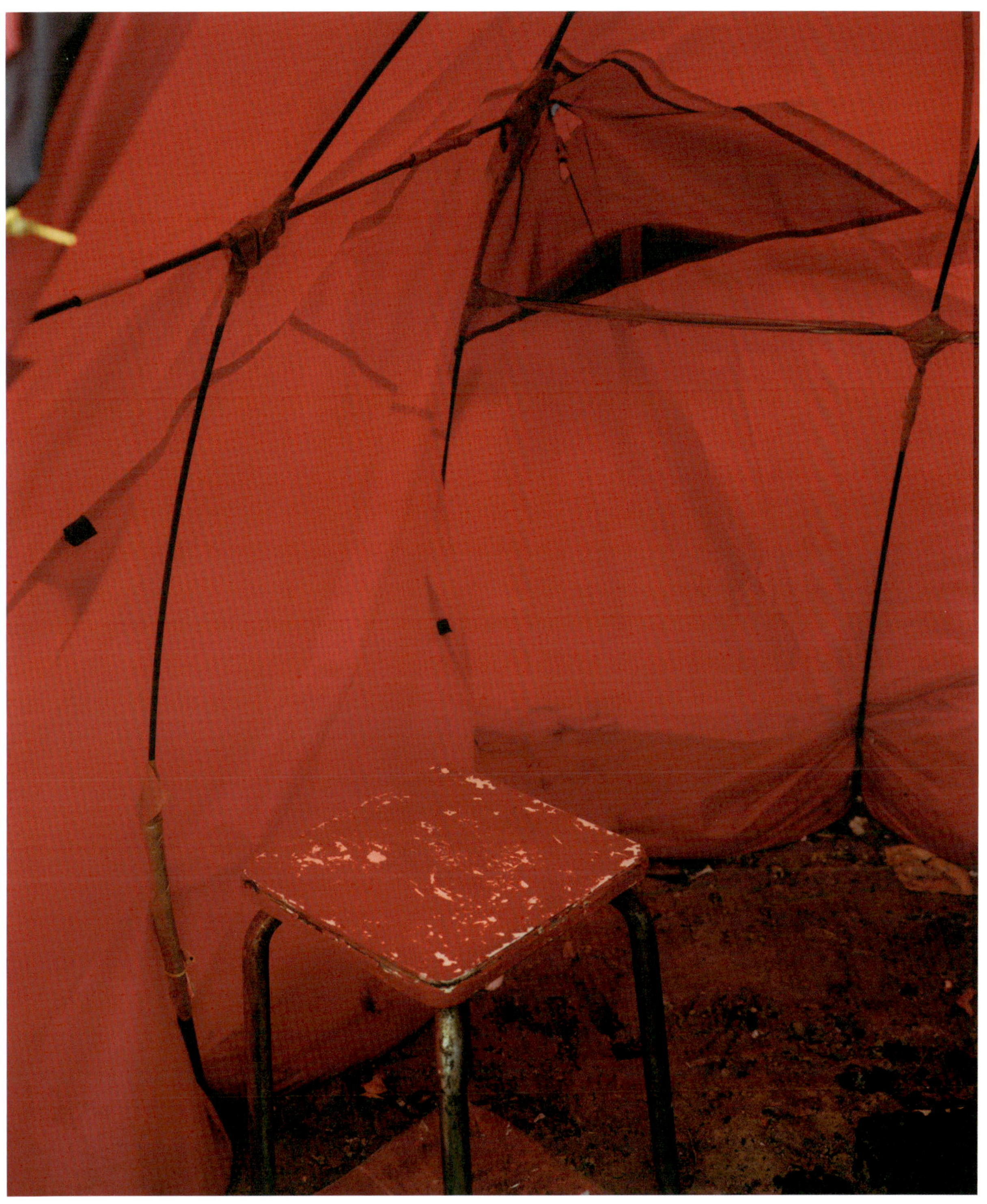

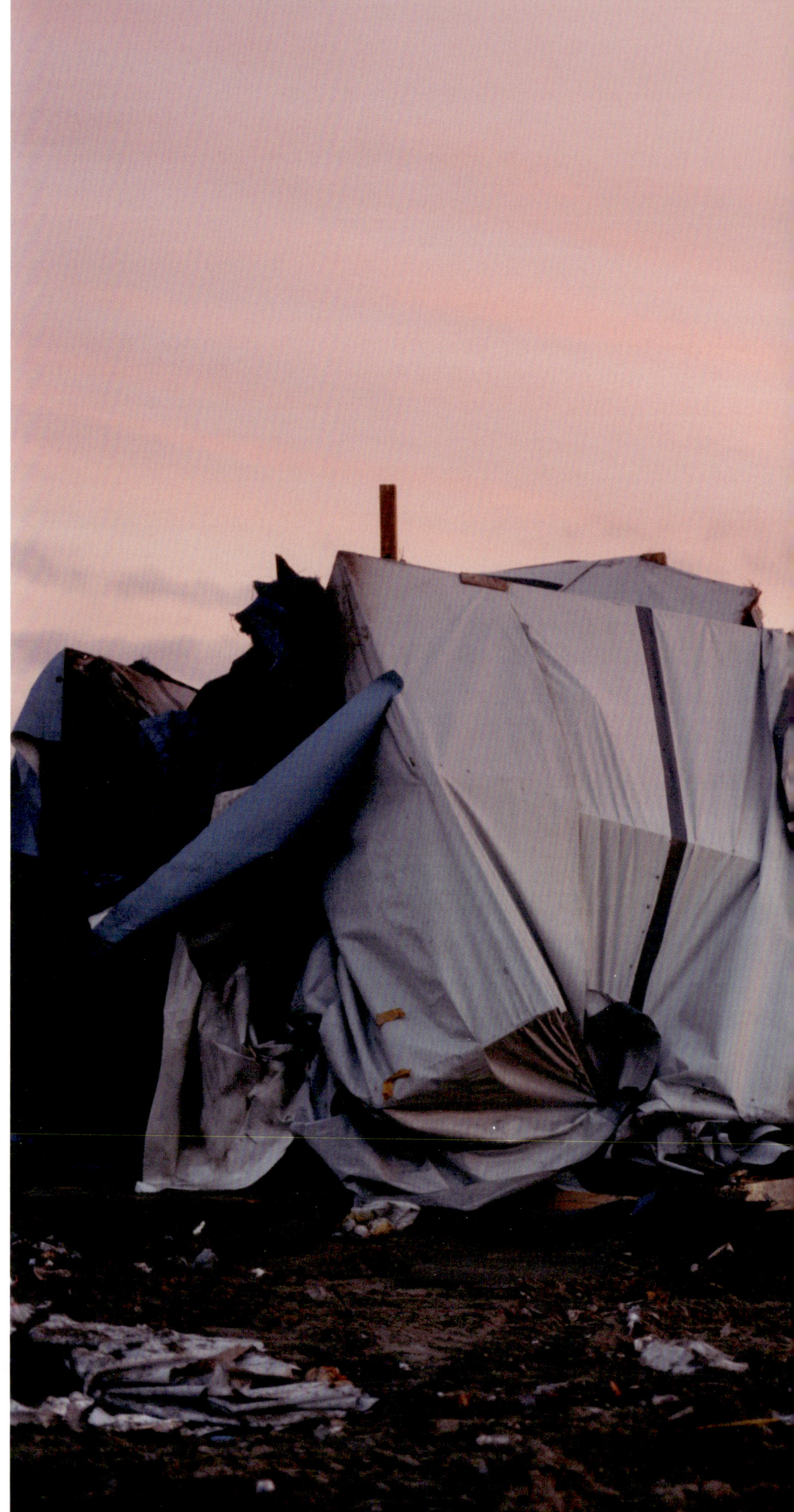

From the series,
Homes, 2016

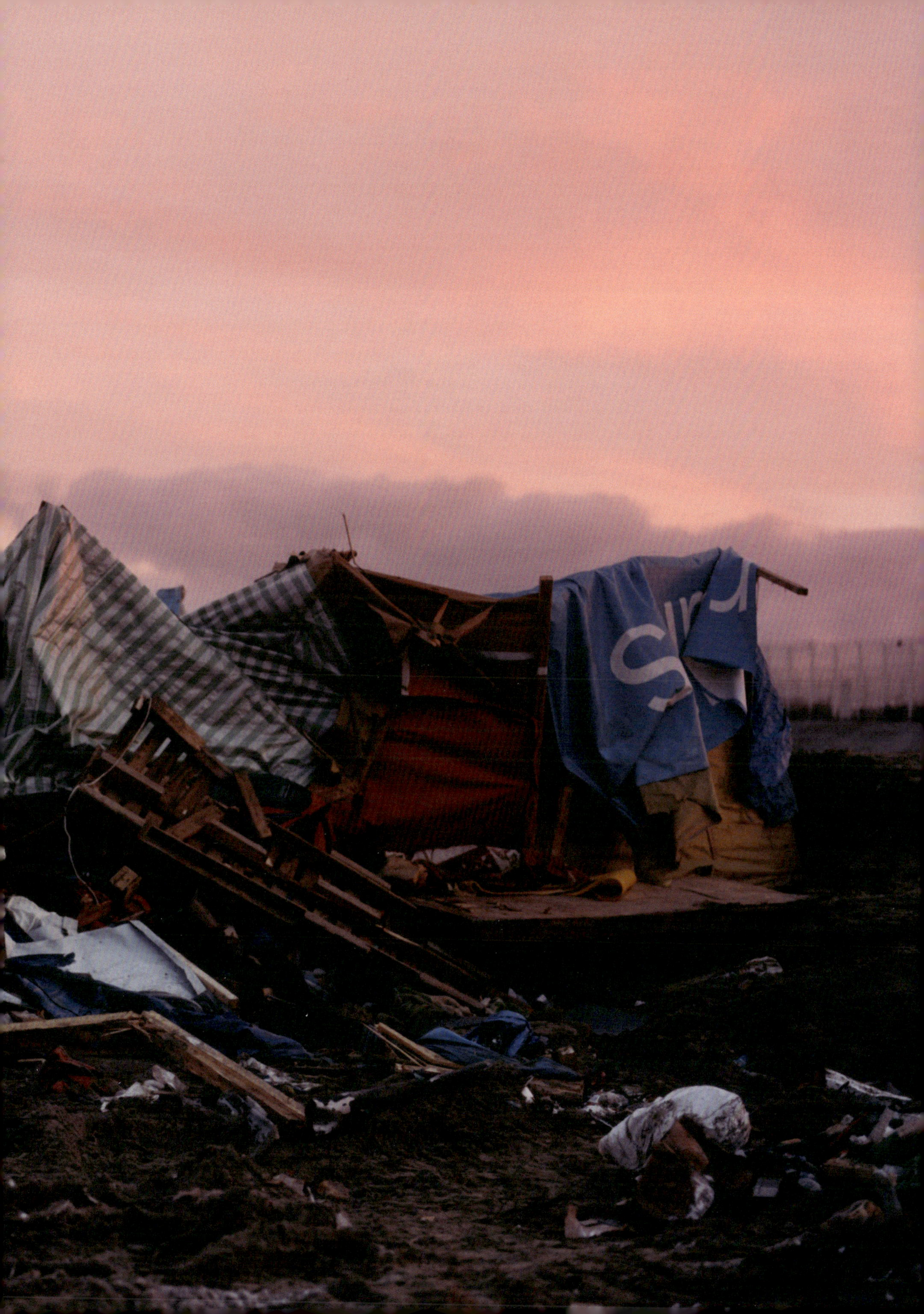

Tereza Červeňová
June

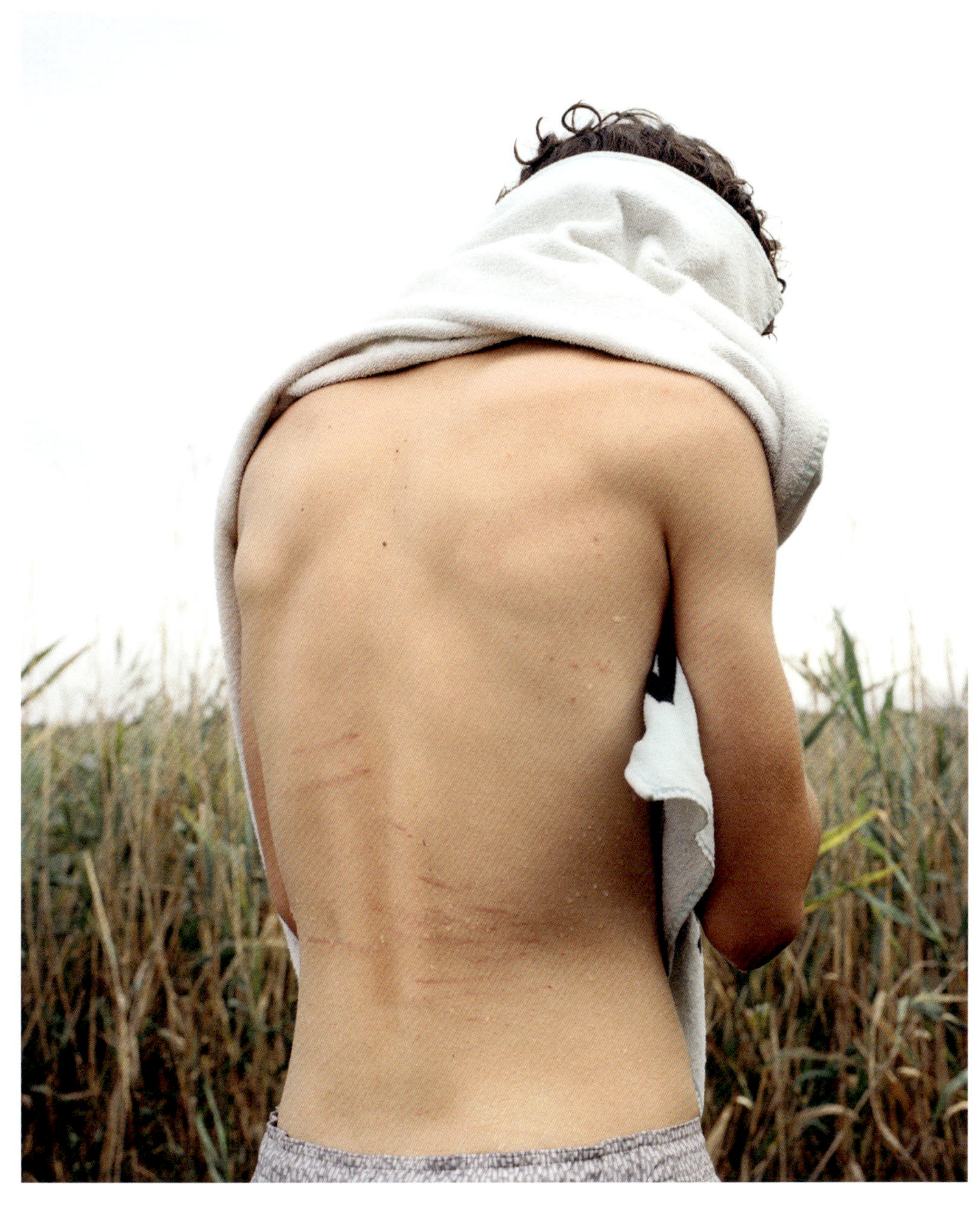

Tomky, Borský Svätý Jur, Slovakia
August, 2016

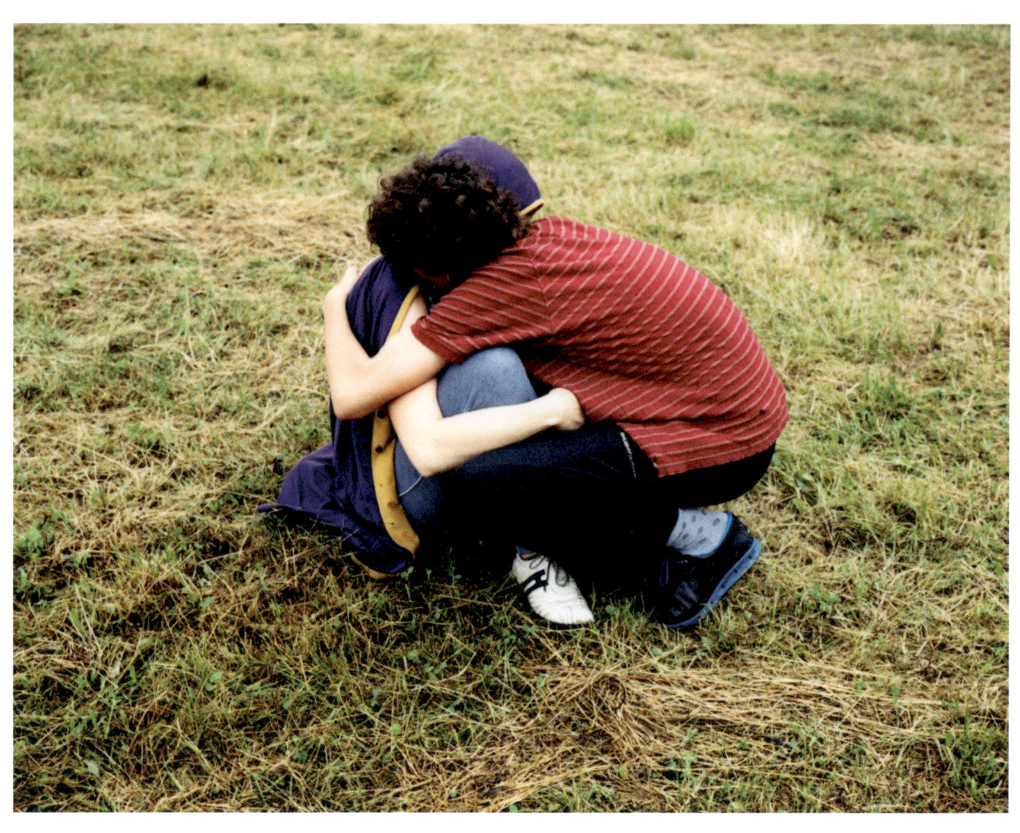

Dlhá nad Oravou, Slovakia
July, 2016

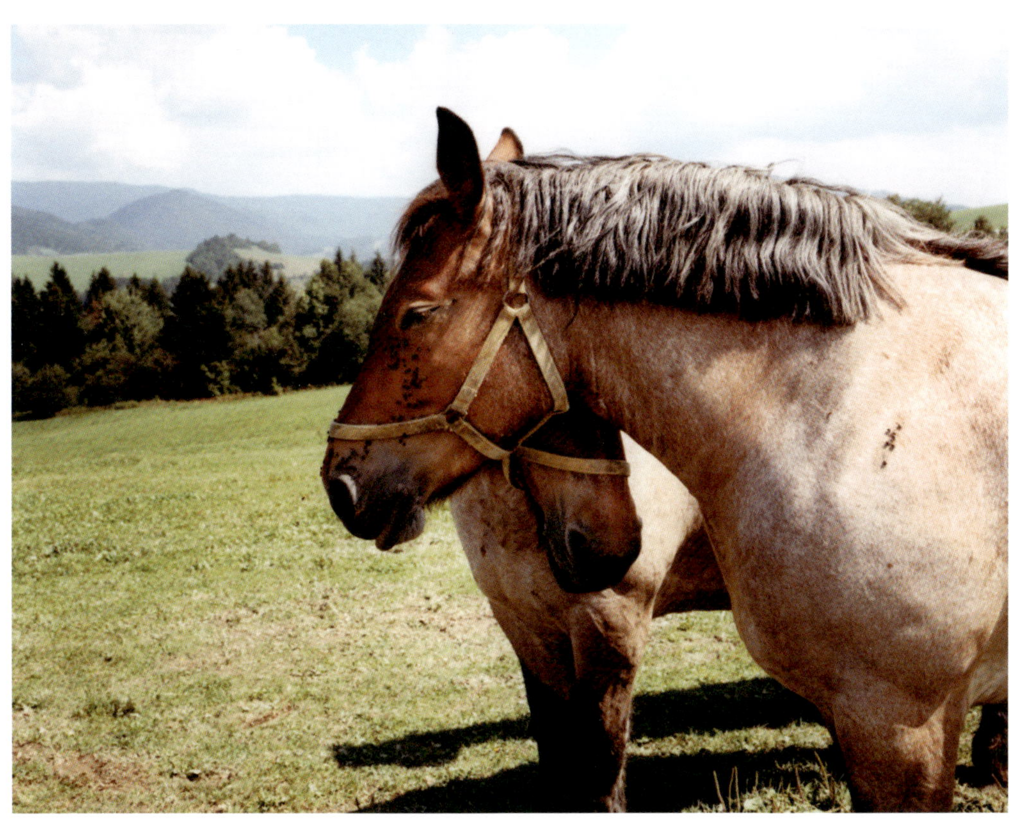

Terchová, Slovakia
July, 2016

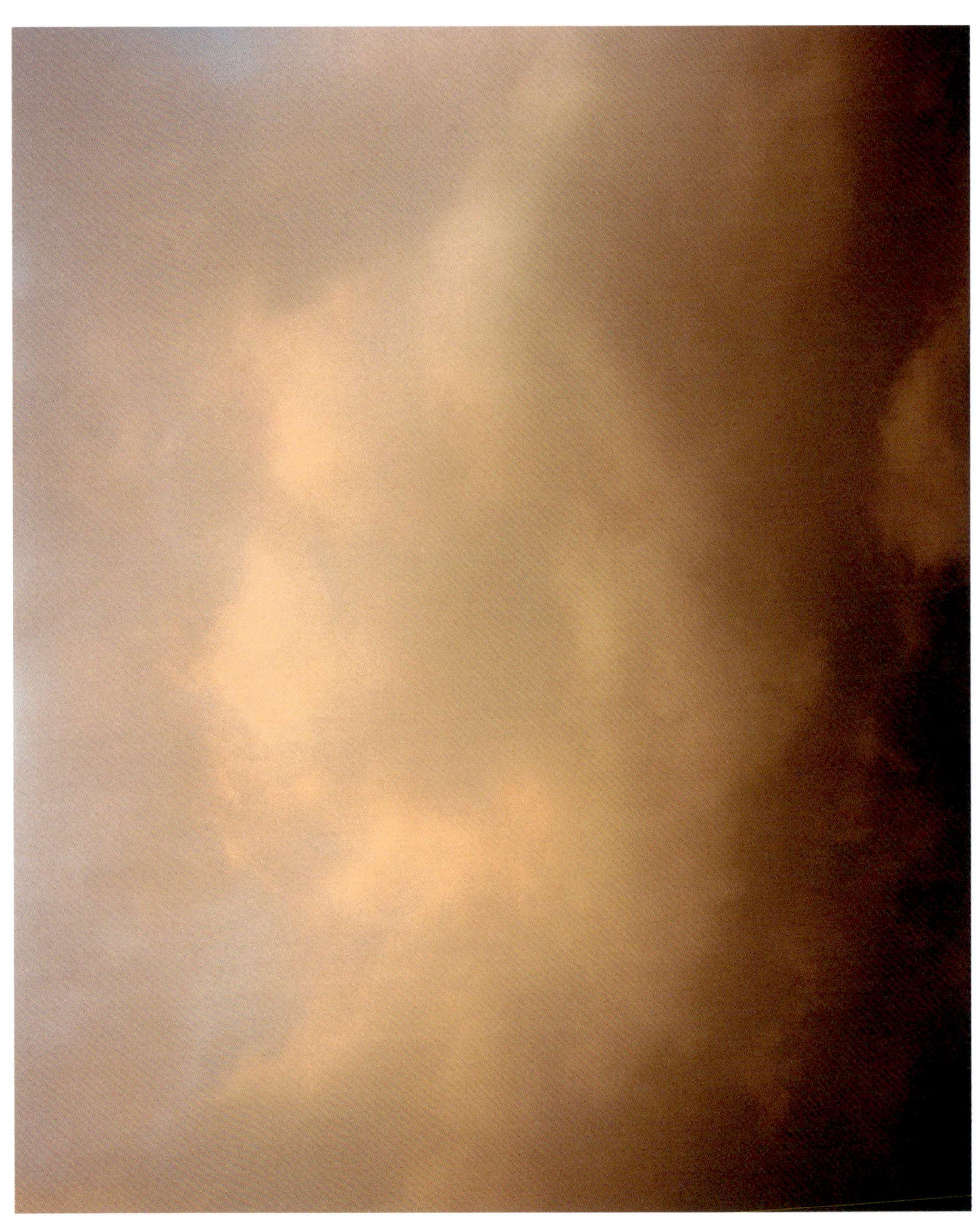

London
8th June, 2017

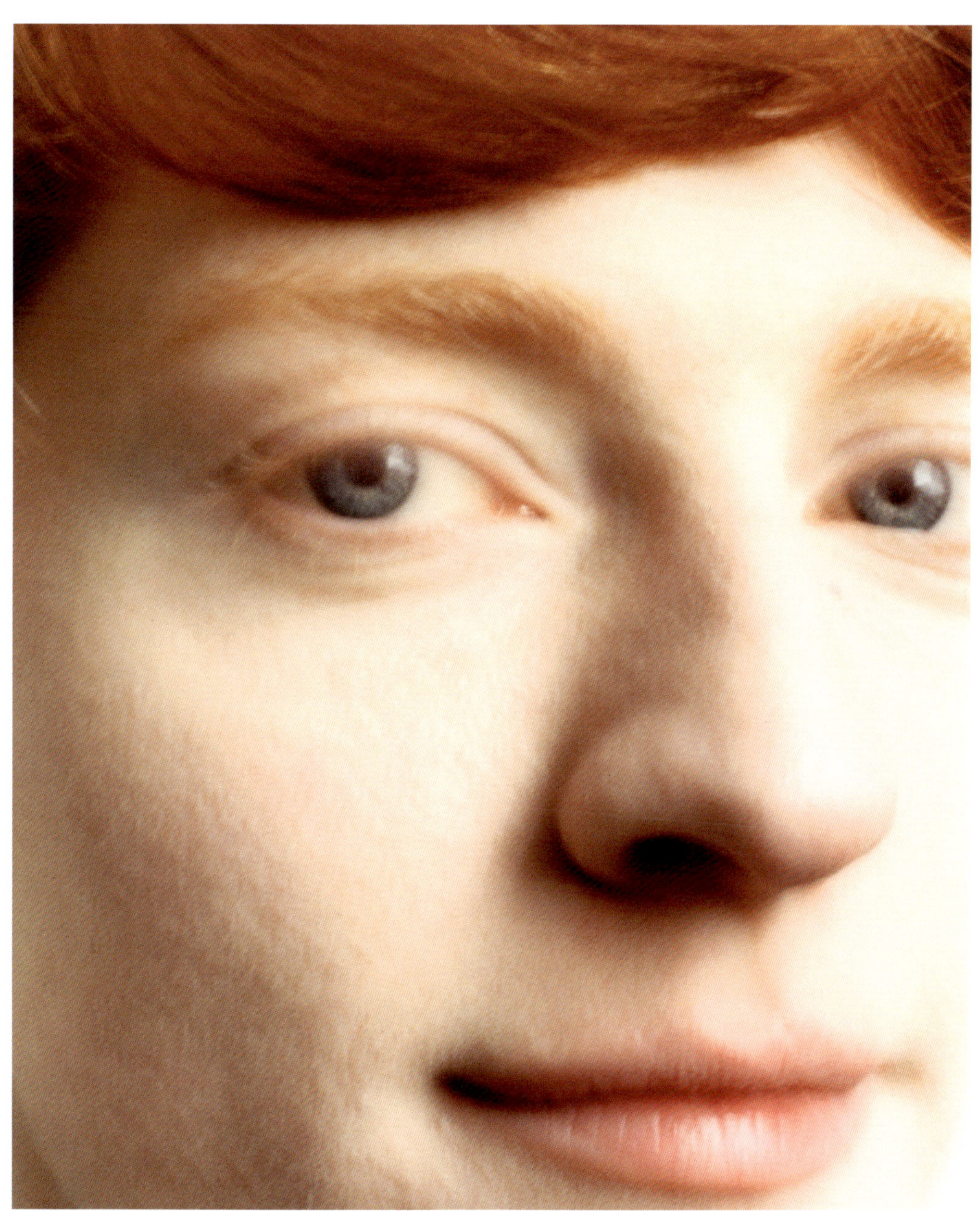

Brixton, London
early December, 2016

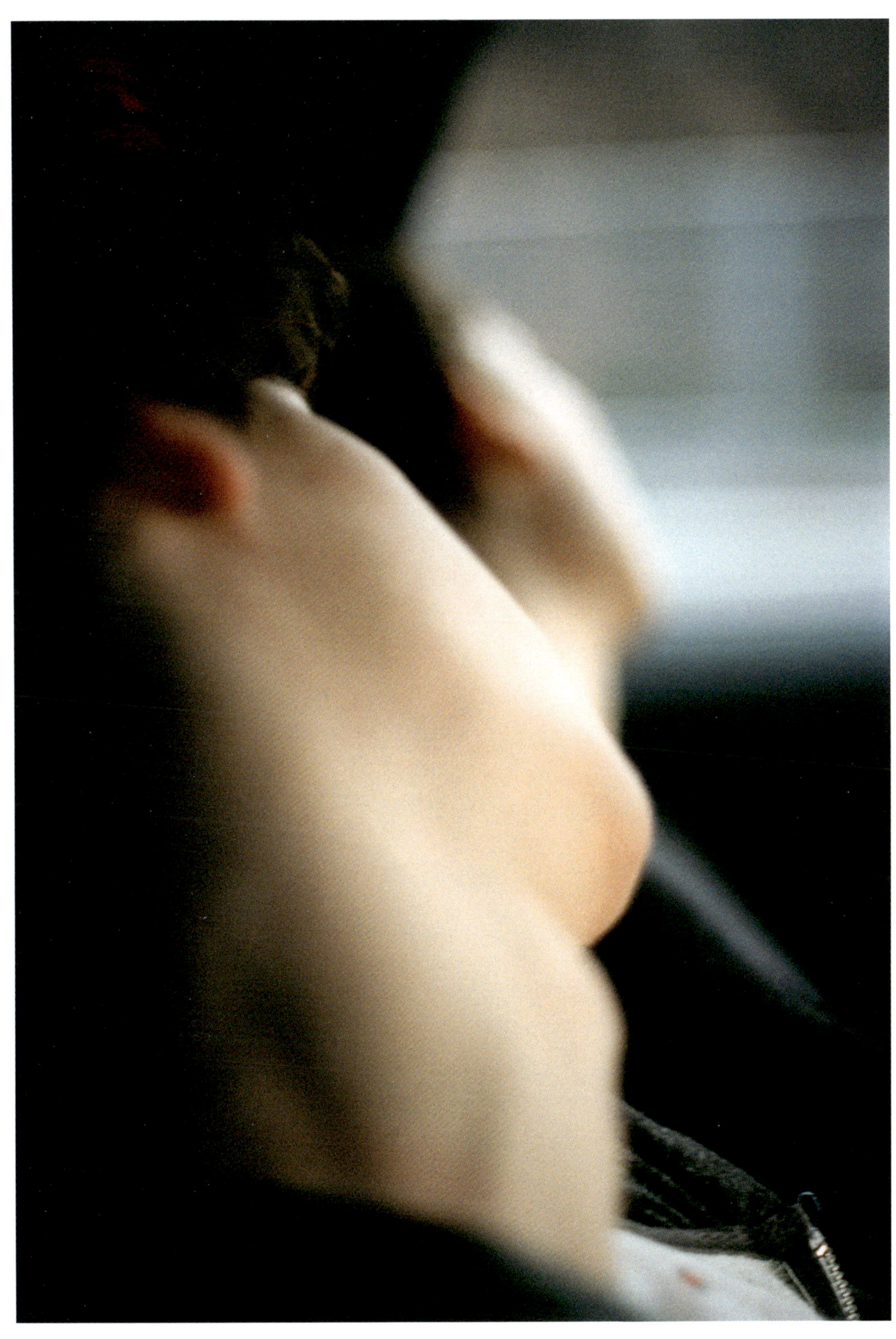

between Slovakia and Austria
late December, 2016

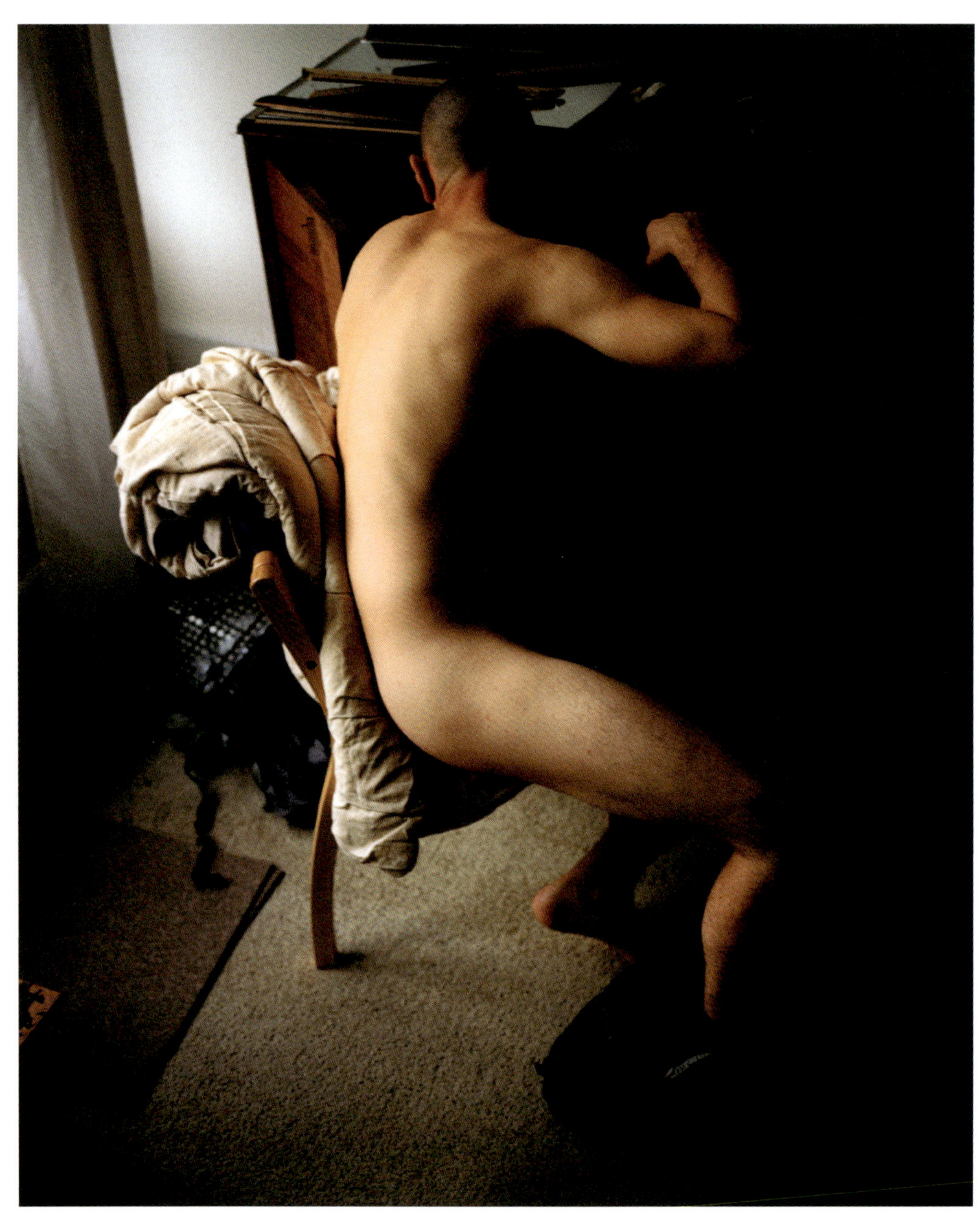

Golders Green, London
November, 2016

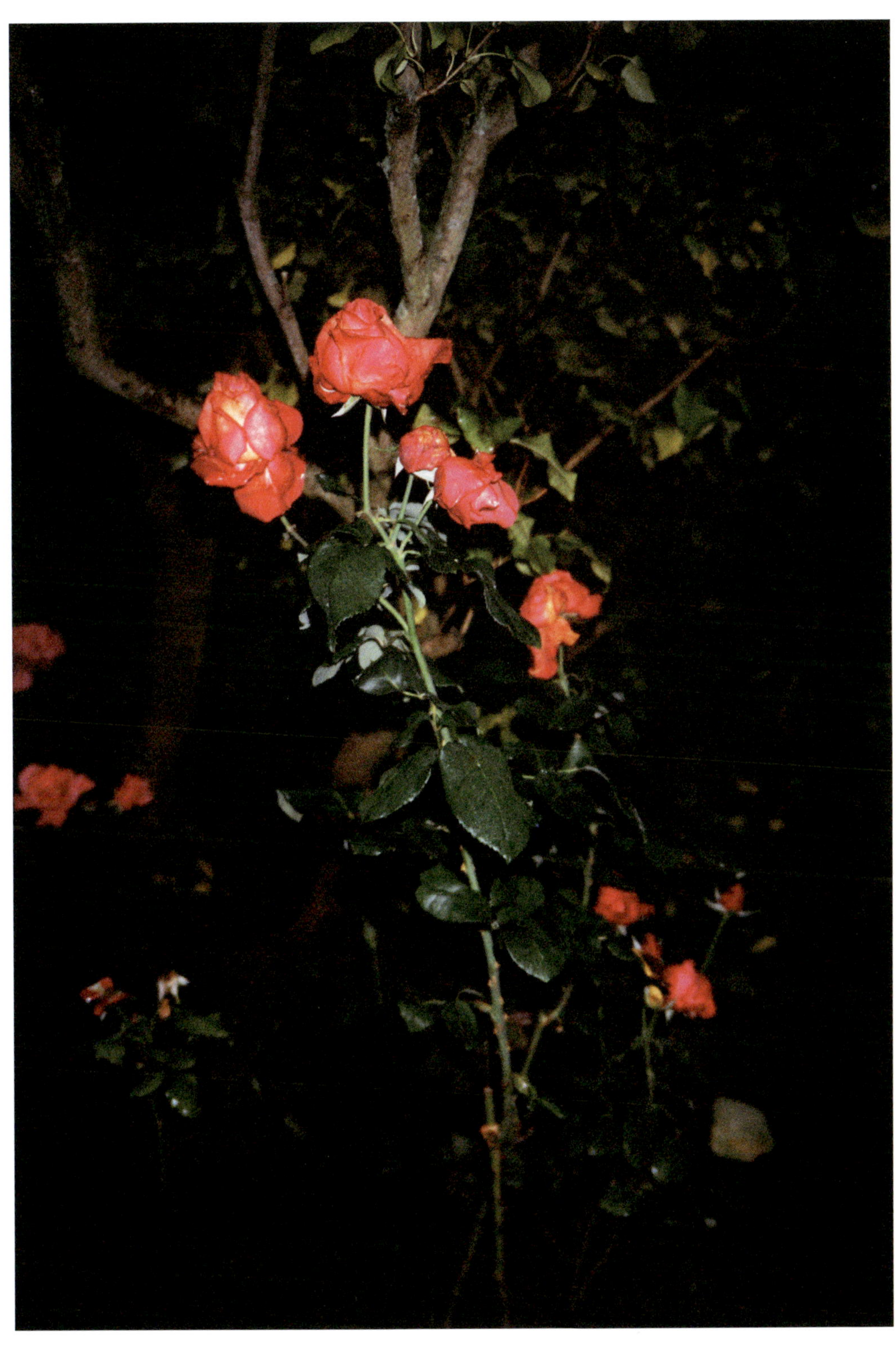

Golders Green, London
November, 2016

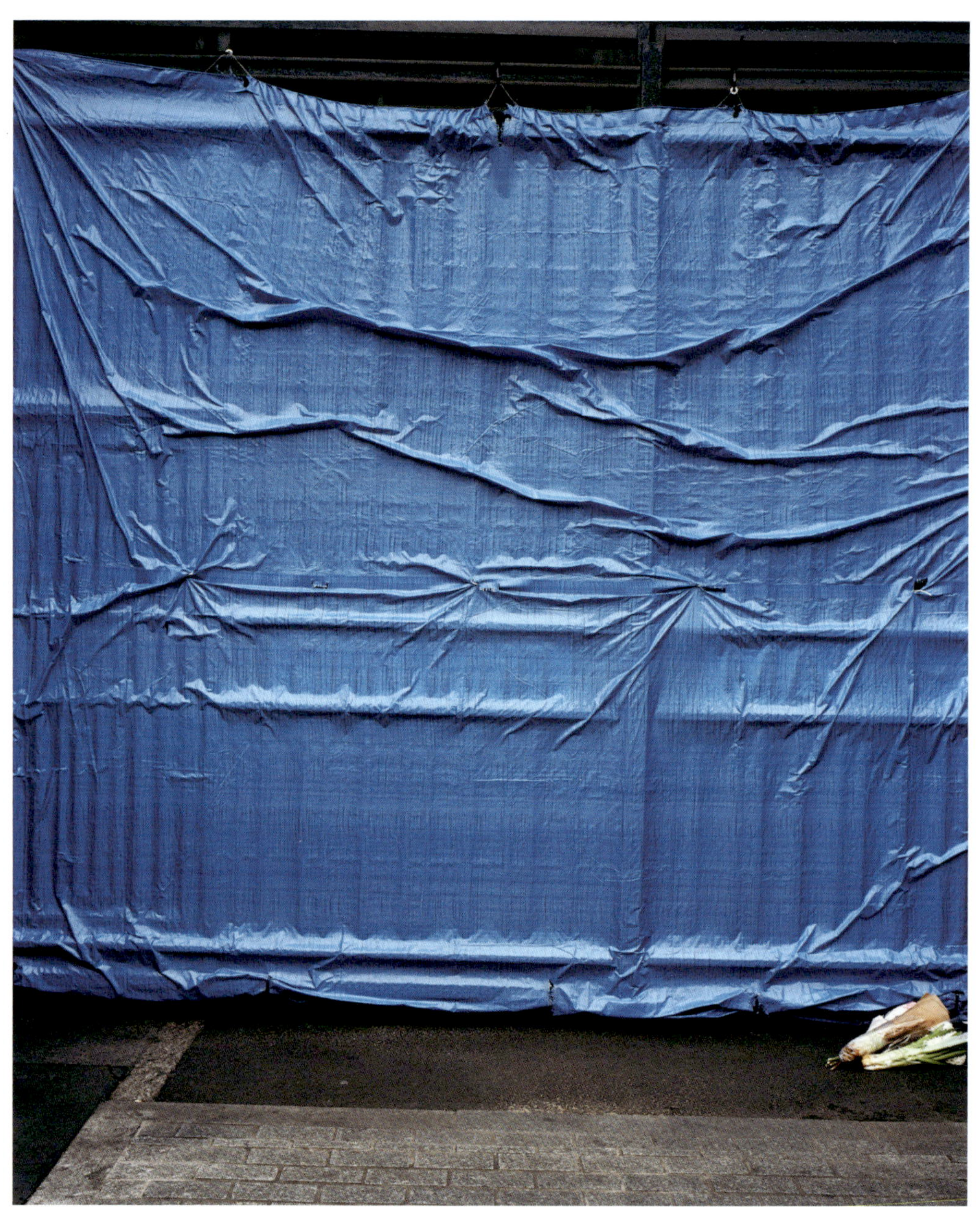

Borough Market, London
8th June, 2017

TEXT

FREEDOM OF MOVEMENT: DANCING TOWARDS A NEW CONCEPTION OF EUROPE
Jamila Prowse, 2019

IMAGES

Ronan Mckenzie
Bernice Mulenga

I find it difficult to think of Europe without Wolfgang Tillmans' archetypal images for the anti-Brexit campaign coming to mind. Landscape photographs of seashores eclipsed by the rolling onset of waves and multicoloured horizons lent themselves as visual signifiers of a construction of Europe as a unified entity, which defies borders in favour of cross-cultural exchange. In 2016, these images could be printed out as posters, to proudly display in front windows or on sitting room walls as a manifestation of Tillmans' rallying cry to 'Say you're in if you're in'. A year later, these same posters were confined to glass cabinets in Tillmans' Tate Modern retrospective, relics of a recent past. It would be easy to look upon these posters today with sighs of nostalgia for the Europe that has been lost, a Europe in which freedom of movement took precedence and we were all one big happy family (as one of Tillmans' slogans stated, 'It's a question of where you feel you belong. We are the European family').

Nostalgia is a dangerous way of looking at the past. It shrouds historical context in a rose-tinted hue, conjuring up an image of a simpler time. In looking to the future of Europe, we must not allow this nostalgia to mask the very construction of Europe as a continent that is unified for some, but not for all. Europe, for all its benefits, is not the antithesis of xenophobia. When we talk about Europe, we rarely acknowledge Europe's vision of itself as a white continent. Social scientist Alana Lentin and journalist and author Reni Eddo-Lodge discussed this concept on Eddo-Lodge's *About Race* podcast, noting that Europe has always had a problem with its 'darker margins'. Centring Europe as an ideal can serve to reinforce a Eurocentrism that is interchangeable with whiteness. Even if one's conception of being European encompasses multiple cultural backgrounds, it is often in direct opposition to non-whiteness.

Blackness – both in Europe as a whole and specifically in the arts – is routinely presented as marginal, a relational value to the dominant norm of whiteness. The dialogues around blackness in the visual arts are contextualised by invisibility. White-walled spaces rarely permit the existence of blackness, and when blackness is positioned within the arts it is frequently discussed through an analysis of its inferiority or lack. The historical construction of Europe as a white continent, as posited by Lentin and Eddo-Lodge, serves to strengthen the othering of blackness within the arts and beyond.

Evan Ifekoya proposes an alternative to this narrative. In their 2018 show *Ritual ~~Without~~ Belief* at Gasworks in London, Ifekoya posed the question 'What would it mean to start from a place of abundance – rather than scarcity?' This question communicates a desire to create and exhibit work pertaining to the complexity and intricacy of experience, as opposed to limiting exploration to one context. Ifekoya also raises the concept of polyvocality, in which they acknowledge that 'there is no objective positionality'. Rather, everything they create is influenced by a myriad of subjectivities, including – but not limited to – their surroundings, upbringing, cultural influences, gender, sexuality, and race. Ifekoya's proposal allows for an analysis in which race is acknowledged but is not required to take precedence over the other subjectivities in the work, which in turn allows for blackness to be expressed through an abundance of meanings and intersections. This abundance connotes breadth, fullness, and overflowing possibility. Moreover, it is an indication of visibility.

To centre blackness within art, it is important to move beyond its construction as a relational value. Abundance proposes a lens through which to read blackness not as marginal, but as multifaceted in and of itself. For *Untitled (Dance Piece)* artist Ronan

Mckenzie invited black women to film themselves dancing. The work – which was created for the 2018 exhibition *I'M HOME* at London's BLANK100, which Mckenzie also curated – was displayed in a room across individual screens with isolated sound, and invited viewers to step into the subject's intimate world. Blurring the division between public and private, each subject captured themselves in a domestic setting, dancing freely to a song of their choice. Some danced alone, others with friends. Some danced while cooking, others in the solitude of their bedrooms. Some filmed themselves for the length of one song only, others over the course of multiple days. The songs selected varied from upbeat to slow and melancholic, yet the series as a whole was characterised by an overwhelming joy. Dance is a medium which exists across borders, a universal language of joy and expression. As such, visual art that speaks through dance establishes the possibility for new languages around blackness. Dance provides an avenue to explore blackness through the lens of abundance – as proposed by Ifekoya – as a site of freedom, expression, and fullness.

#friendsonfilm is a project that photographer Bernice Mulenga has been producing since 2015. Often situated within their hometown of London, the images capture the experiences and interactions of Mulenga's friends. Within the series, Mulenga's loved ones are often presented in moments of ecstasy. With a trusted peer behind the lens, the subjects are unperturbed by the exchange of having their photo taken – they exist in a moment of freedom, uninhibited. Dominating the series are smiling faces, friends held in embraces, and flowing bodies, frozen momentarily within the frame of a photograph. Movement and dance are ever present in Mulenga's practice. A member of the club collectives Pxssy Palace and BBZ, Mulenga is routinely present at their nights, immortalising specific moments within their and their peer's experiences. Both Pxssy Palace and BBZ centre queer, trans, and non-binary people of colour. Situated in this context, *#friendsonfilm* encapsulates a moment and a space that is held for a community, in which the bodies that exist on the dance floor are not marginal. In dance, they collectively communicate through a language of abundance.

Towards the end of last year, I ran a programme called *Reflections of Us* for Brighton Photo Fringe, the fringe festival accompanying Brighton Photo Biennial. *Reflections of Us* created an opportunity for Brighton-based people of colour aged 14–25 to be trained in curation and to contribute to an evolving exhibition that ran for the month of the festival. Within this space, we had many discussions about where we could see ourselves reflected in the cultural landscape. Music often featured in these conversations, as a medium that felt – at least partially – representative of some of our lives. But many of us felt that our identities were not mirrored in the visual arts. In one of the first sessions, I asked the group to bring in a photograph that they felt represented or spoke to a part of their identity. One of the photographs shared came from the *#friendsonfilm* series. Despite this project being personal to Mulenga, the images still communicate an experience that the wider black community can relate to. Chowa, who brought in the photograph, explained that the series felt akin to moments she had shared with her own friends. For her as well as many other members of our group, dancing is a commonality that unifies our experiences. Chowa expressed the joy she observed in Mulenga's images, and when looking at them felt as if she was looking at her own friends. A pervasive whiteness within the visual arts means that we often have to scour images to find experiences that parallel our own. In their depiction of the universal language of dance, Mulenga carves out a space not only for their friends, but for an abundance of people, who can look upon the images and see themselves reflected back. Black people seldom have control over their self-image in a gallery setting. Mckenzie's project, when situated on the white walls of a gallery, allowed for the black body to exist in what is a traditionally homogenous space and to emanate freeness and possibility. Mulenga in turn engages in a position of agency as a maker of images. Taking the camera into our own hands, or putting it in the hands of a trusted friend, affords the black community control over the way in which our bodies are represented, something that we have long been denied. Bodies that move – despite that which attempts to bind them, restrict them, and hold them down – will always connote freedom: a freedom to move, to express joy, and to exist as more than a relational value. Bodies which are expressed through abundance as opposed to inferiority.

Writing about the *New Europe* is a task that feels loaded with responsibility. There is an inherent weight in orientating oneself towards an undecided future, while looking back at a past that remains convoluted. One thing I am certain of is that we cannot let a longing for a lost Europe cloud the continent in a nostalgia akin to forgetting. The present state of flux in the United Kingdom's positioning within Europe provides an opportunity to envision a *New Europe* that is not reliant on inferiority or lack to survive. This *New Europe*, in the arts sector and beyond, should be a space that not only acknowledges the existence of blackness, but also discusses it through a lens of abundance, fullness, and possibility. Dancing, as a cross-cultural signifier of freedom of expression, is a site through which this new perspective can be articulated – a body that is not contained in relation to another, but instead is free to move and evolve, to dance towards a new conception of Europe.

Ronan Mckenzie
UNTITLED for I'M HOME

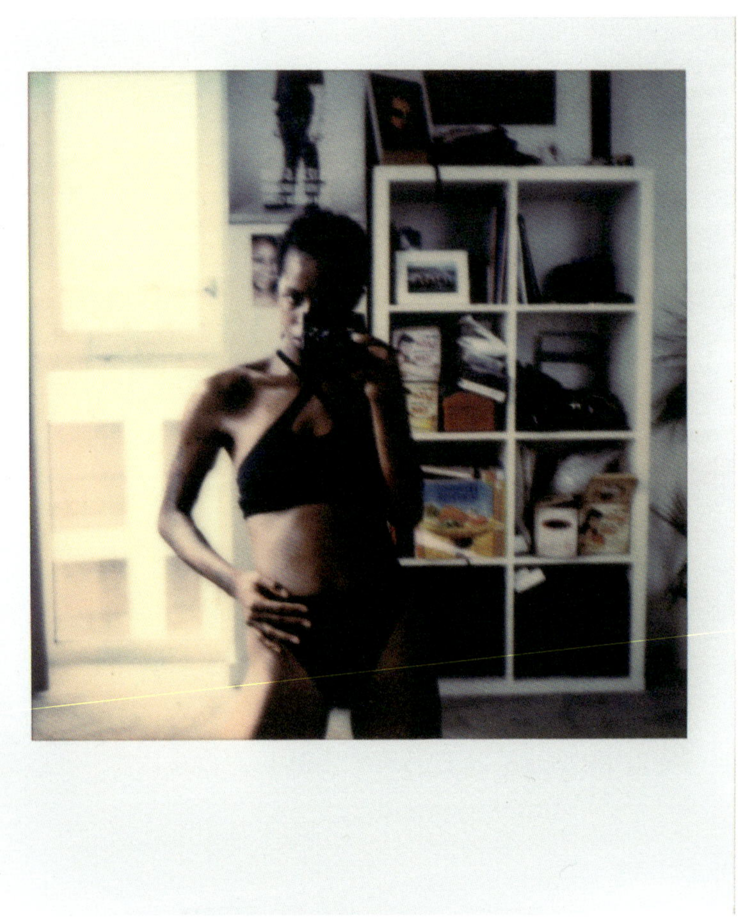

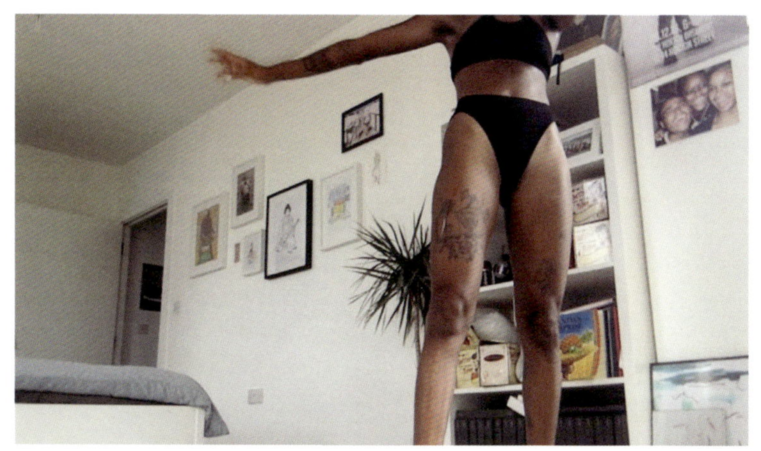

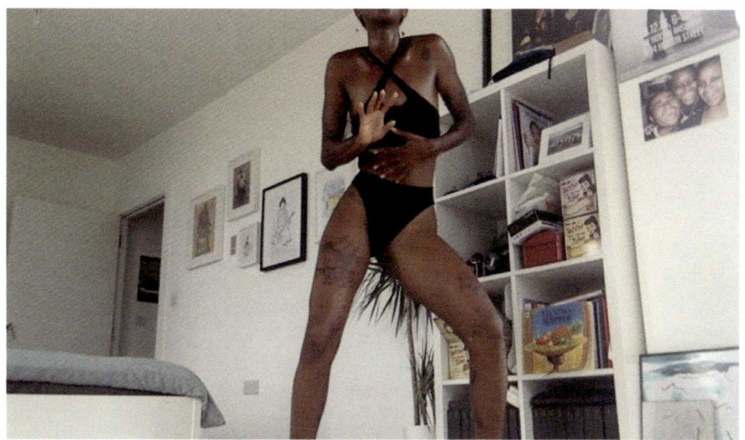

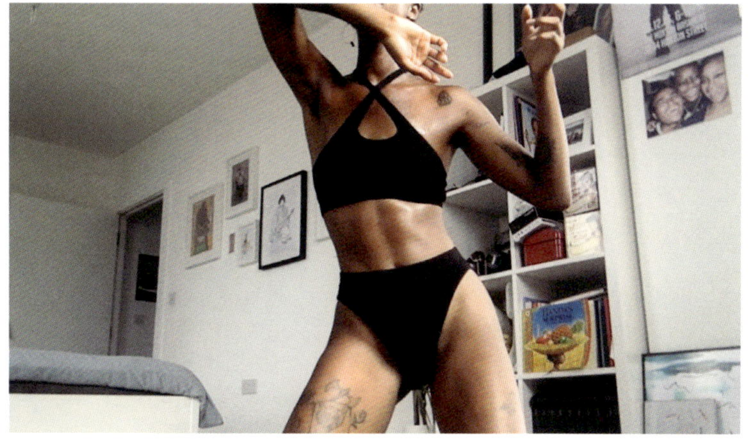

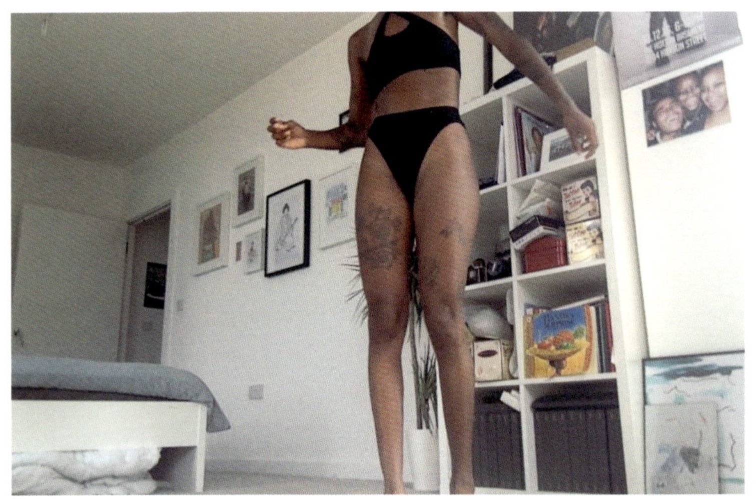

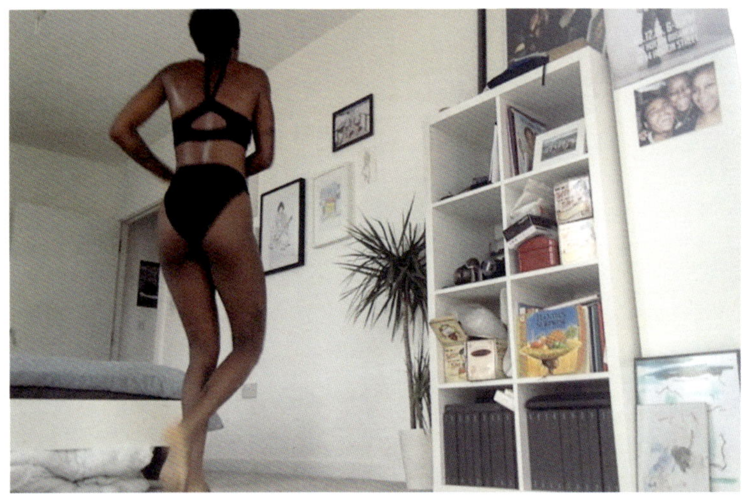

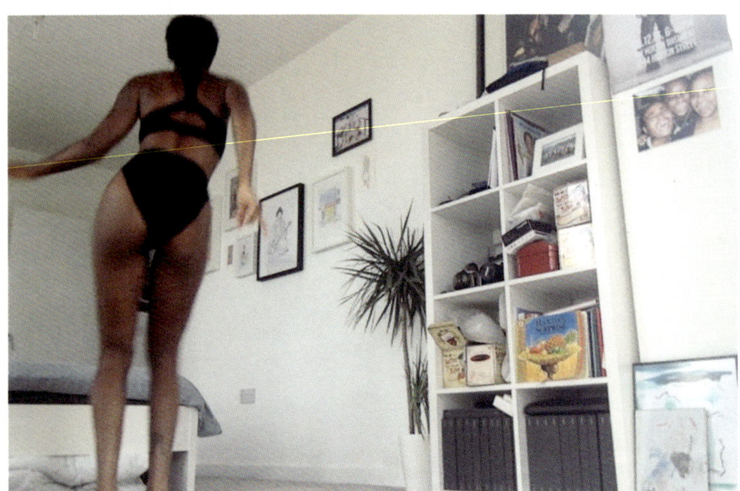

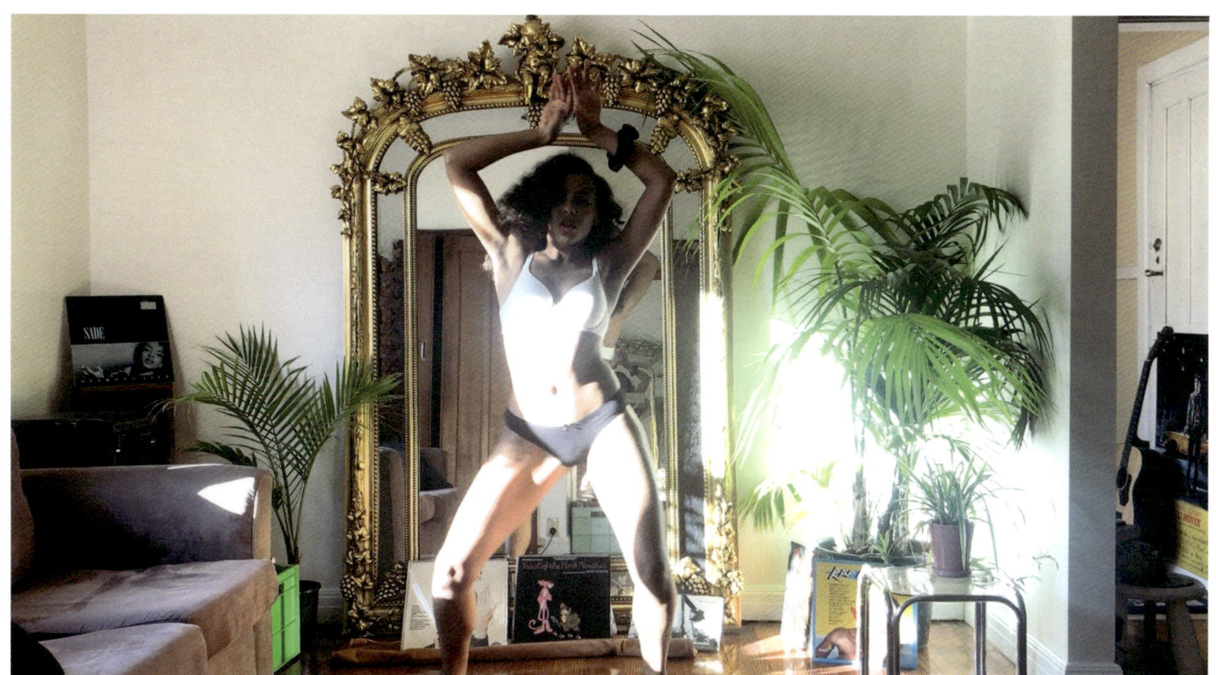

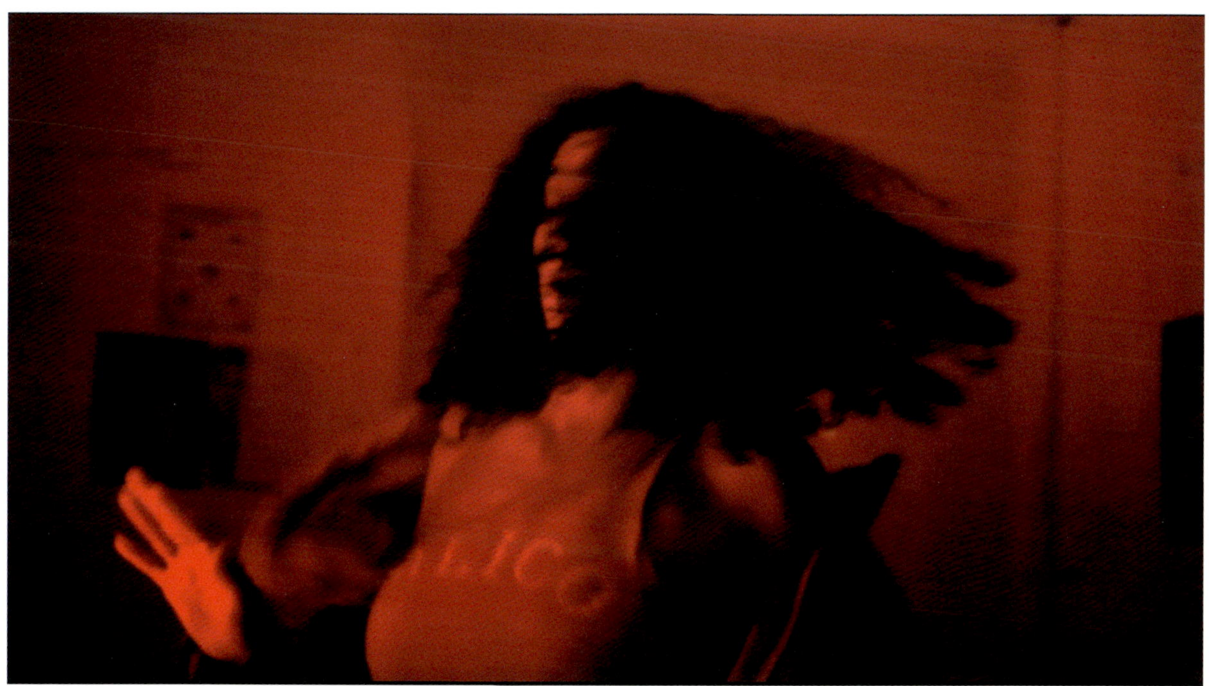

Untitled. From the series,
UNTITLED for I'M HOME,
2018

114–116: Ronan
117: Top Right: Zeina
Bottom Right: Cosima

Bernice Mulenga
#friendsonfilm

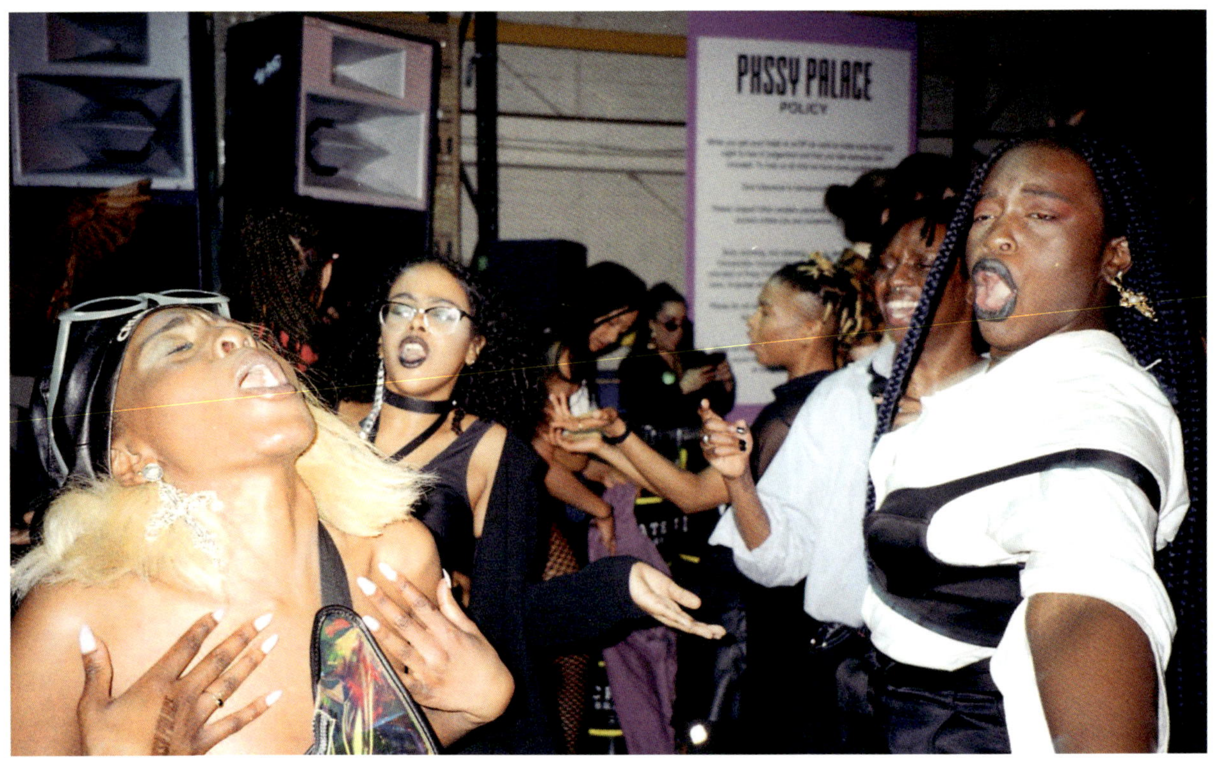

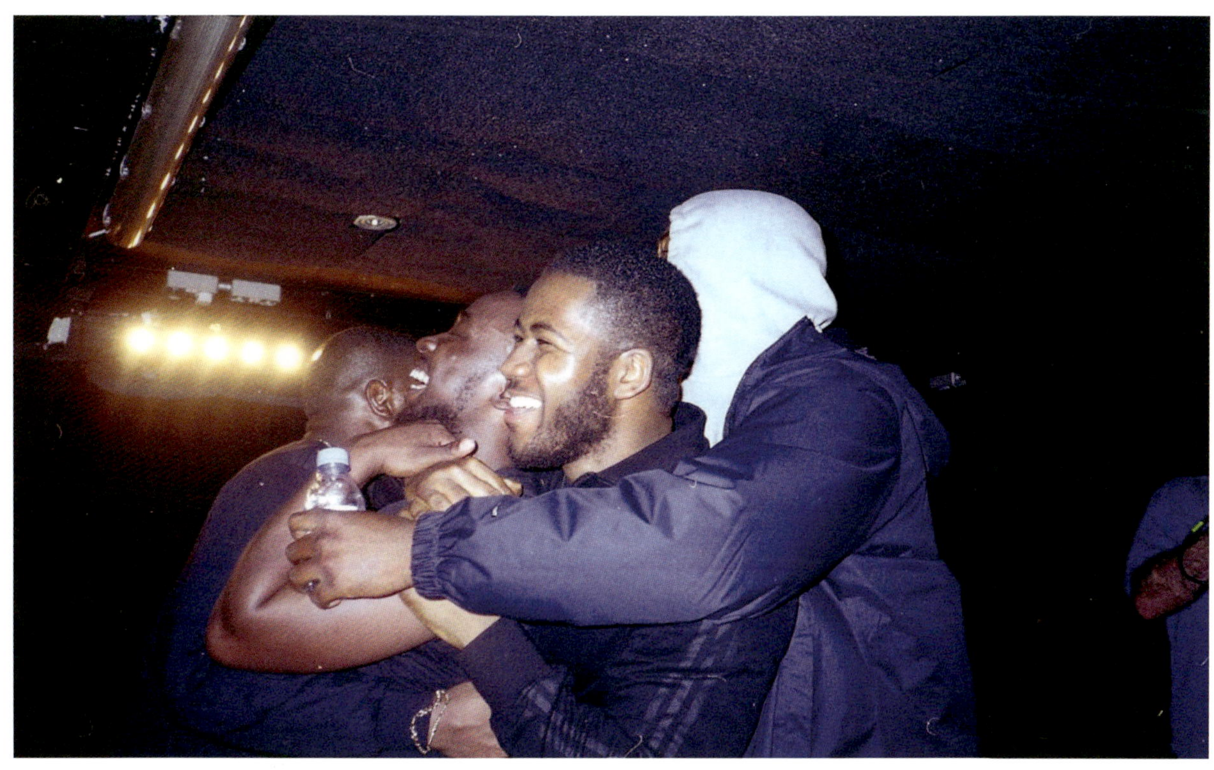

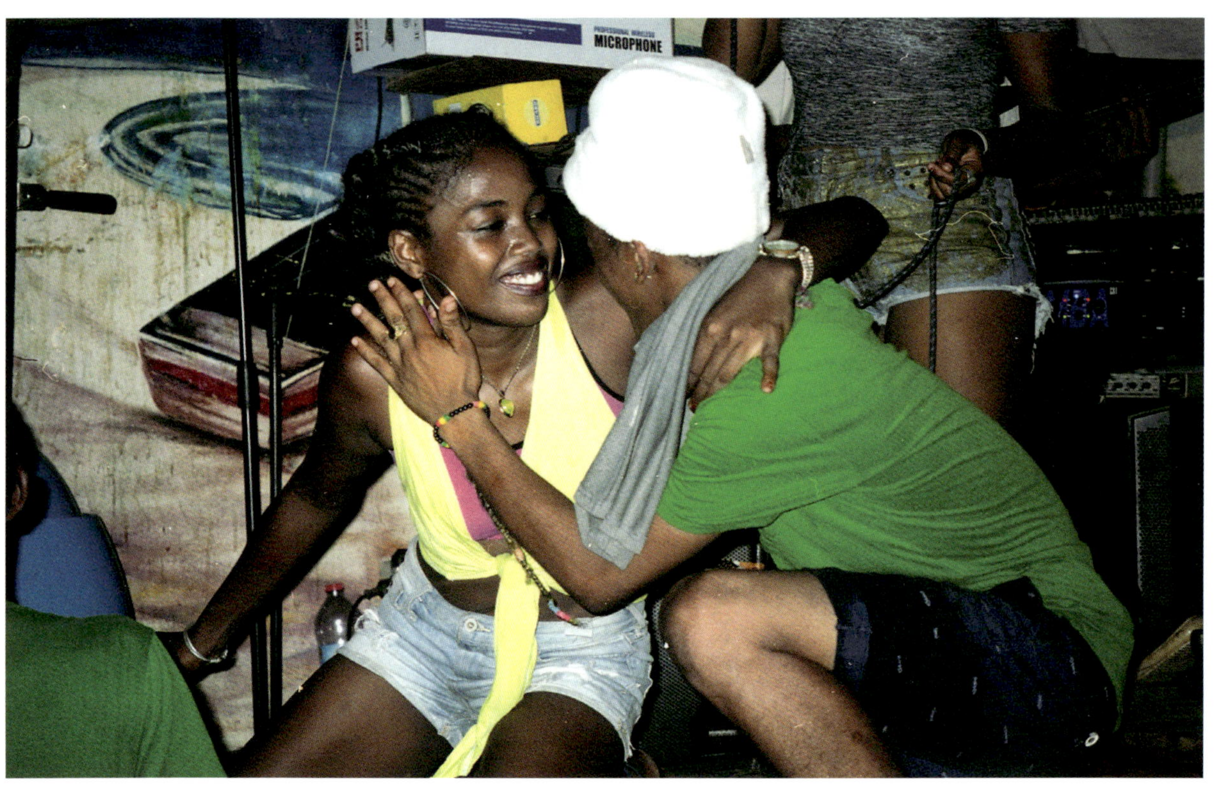

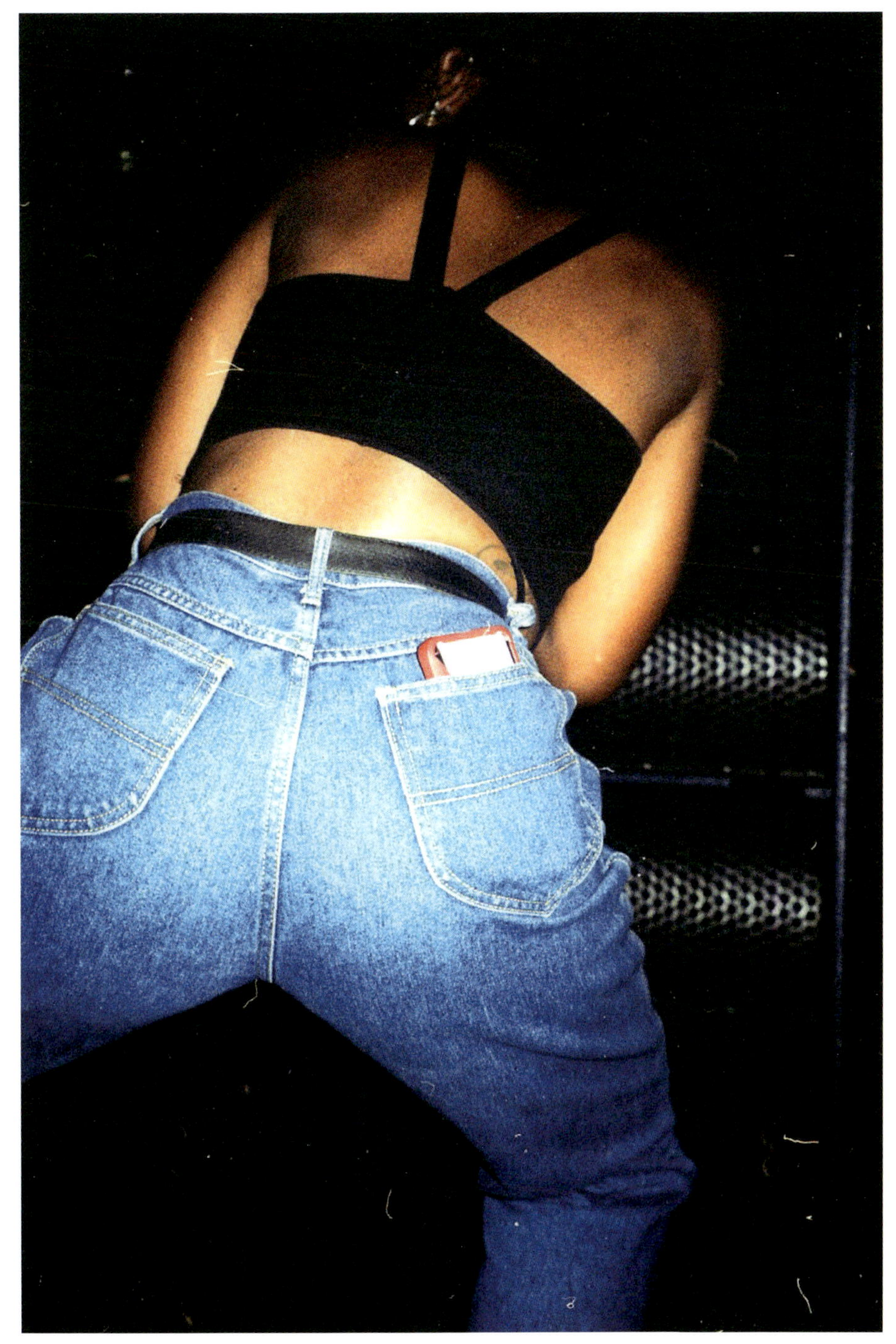

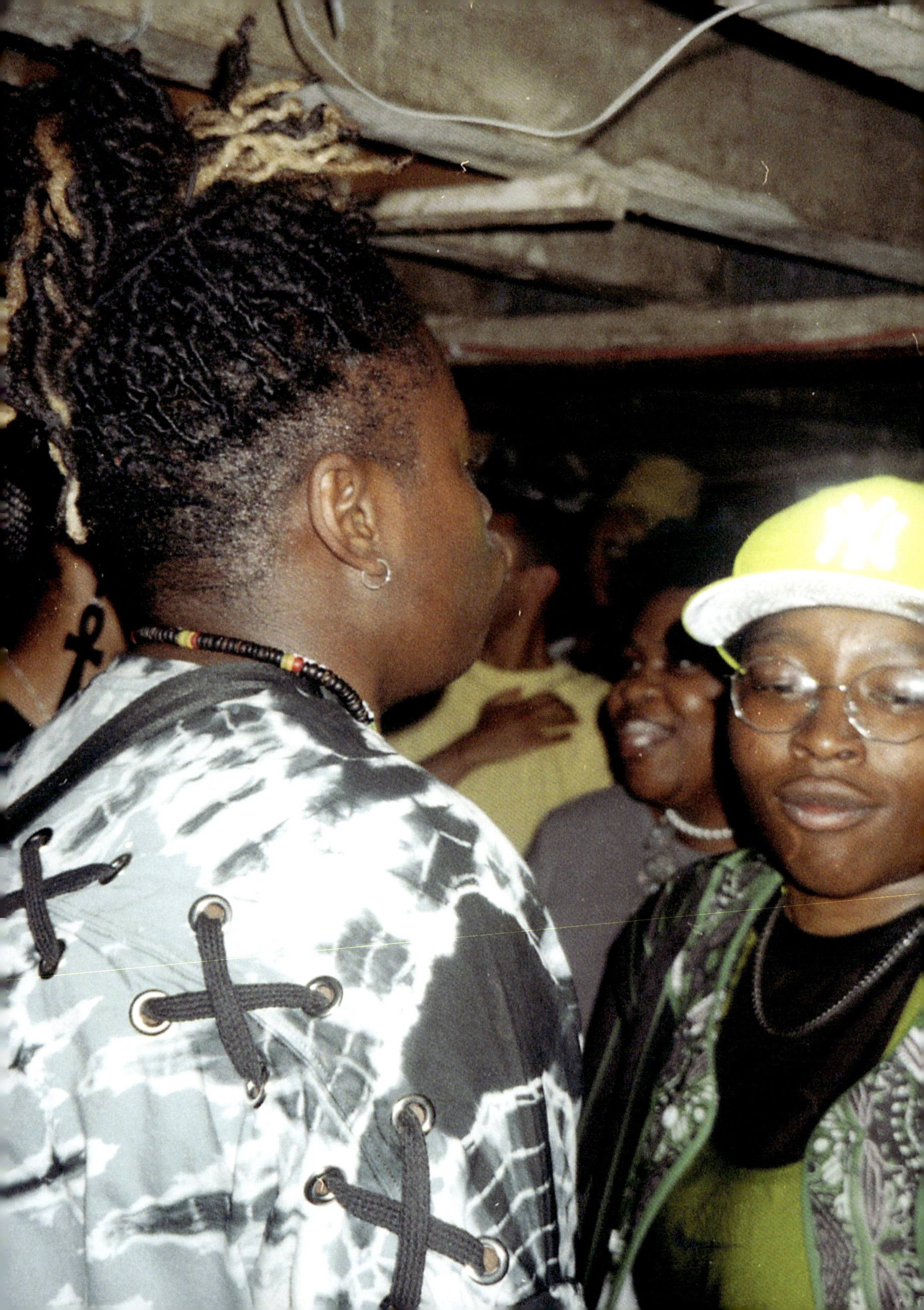

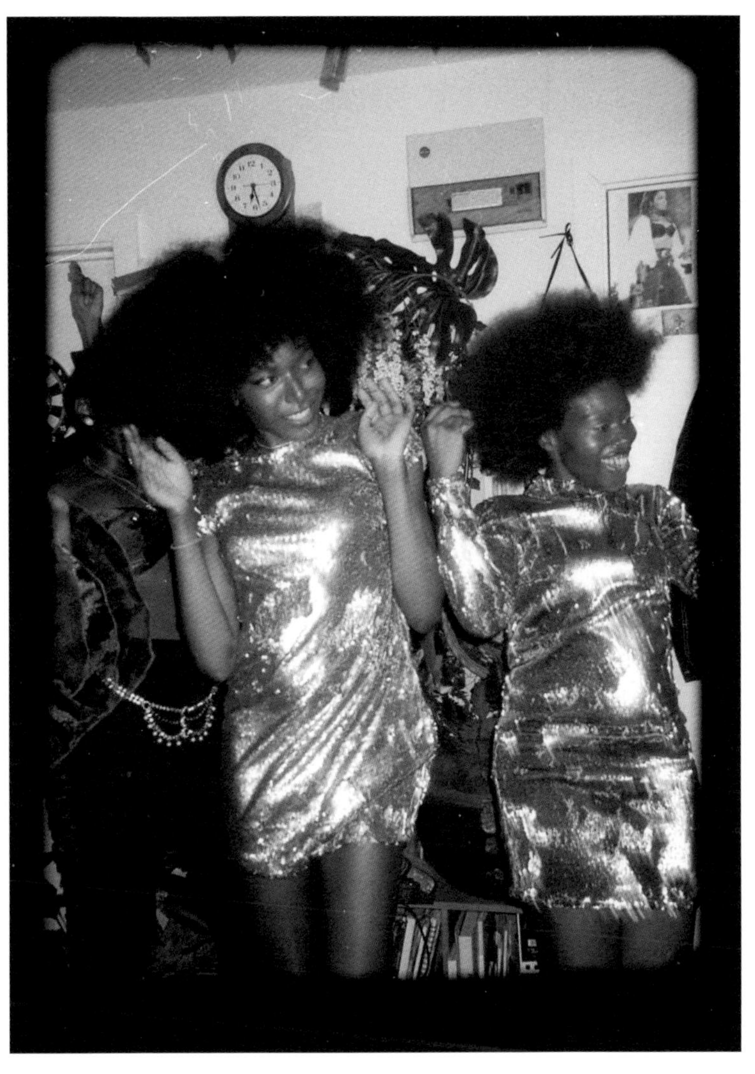

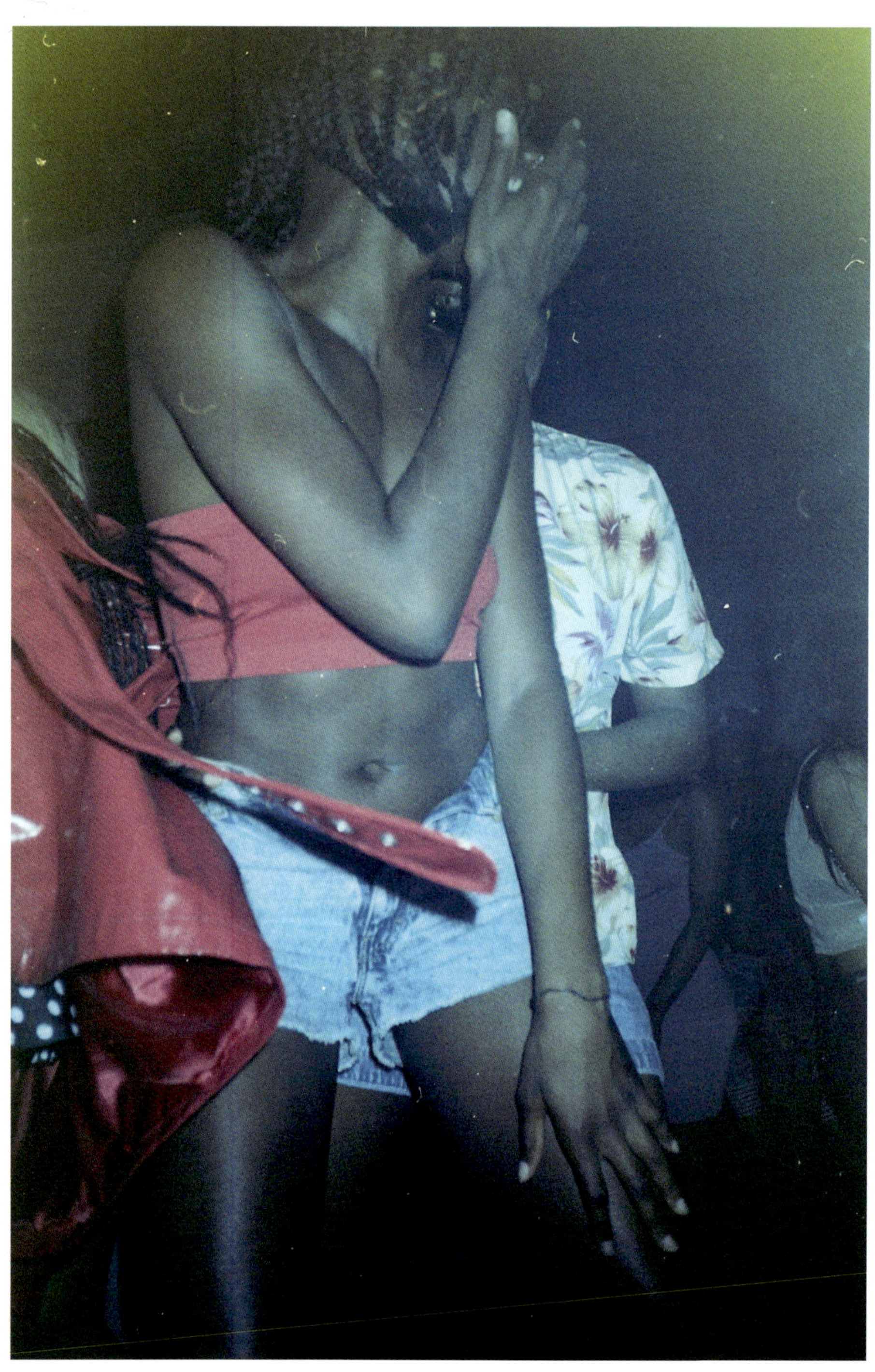

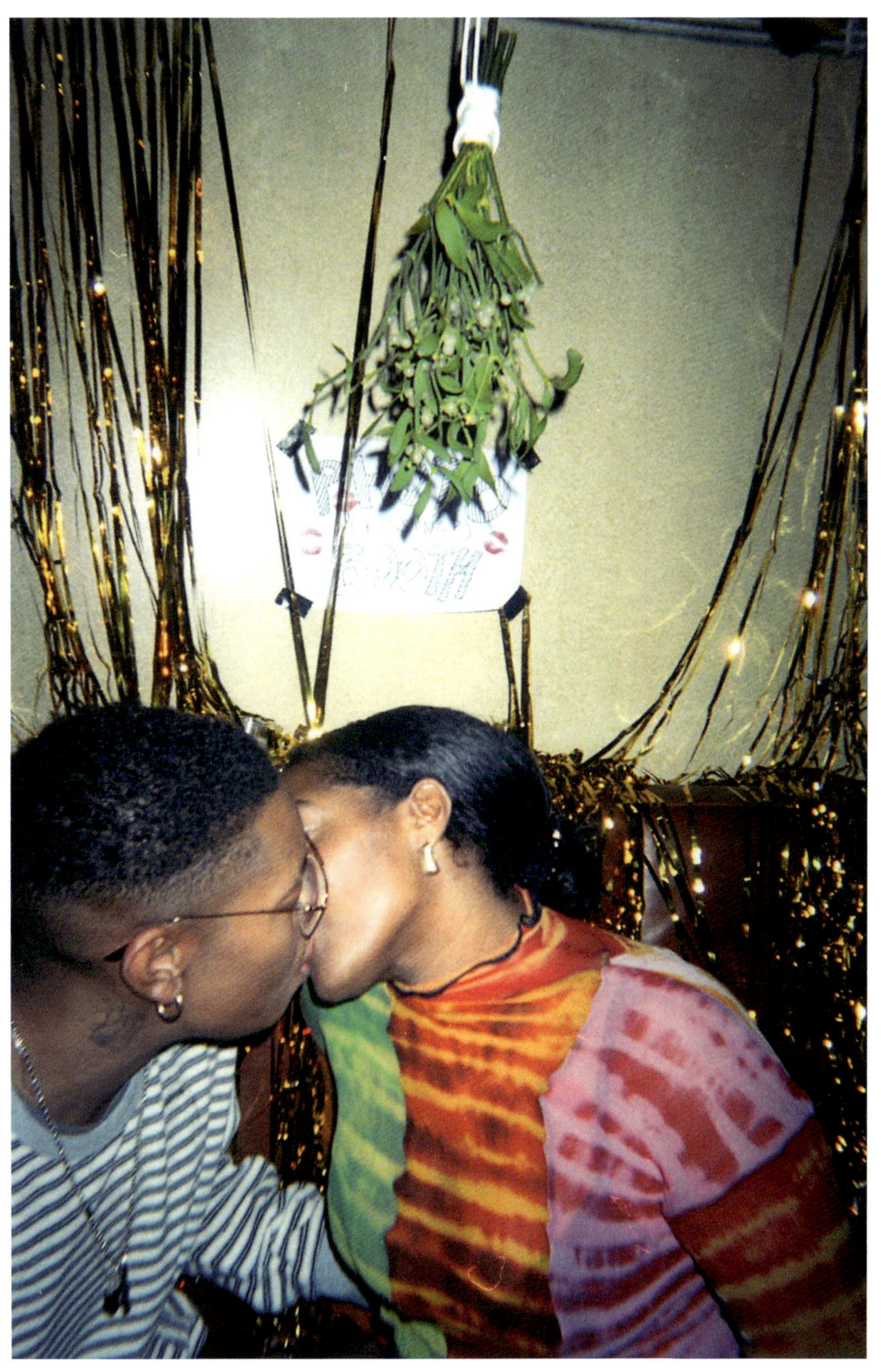

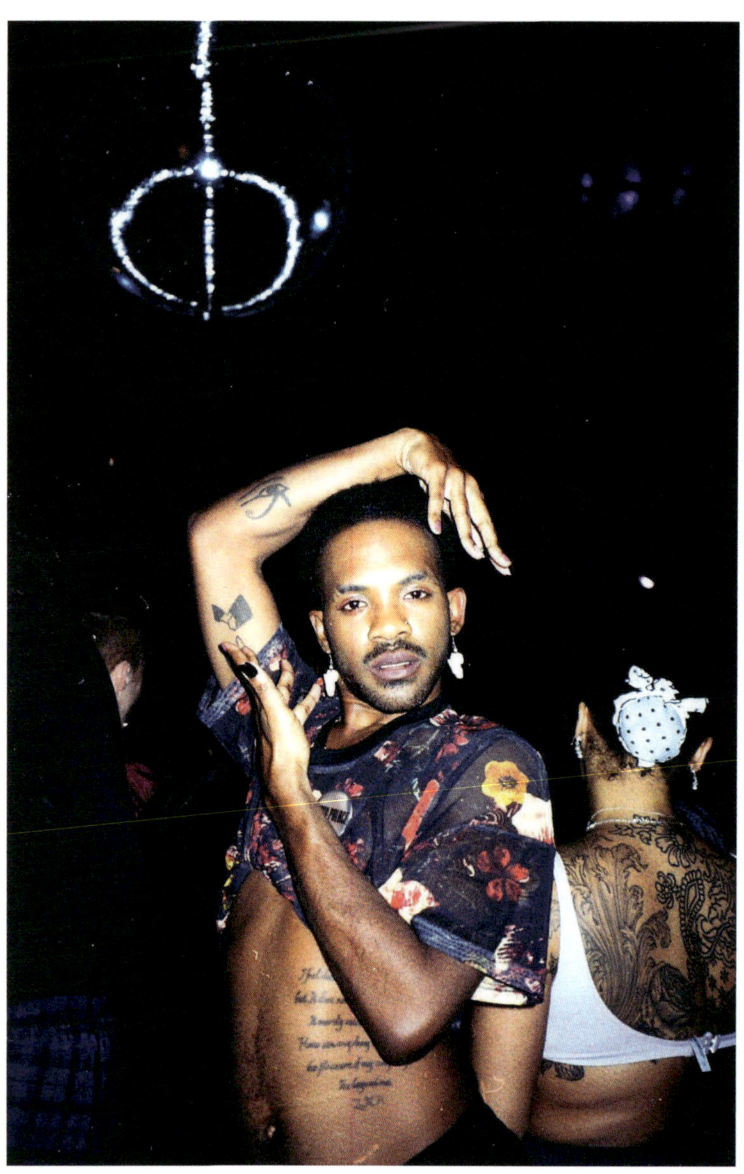

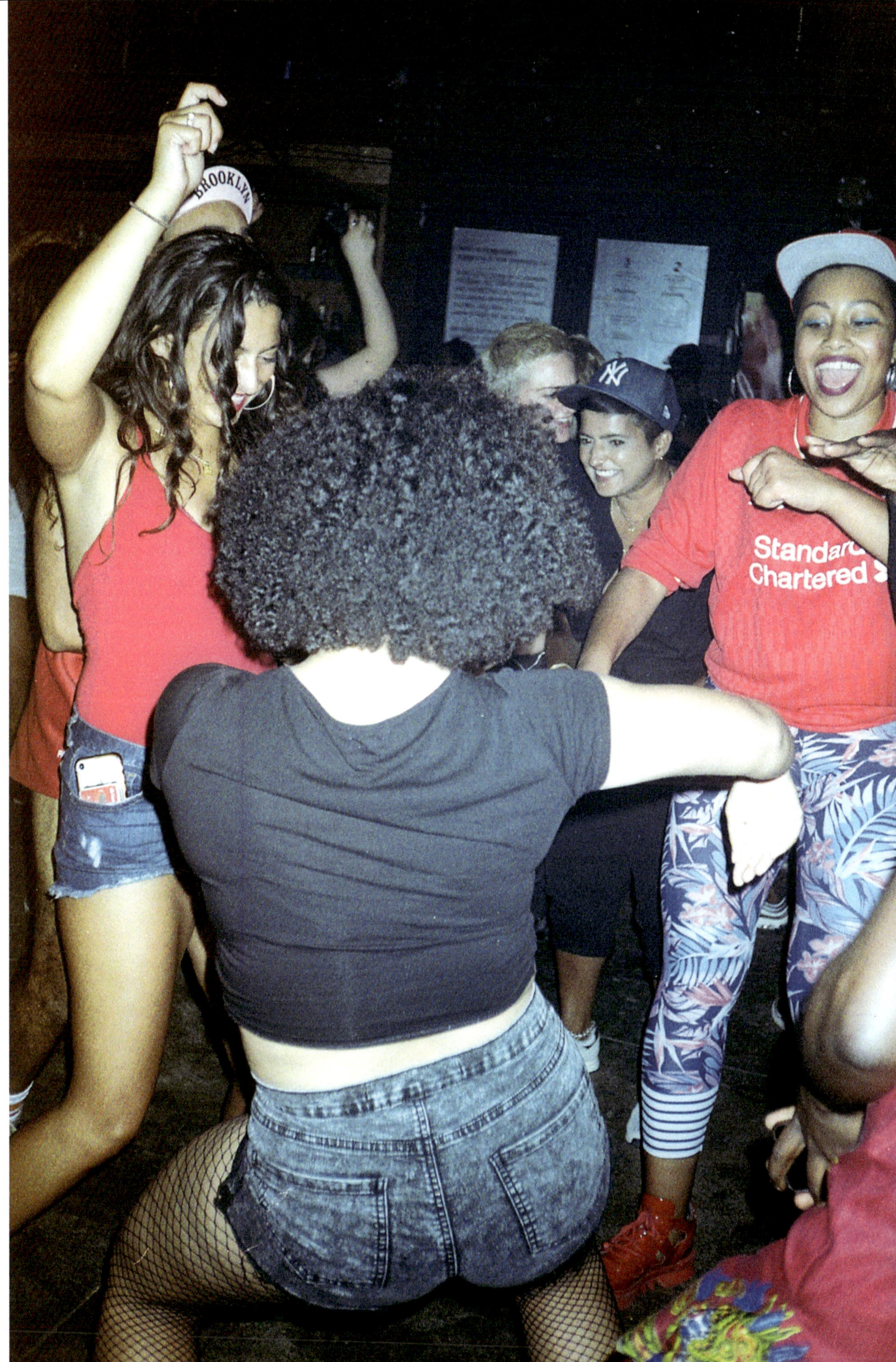

BROOKLYN
NY
Standard
Chartered

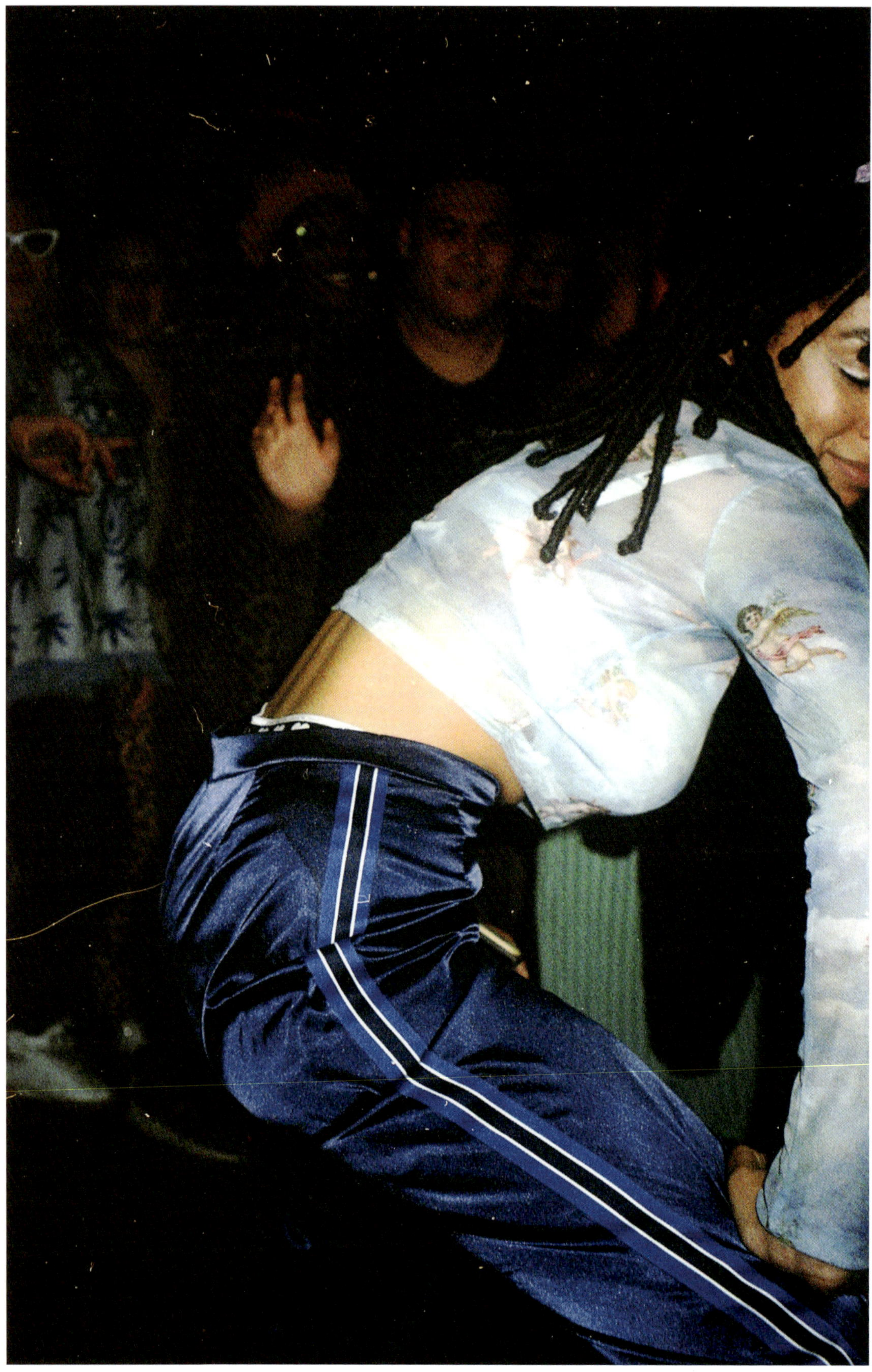

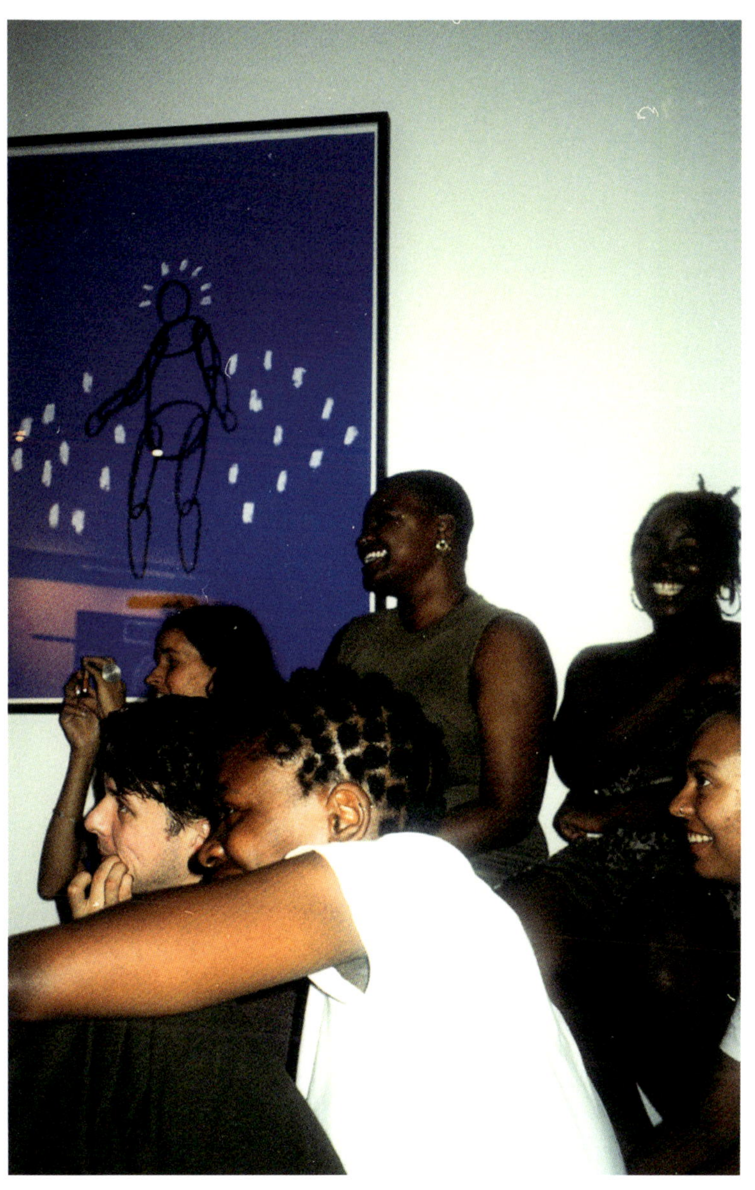

From the series,
#friendsonfilm, 2015

The Last Song, 2018
Oscars Embrace, 2017
Taxi-Be, 2018
Yoyo's Dip, 2018
Adae's Glow, 2018

Afro Sheen, 2018
Mulan's Groove, 2018
Babez Mistletoe, 2018
Follow Me, 2018
Bae Watch, 2018
The Second Walk Off, 2018
Joy's Middle, 2018

TEXT
HOMECOMING
Eliel Jones, 2019

IMAGES
Joanna Piotrowska

Although the Government has committed in principle to allowing EU migrants to remain in the UK after Brexit, there are still many unresolved questions about their longer-term status. One of the groups most affected by this uncertainty are migrants from Poland, who in 2017 comprised 25% of the total EU-born population living in the UK. Although Polish migration to the UK has historically taken many forms – and has often included socially and politically motivated seeking of refuge spanning several centuries – the movements that are most prevalent in the British psyche relate to a more modern tale of global economic migration. This tale has its origins in 2004, with the EU's enlargement to include Poland and several other Eastern European countries, and the UK's decision not to restrict the employment rights of workers from newly acceded states, making it one of only three member states (along with Sweden and Ireland) not to impose temporary labour restrictions. In initial studies of the Brexit phenomenon, academics including Peter Hall and Livia Ortensi have drawn parallels between Britons' aversion to migrants from other European countries and this aspect of the UK's management of the 2004 EU enlargement.

Many young, educated, and variously skilled Poles were drawn to move to the UK by the country's initially welcoming policies and the possibility of higher rates of pay. But the main image that quickly formulated in the minds of some Britons and other EU15 citizens – the so-called original member states – was that of the 'Polish plumber'. This term was first used by Philippe Val in *Charlie Hebdo*, the French satirical weekly magazine, and was popularised thereafter by Philippe de Villiers, leader of the Eurosceptic political party *Mouvement pour la France*, as an emblem of cheap labour coming from Eastern Europe. 'Polish plumber' soon became an umbrella term symbolising a threat to the jobs of Western Europeans. The Polish tourism board attempted to fight back against this damning rhetoric by reclaiming the phrase in a seductive ad campaign specifically targeted at French citizens. The first poster released featured the figure of the Polish plumber (fig.1), here embodied as a godlike, hunky male model, with the slogan 'I'm staying in Poland – do come over.' A second poster featured the plumber's female counterpart: the nurse (fig.2). In this version, a female model suggestively poses, peering over her glasses as if checking someone out, with the slogan 'Poland: I'm waiting for you', her own faithful promise.

If the appropriation of the negative stereotypes paid off somewhat, with many French audiences praising the ads' humour, today's anti-immigrant sentiment in the UK feels far from reparable with savvy – albeit a little dodgy – marketing. If anything, the Brexit referendum dangerously brought back into public consciousness the figures of the plumber and the nurse, to the Leave campaign's advantage, but they were no longer *only* Polish. According to the Migration Observatory at the University of Oxford, between 2006 and 2015, the population aged 20–34 years in Poland, Romania, Spain, Italy, Hungary, and Portugal declined by about 15%, an exodus powered by the high rates of unemployment and the continued weak labour market conditions in the EU countries that were most affected by the 2008 financial crisis. These countries made up only 40% of the total EU-born population in the UK in 2011, but would be responsible for almost 80% of the *growth* in numbers over the next 4 years.

In Spain alone, youth unemployment reached an all-time high of 56.1% in 2013. Only a few years previously, I finally moved from Malaga to London, still closeted, at the age of seventeen. I say *finally* because, having grown up between England and Spain, the son of a British father and Spanish

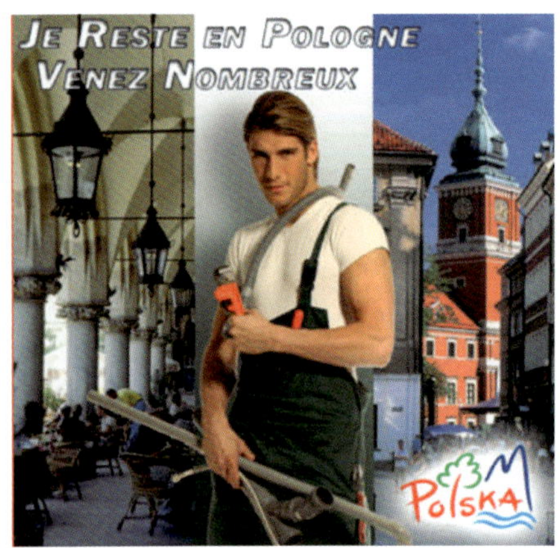

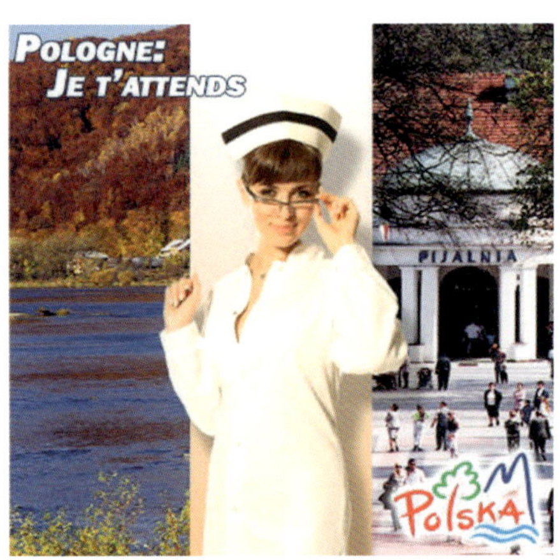

Left: (fig.1) *Polish Plumber*, 'Je Reste en Pologne Venez Nombreux' (I'm staying in Poland – do come over), Polish Tourism Organisation (POT), 2005

Right: (fig.2) *Polish Nurse*, 'Pologne: Je t'attends' (Poland: I'm waiting for you), Polish Tourism Organisation (POT), 2005

mother, burdened by religious and patriarchal traditions (I grew up in a small fishing town, as a member of an outsider Christian Evangelical community that was largely against homosexuality), London had always seemed to me to be the land of milk and honey – and it indeed would prove to be, in many, many, ways. The only divulged reason for my departure was to go to university – an excuse of sorts to allow for a smooth and friendly transition, one that alleviated the need to express my anxieties about not belonging and my desire to extricate myself from an environment that had been painful and damaging. The dire financial situation in Spain was a further key reason for me and those around me to justify leaving the country. The few artists and writers whom I knew in Andalusia were barely surviving, sustaining their practice while working multiple precarious and underpaid jobs.

Over the years, I would visit my hometown and meet with my high school friends. They would tell me about the perils of living under their parents' roofs, but mostly about their frustrations with their inability to secure stable jobs, irrespective of their degrees and extensive training. Many of them said that they would consider moving to other European countries, but only if they secured a job in their field. One of their main impediments was that they lacked a full command of English, but often the real problem was the idea of leaving their lives behind. Their families would be devastated to let them go, and they would be heartbroken to say goodbye themselves. It took my Spanish grandparents a

long time to stop asking me if I was ever planning to come back. Since the Brexit vote, however, they have resurrected their questioning, and their interrogation now seems more like an imperative. It makes me wonder who else is being asked the same question.

How many people will soon choose – or be forced to – return home, Brexit reuniting them with their friends and families, and perhaps leaving them, for the first time, with better prospects in their home countries than on the lonely island they'll be leaving behind? Some of them might have supported their spouses' or children's care, their parents' wellbeing or their brothers and sisters' educations with money sent from afar. Their return home would be akin to that of heroes, yet the realities of the day-to-day happenings that they've missed out on will also potentially become clearer – the growing of their children, the longing of their partners, the love of their siblings, the mocking of their friends. Others, myself included, will be tempted to suffer the impending consequences of Brexit, whatever they may be, rather than return to a life that seems long gone. We choose to continue managing our relationships from afar, constantly negotiating the various terms and conditions of this entanglement – FaceTime appointments, holiday dates, various family members' birthdays. Information will continue to be carefully shared and passed on, small, intimate facts being laid bare on screens.

In either case, photo albums from the years of absence would be incomplete, the overseas family members represented only in digital single portraits, passport pictures, and selfies, all artefacts of life on the other side. Upon our various returns to the family home, whether they are temporary or permanent in nature, Joanna Piotrowska's series of staged family photographs, *Frowst* (2014), could serve as a visual instruction manual for homecoming – for reinstituting relations, habits of care, physical connections, and touch, facilitated by the process of taking a photograph. It is possible to imagine Piotrowska as the official family photographer for these reunions, crossing countries to revisit moments that could have been captured but never were, and re-examining those that were immortalised but are now perhaps in need of healing because of the passage of time, the changing of circumstances. In her use of movements and gestures influenced by German psychotherapist Bert Hellinger's concept of 'Family Constellations', which attempts to expose and heal multigenerational trauma, Piotrowska's photographic restagings could alleviate – or at least make visible – the emotional baggage that was previously excluded by the lens of the camera. When family members become uncomfortable, or are on the verge of tears, Piotrowska could move them and place them close together, their chests tight, their arms interlocked, their lips on each other's cheeks, their bodies made vulnerable to one another. Mothers could touch their grown sons, fathers hold their daughters, estranged brothers and sisters awkwardly revisit the playfulness of their childhood intimacies, only to later find their bodies charged with a confused sense of eroticism. Piotrowska's family albums would thus be filled with paradoxical images of love and heartache, celebration and mourning, proximity and distance. They would comprise both genuine and performed moments of *being* a family, and help to redefine what 'family' means, by emphasising the need for complication, awkwardness, difference, and pain.

Piotrowska would also be the ideal choice for official Brexit photographer, if such a role existed, coming in to chart the break-up of the EU family, to unmask the hidden intentions, the many wrongdoings, structural social divisions, and unbalanced power dynamics. Neither the EU nor the UK is a single group of people or a family in any traditional sense, but that doesn't make the separation any less painful. What happens next is down to *us:* a complex mix of different people that make up the European body politic, bound by history, geography, and ancestry – and not least by our humanity. What we say and do to and for each other from here on out, both inside and outside the UK and the borders of Europe, will determine the next chapter in our relationship. If Piotrowska, who is Polish-born, and the many other EU-born artists, photographers, writers, film-makers, theatre-makers, and choreographers who are based in the UK choose to stay, they might consider lending a hand with these impending changes – reconfiguring and making visible the many social, political and interpersonal realities that, in the words of Nina Simone, 'reflect the times'. Like Piotrowska's *Frowst*, it will be a matter of healing as much as of redefining what is possible, sayable and doable, ultimately facilitating a practice of seeing and feeling what may all too often be left outside the frame.

Joanna Piotrowska
Frowst

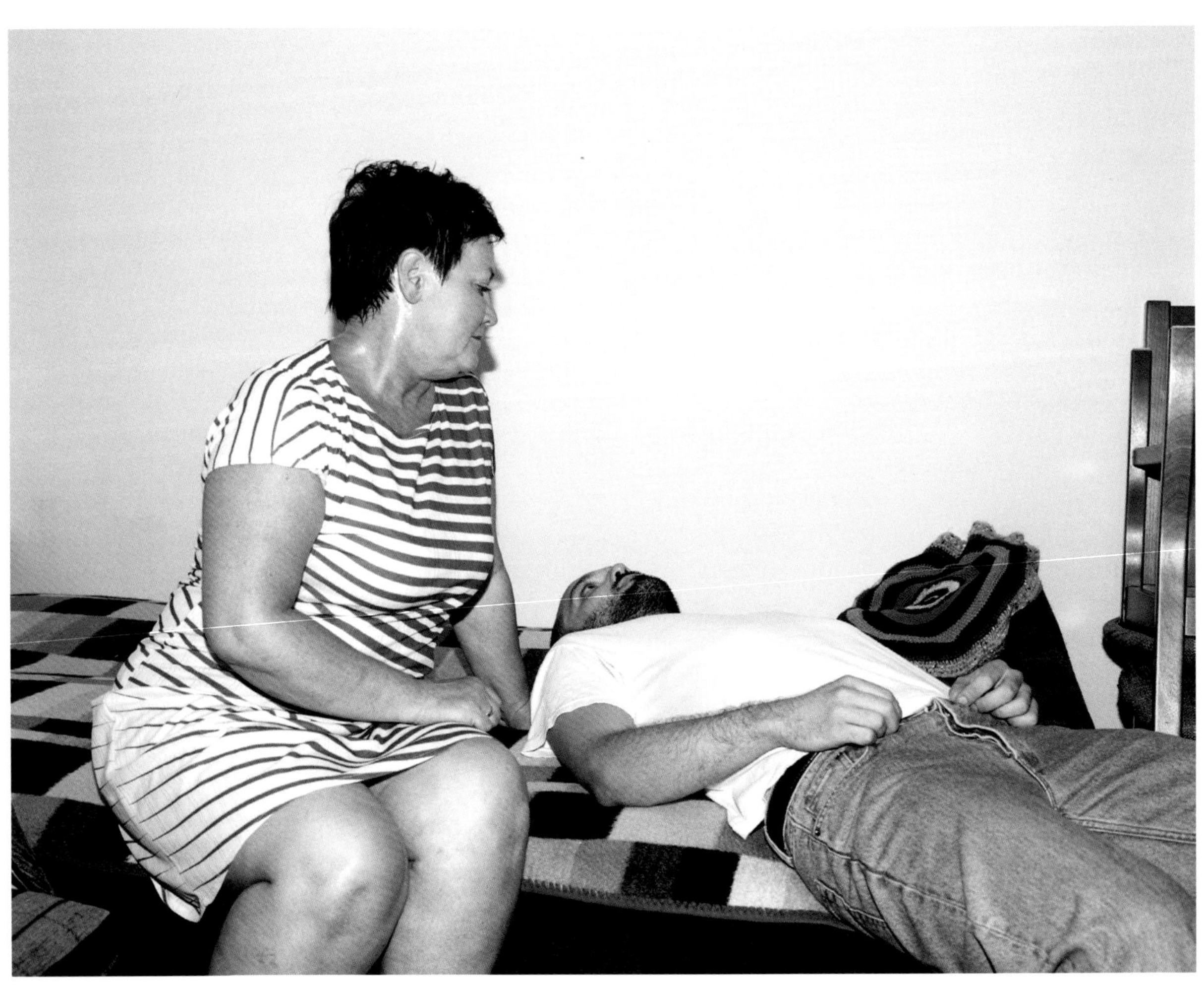

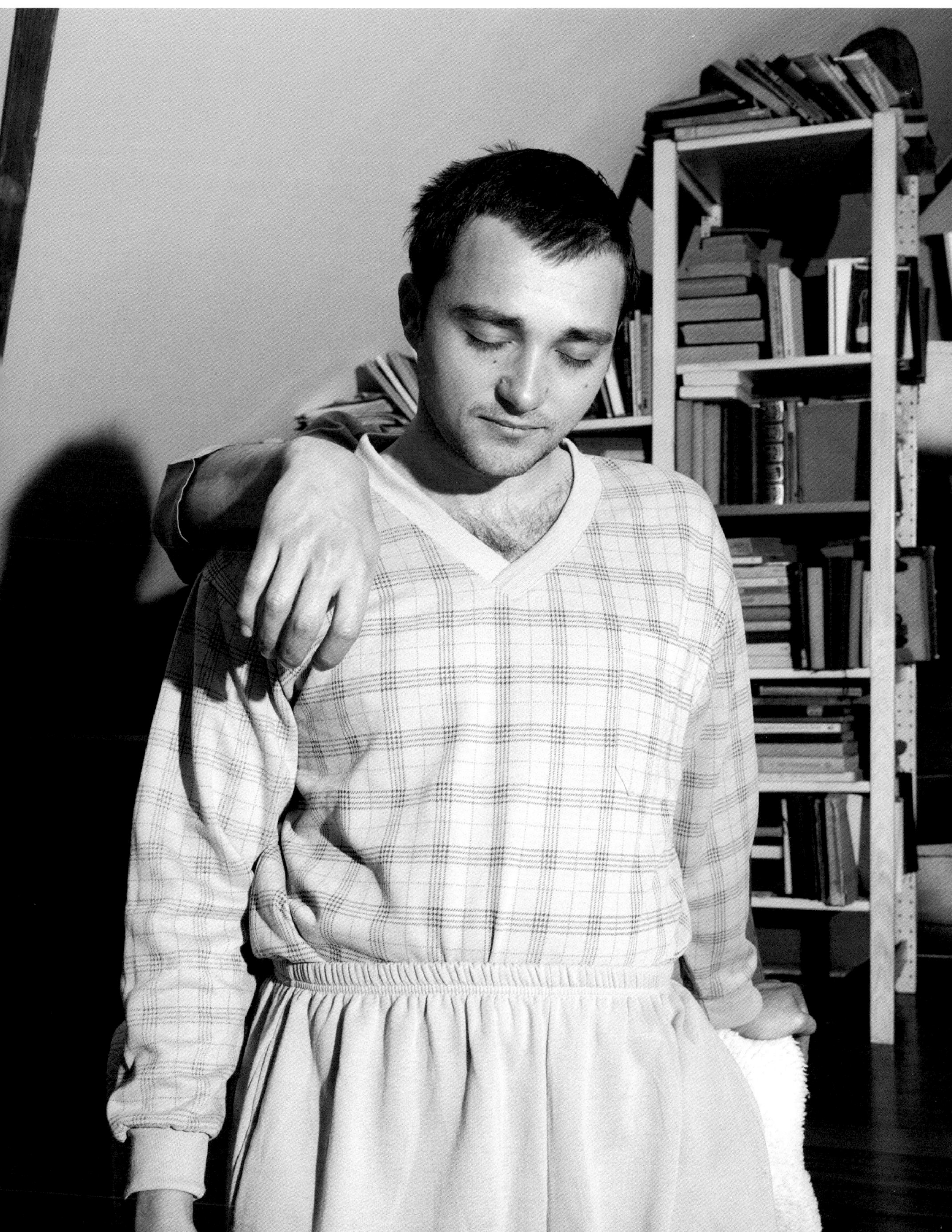

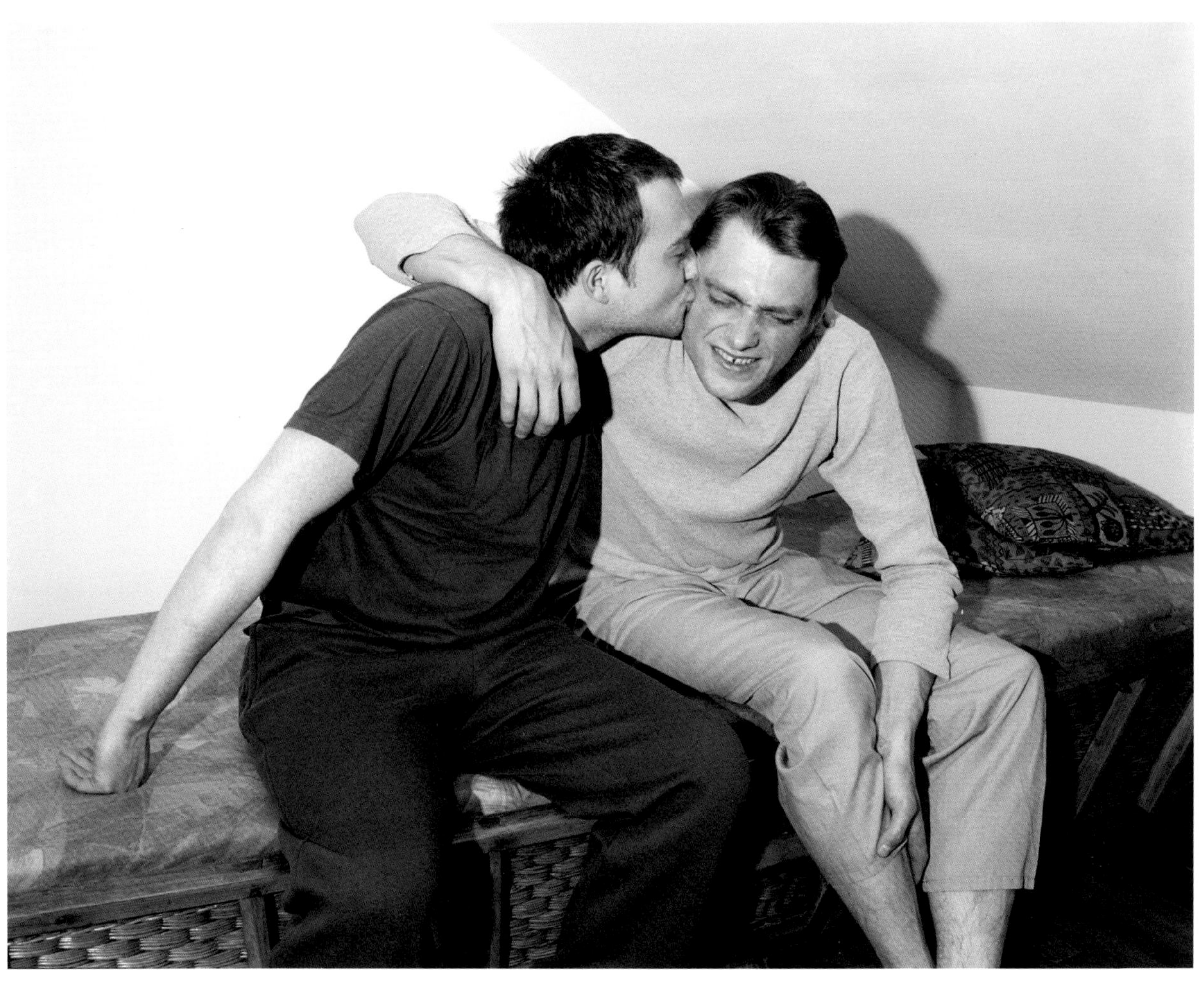

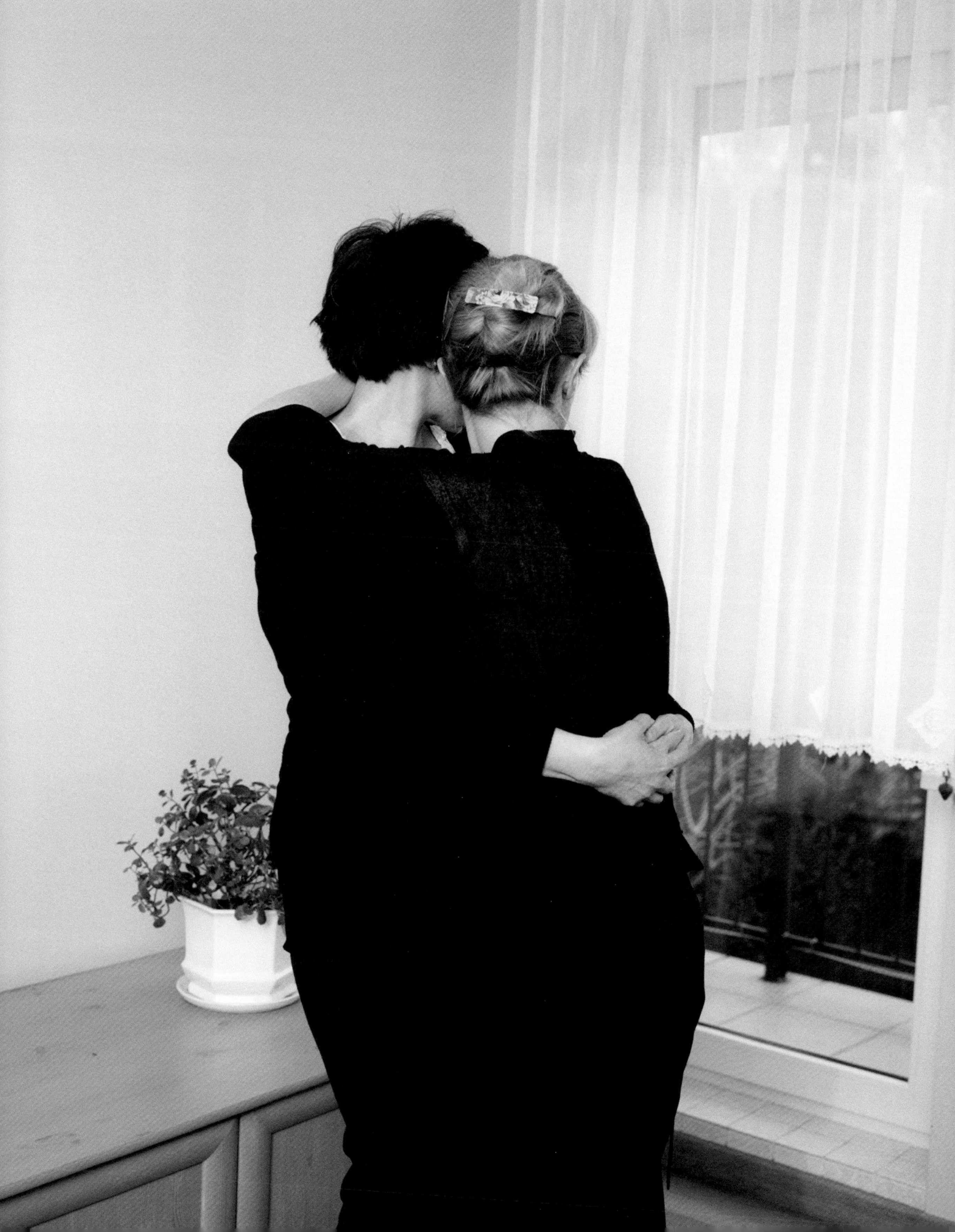

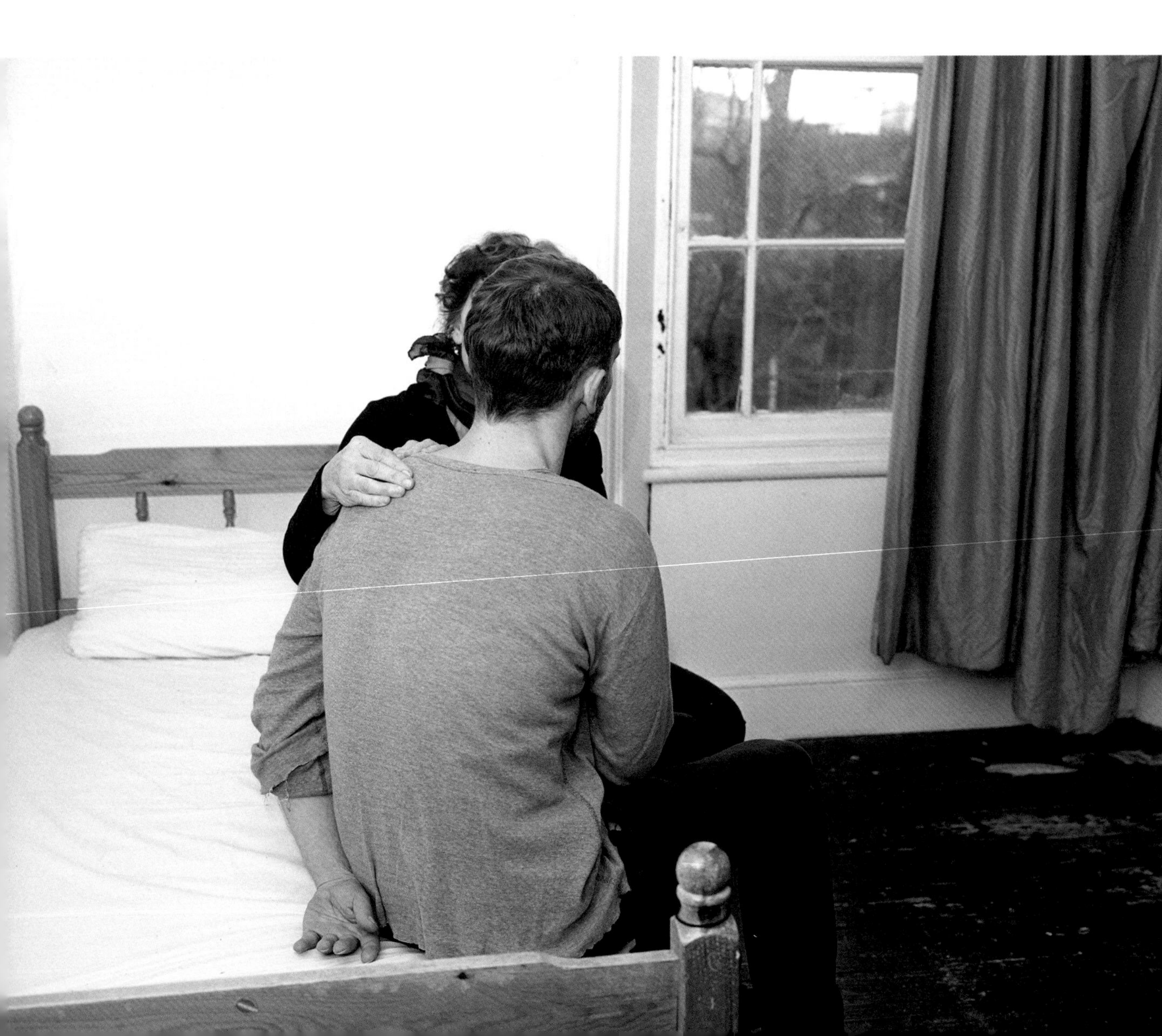

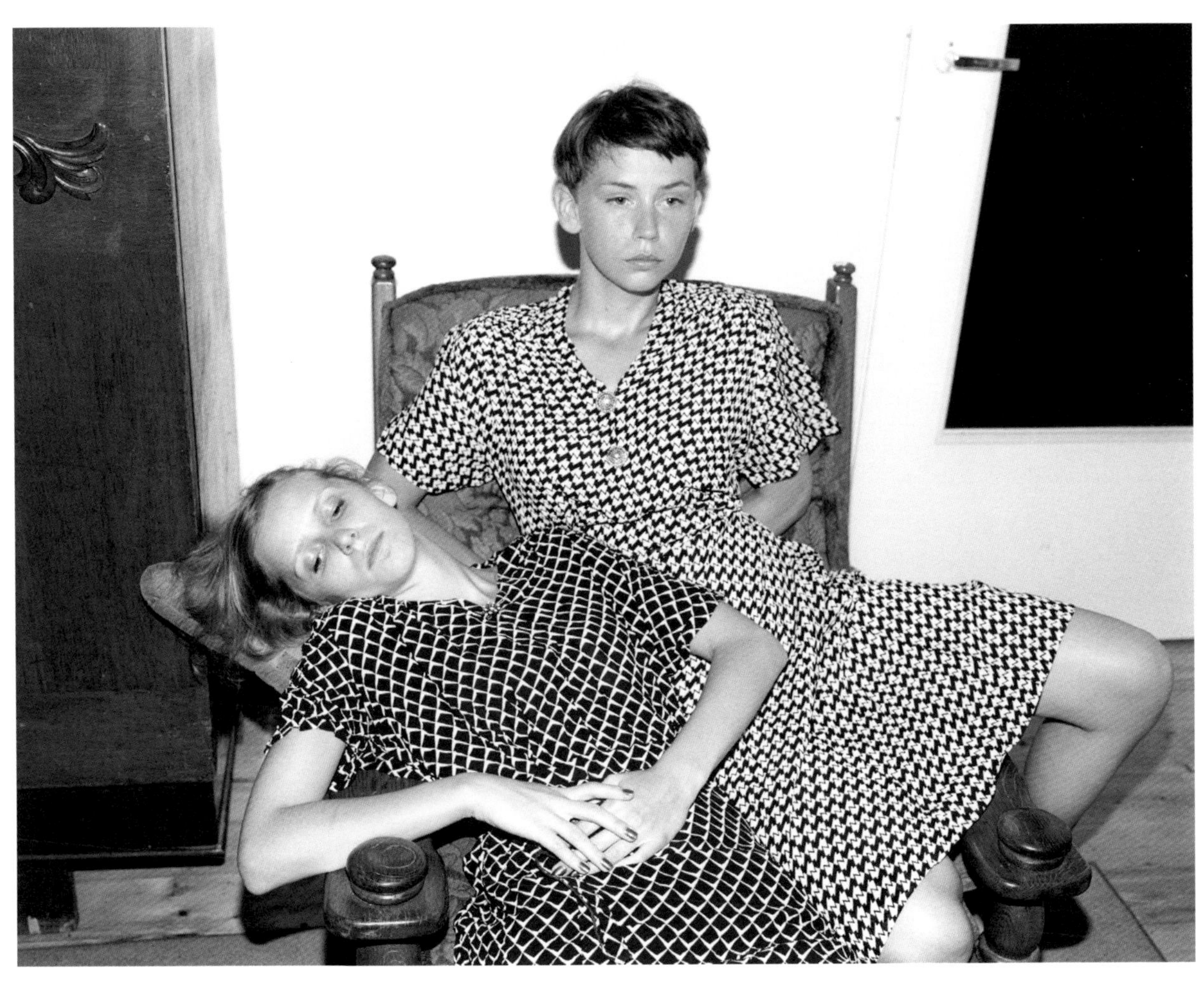

From the series
FROWST, 2013–14

II; IV; X; XIII; XXIV; XXXI

Folio

Aikaterini Gegisian

Robin Maddock

A SMALL GUIDE TO THE INVISIBLE SEAS

TEXT

Allison K. Young, 2019

IMAGES

Aikaterini Gegisian

A Small Guide to the Invisible Seas (2015), Aikaterini Gegisian's seven-part visual narrative, comprises a series of 65 photo collages in which found images of Soviet-era Armenia, Greece, and Turkey are overlaid, juxtaposed, and poetically reassembled. Sourced from mid-20th-century tourist catalogues and photographic albums, each photograph once served as a conduit for the expression of nationalist mythologies. Scenes of leisure and labour, for instance – variously mapped onto picturesque seaside villages or looming concrete towers and industrial infrastructure – promote the triumphs of the modernist project, while representations of nature and the ancient past – crumbling ancient ruins, flowering meadows, and folkloric depictions of rural life – offer a sense of comfort in rootedness and collective histories. In Gegisian's collages, however, these images are decontextualised and disrupted, which erases their ideological assertions. The images are infused with an aesthetics of ecstasy and embodiment, or destabilised through allusions to migration.

Throughout her practice, Gegisian, whose familial lineage spans the geographies of Greece, Armenia, and Turkey, has interrogated notions of cultural filiation and collective identity. In *Self Portrait as an Ottoman Woman* (2012–16), she searched for belonging amid contradictory ethnic, social, and religious formations across a diversity of territories that were once united under Ottoman rule. Taking the form of a gridded matrix of vintage postcards depicting female subjects from Cairo to Thessaloniki, this work calls attention to the ways in which imperialist and Orientalist fantasies are projected onto the female body.

A Small Guide to the Invisible Seas likewise envisions the body, the city, and the sea as complex sites of ideological formation. The series was produced for the exhibition *Armenity* at the 56th Venice Biennale, which commemorated the centennial anniversary of the Armenian Genocide by re-examining Armenian identity through the lens of diaspora and deterritorialisation. Gegisian's project, likewise, transcends the strictures of the nation state. In the first image of the first chapter,

The Sea of Echoes, she overlays two photographs of Mount Ararat, seen from either side of the Turkish–Armenian border, highlighting the incongruity between topography and geopolitics and acknowledging how natural phenomena are translated into nationalist monuments.

Each chapter in *A Small Guide to the Invisible Seas* centres on the image of the sea as a borderless, generative zone of contact and relation, fluidity and circulation. In chapter six, *The Sea of Waves* (reproduced here), which addresses metamorphosis and change, the first few collages make water visible within urban and social space. Like roadways and cities, bodies of water engender the circulation of images, ideas, and people across space and time. In the final collages, Gegisian celebrates water's resistance to fixity and containment, its relationship to the body. There is an explicit embrace of sexual energy in repeated images of waterfalls, as white rapids cascade over rocky terrain, beyond the boundaries of the photographic frame. Such images emphasise the gendered symbolism in myths of national origin – the *birth* of the nation, the founding *fathers*.

In one collage, two young divers swim in Cleopatra's Pool, gliding above the submerged ruins of classical columns. From our contemporary vantage, it is difficult not to interpret the scene as a harbinger of the rise and fall of civilizations, the threat of rising sea levels, and environmental cataclysm. The sea has become an assurgent symbol of the stateless, the fugitive. The so-called migrant crisis is communicated through affective images of boats carrying refugees to European shores. Amid the ensuing global rise in nationalist isolationism, the UK braces for Brexit, and the symbolic import of the nation's identity as an island grows increasingly potent, prompting questions about the sustainability of transnational unity. Gegisian's *The Sea of Waves* reminds us, however, that history moves in cycles. Social and political movements come in waves that swell, dissipate, and re-emerge anew. Engagement with the past can help us to better shape the future, to set transformation in motion.

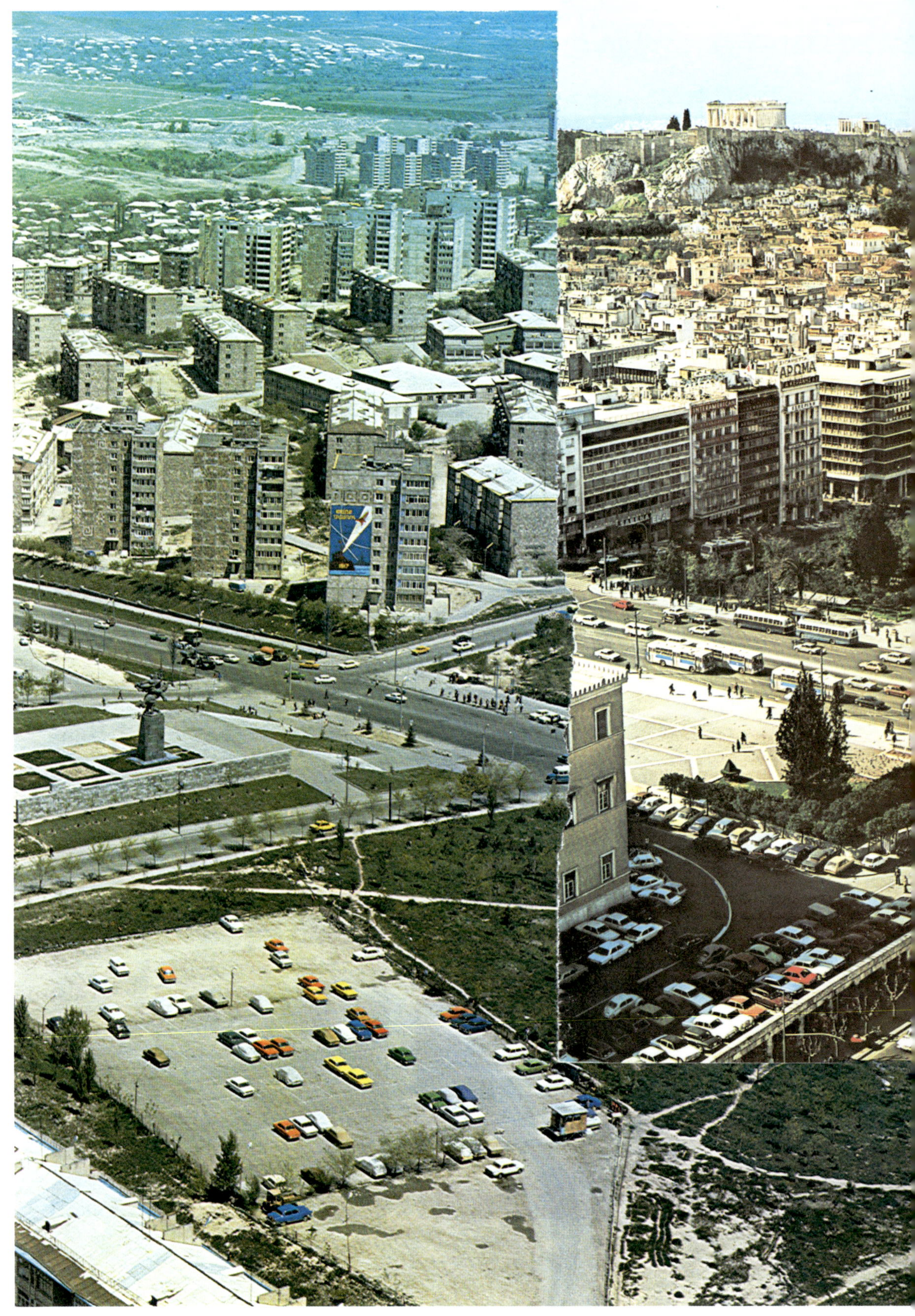

ΑΡΩΜΑ

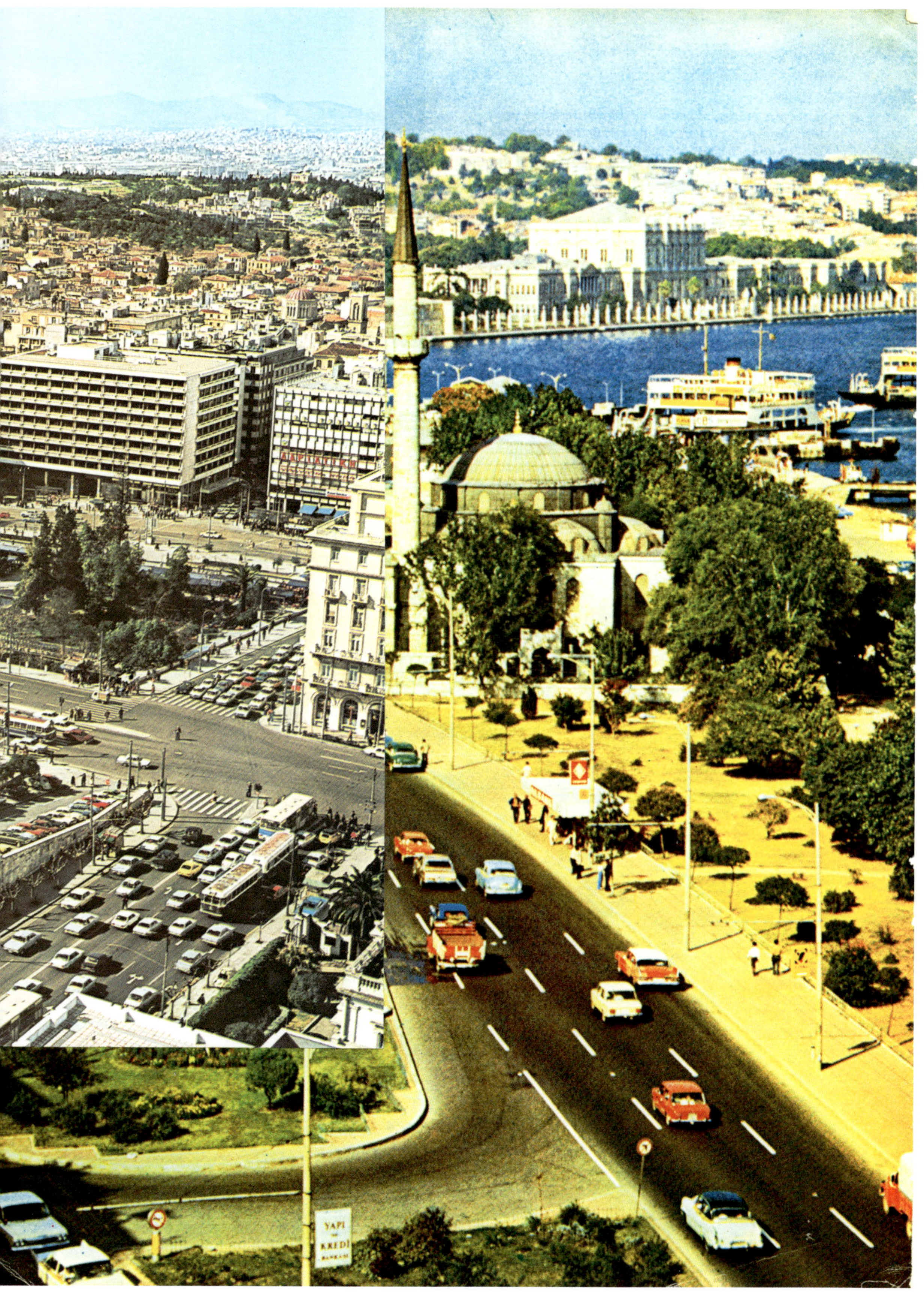

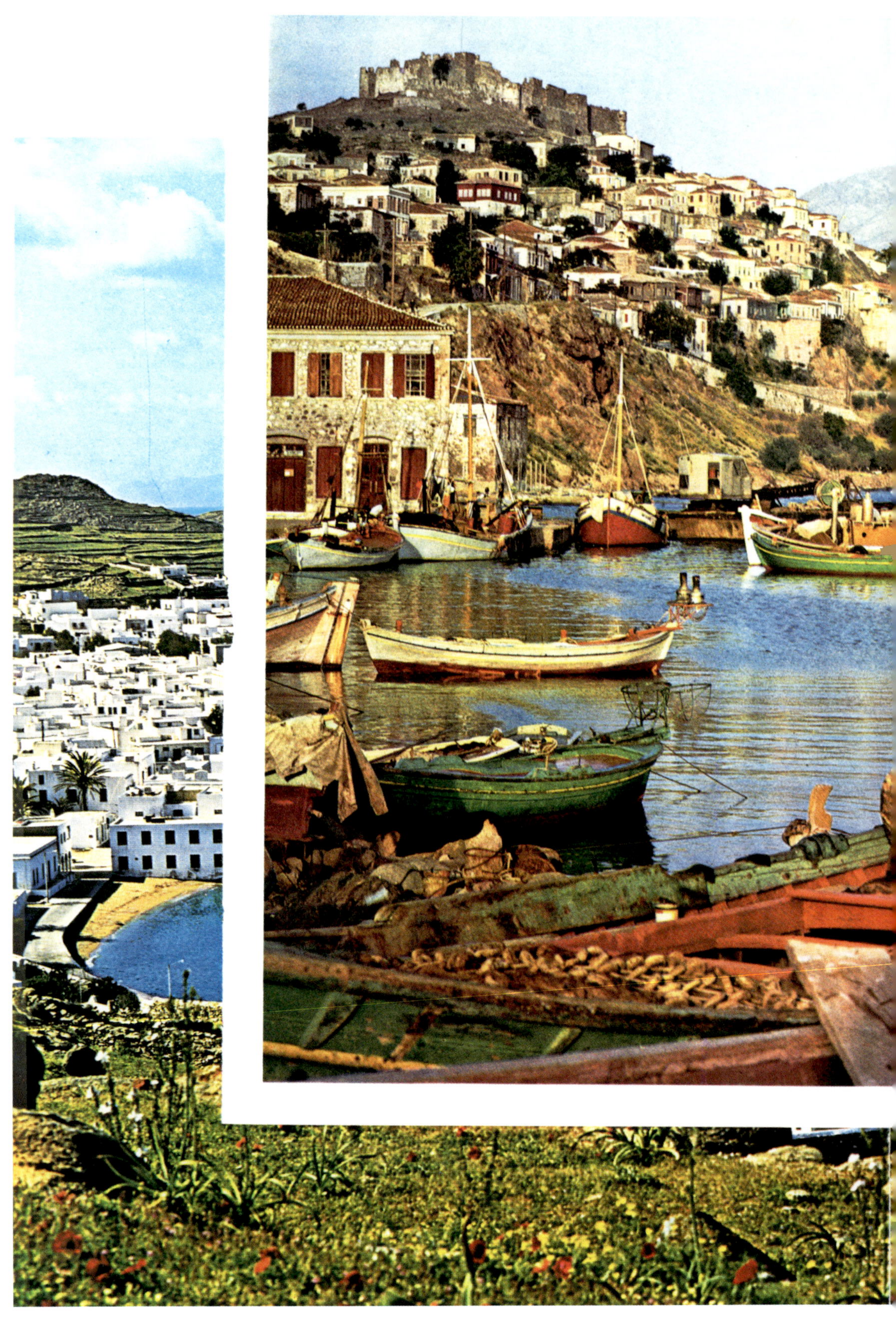

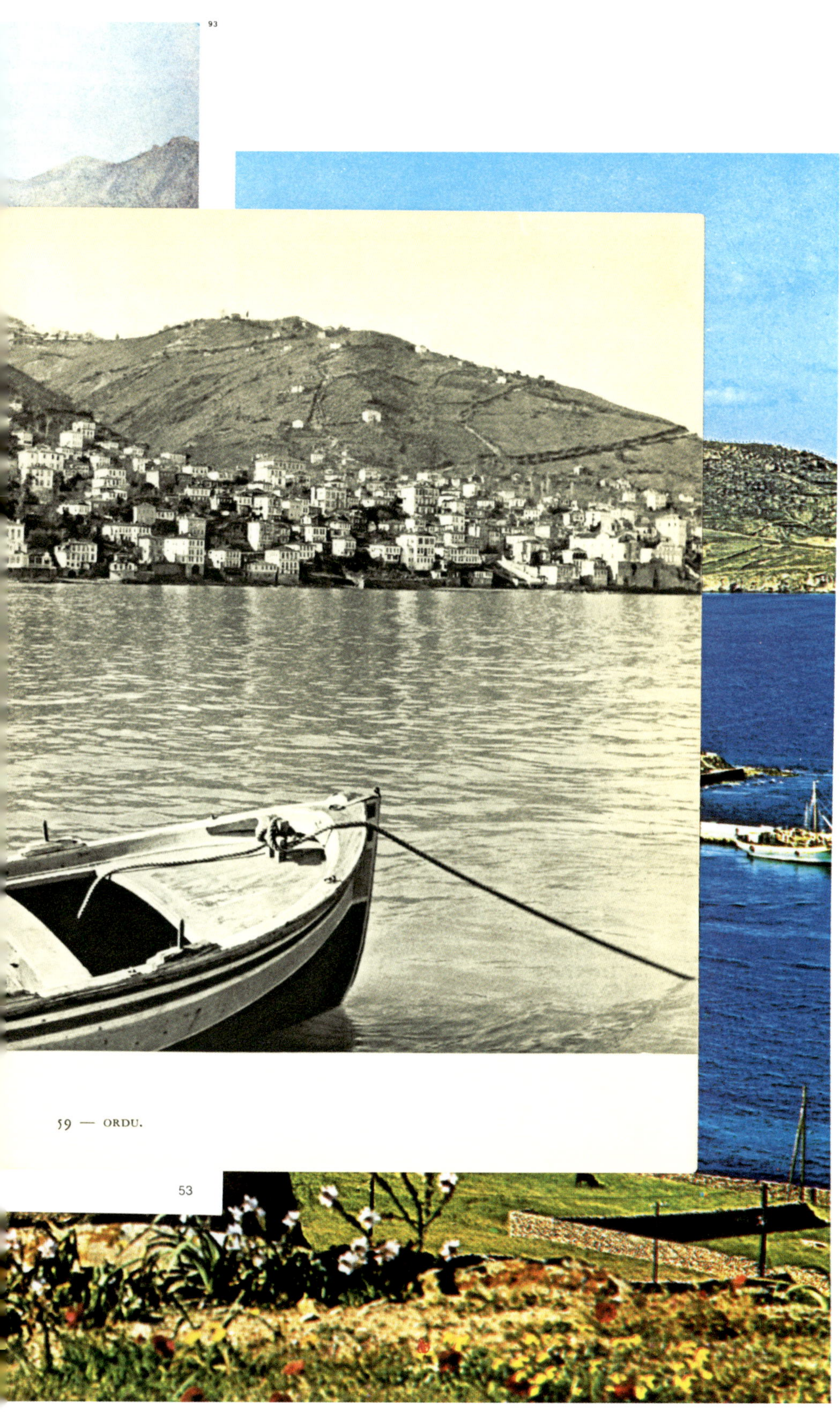

59 — ORDU.

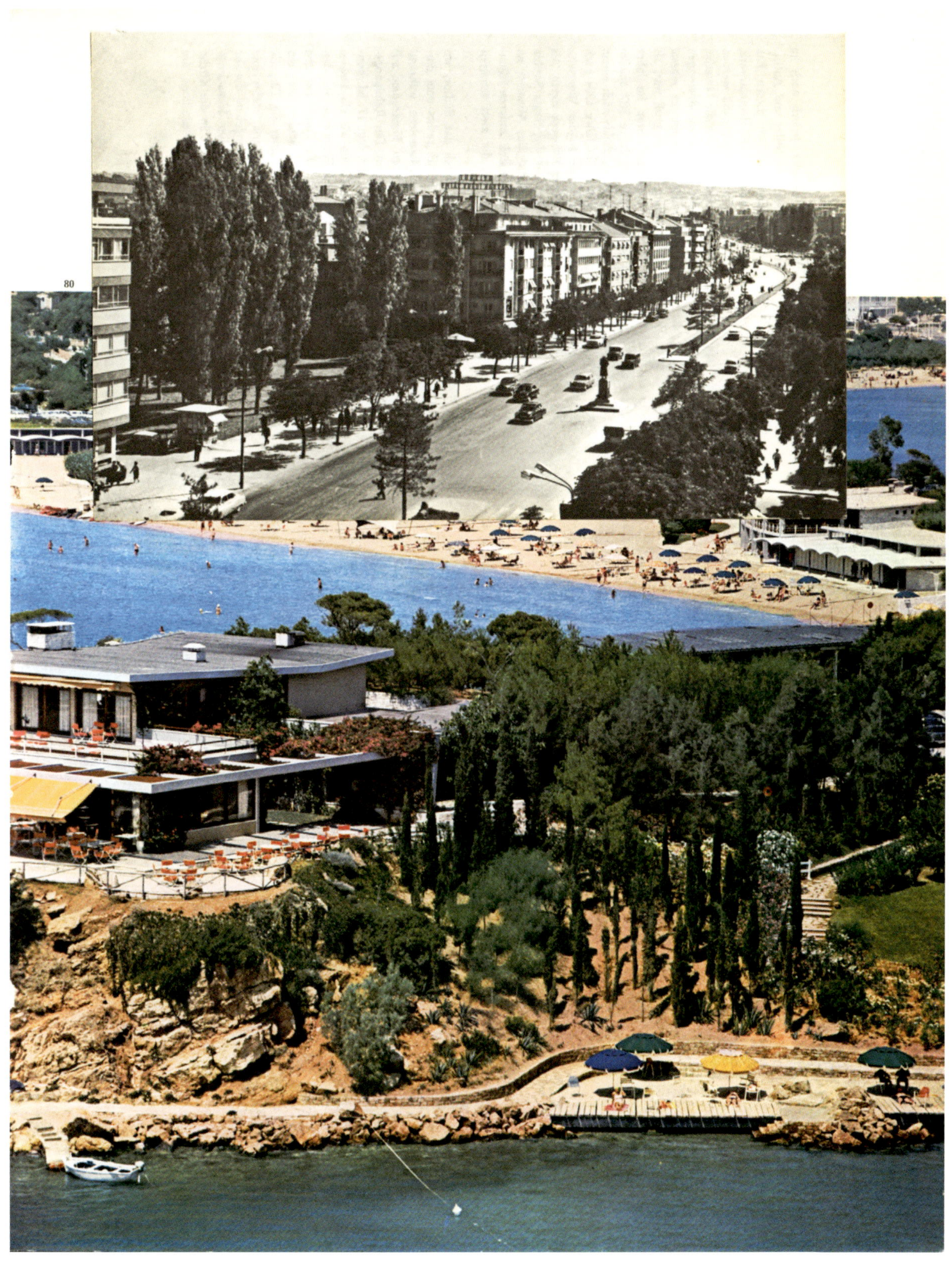

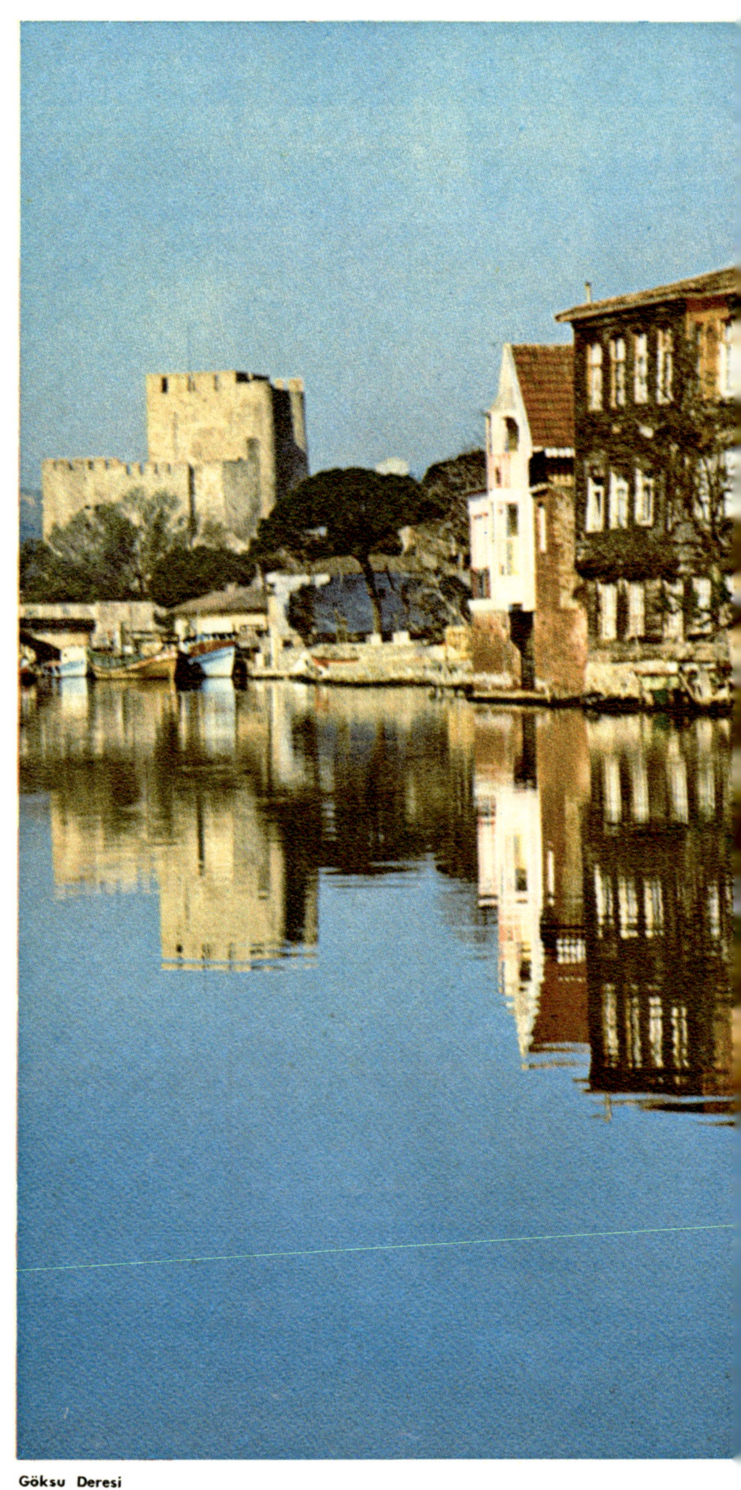

Göksu Deresi

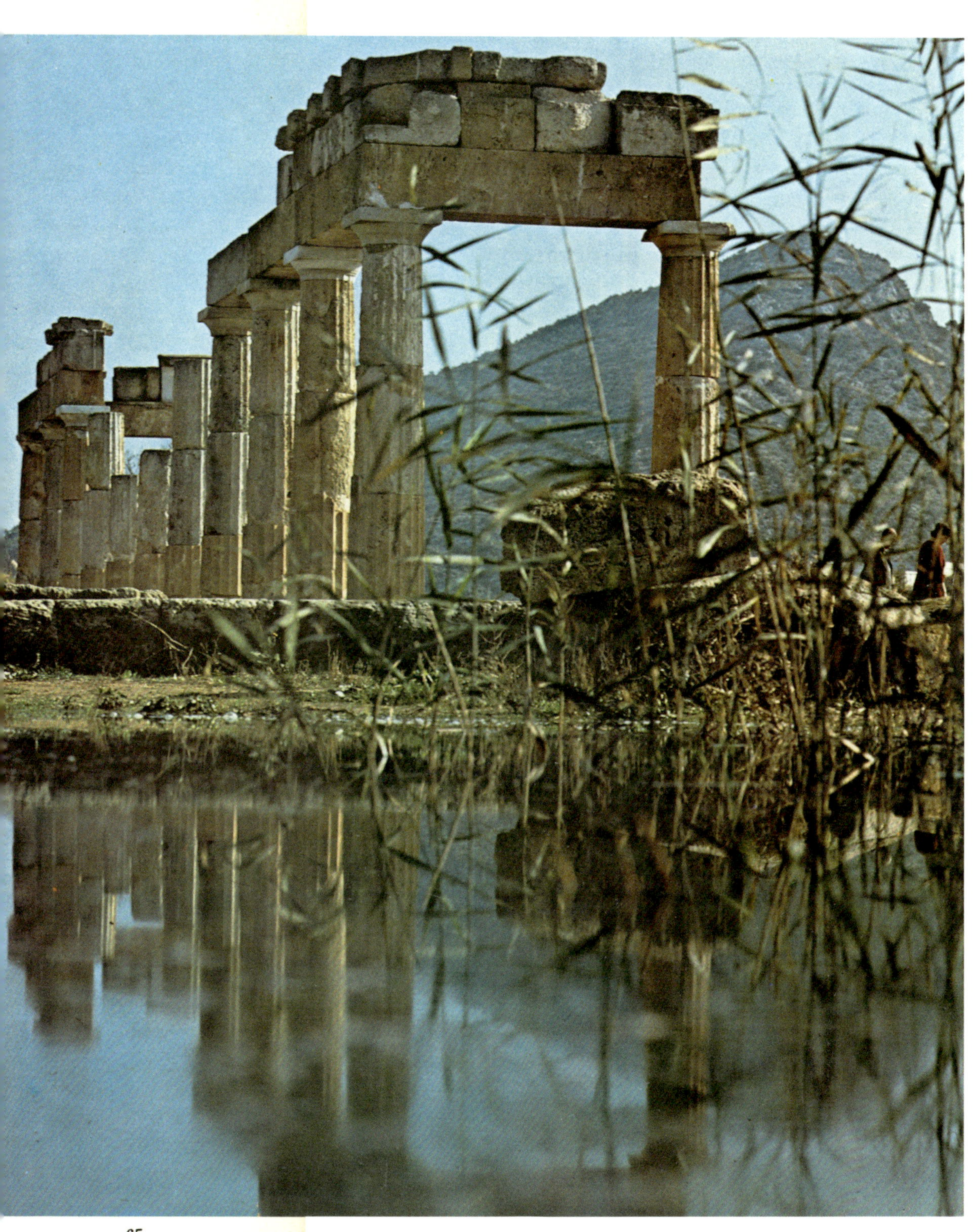

65

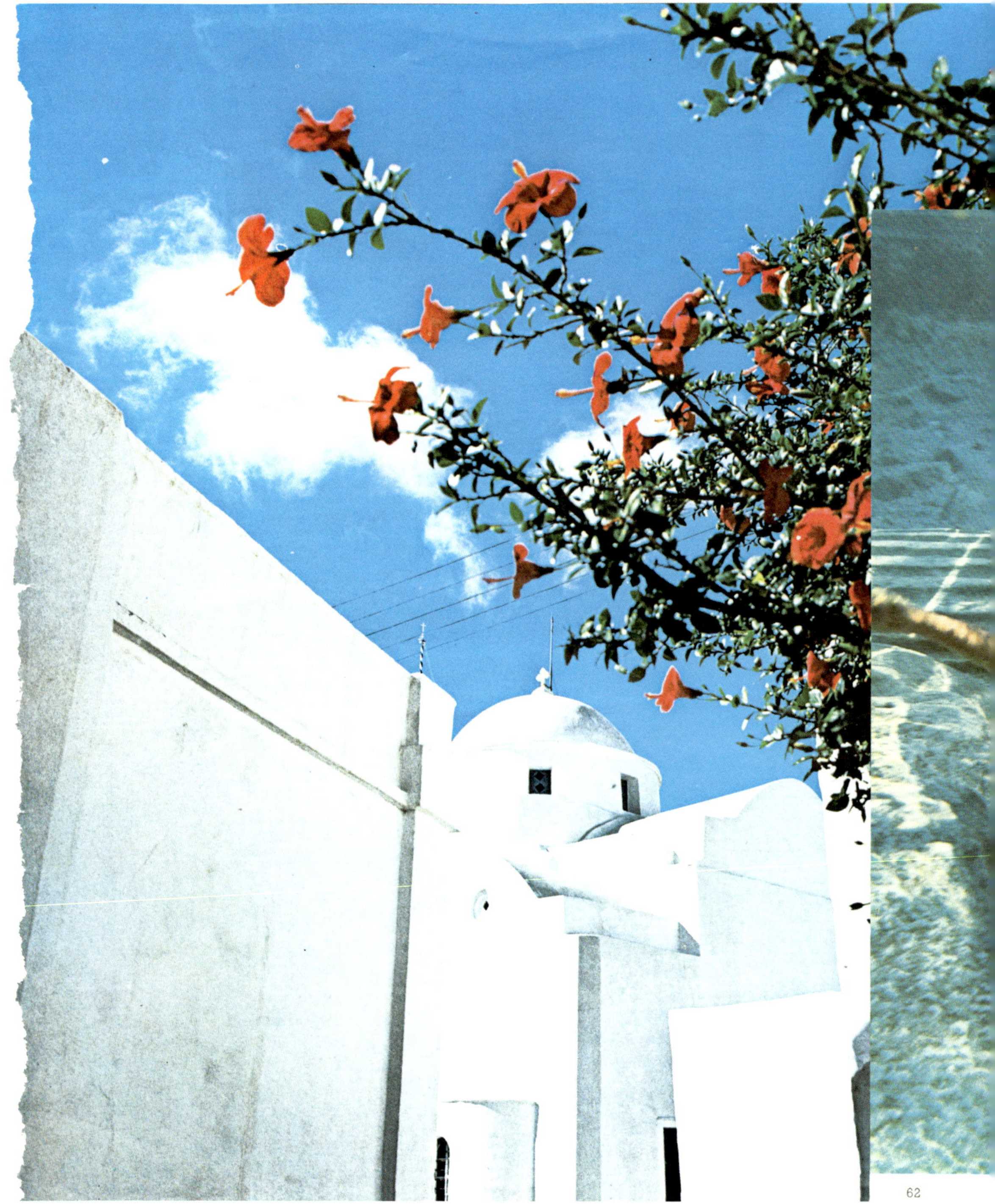

62

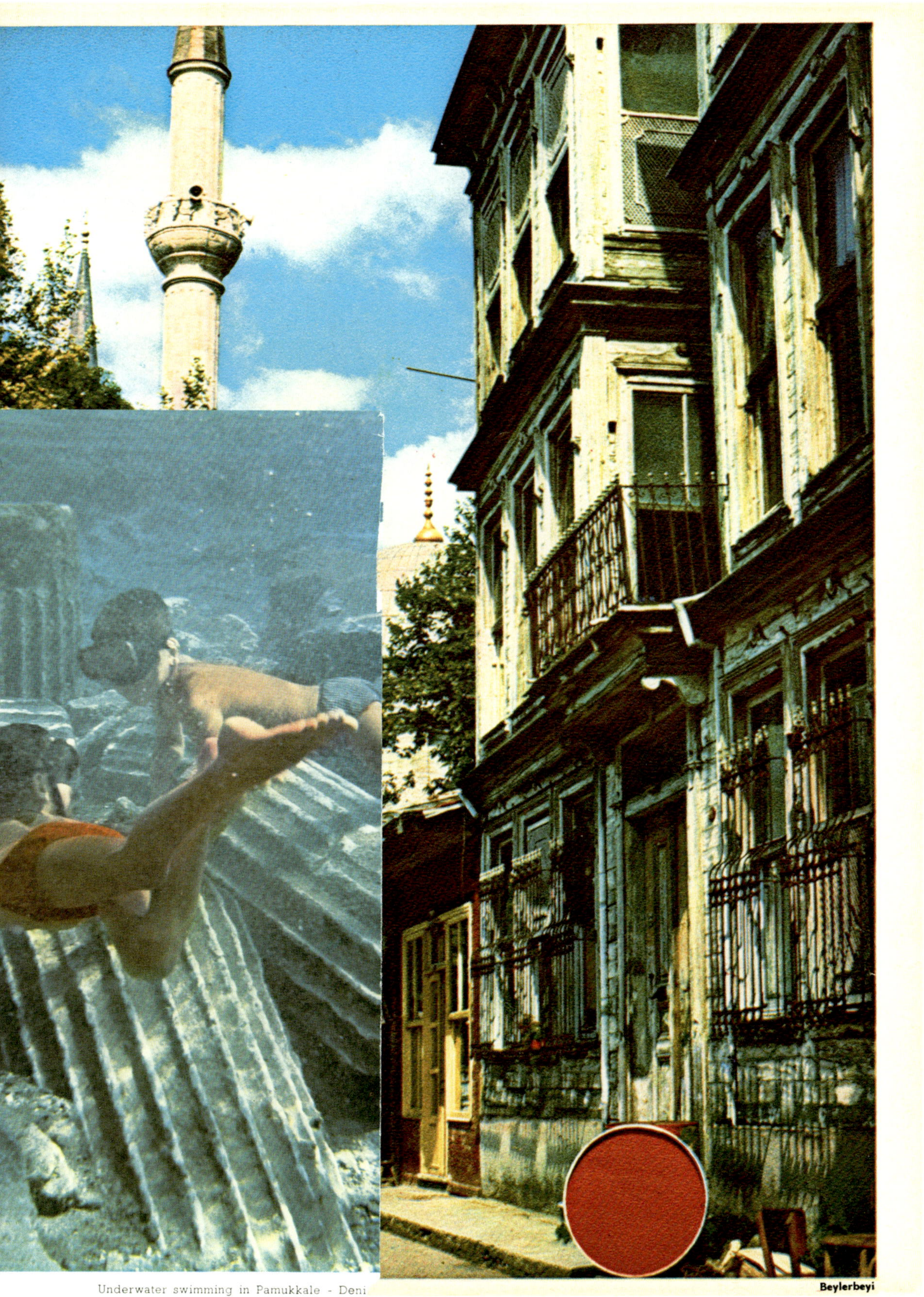

Underwater swimming in Pamukkale - Deni

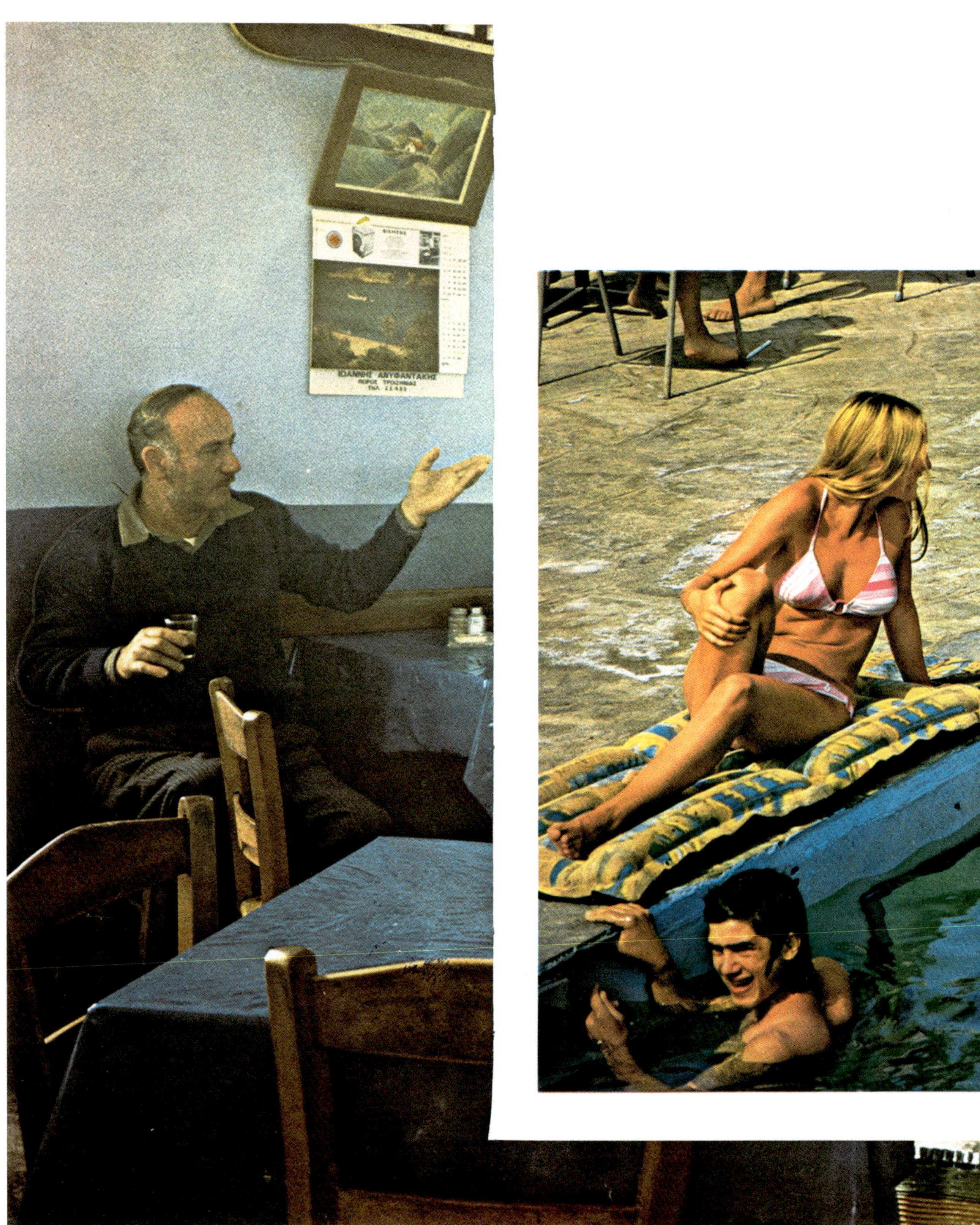

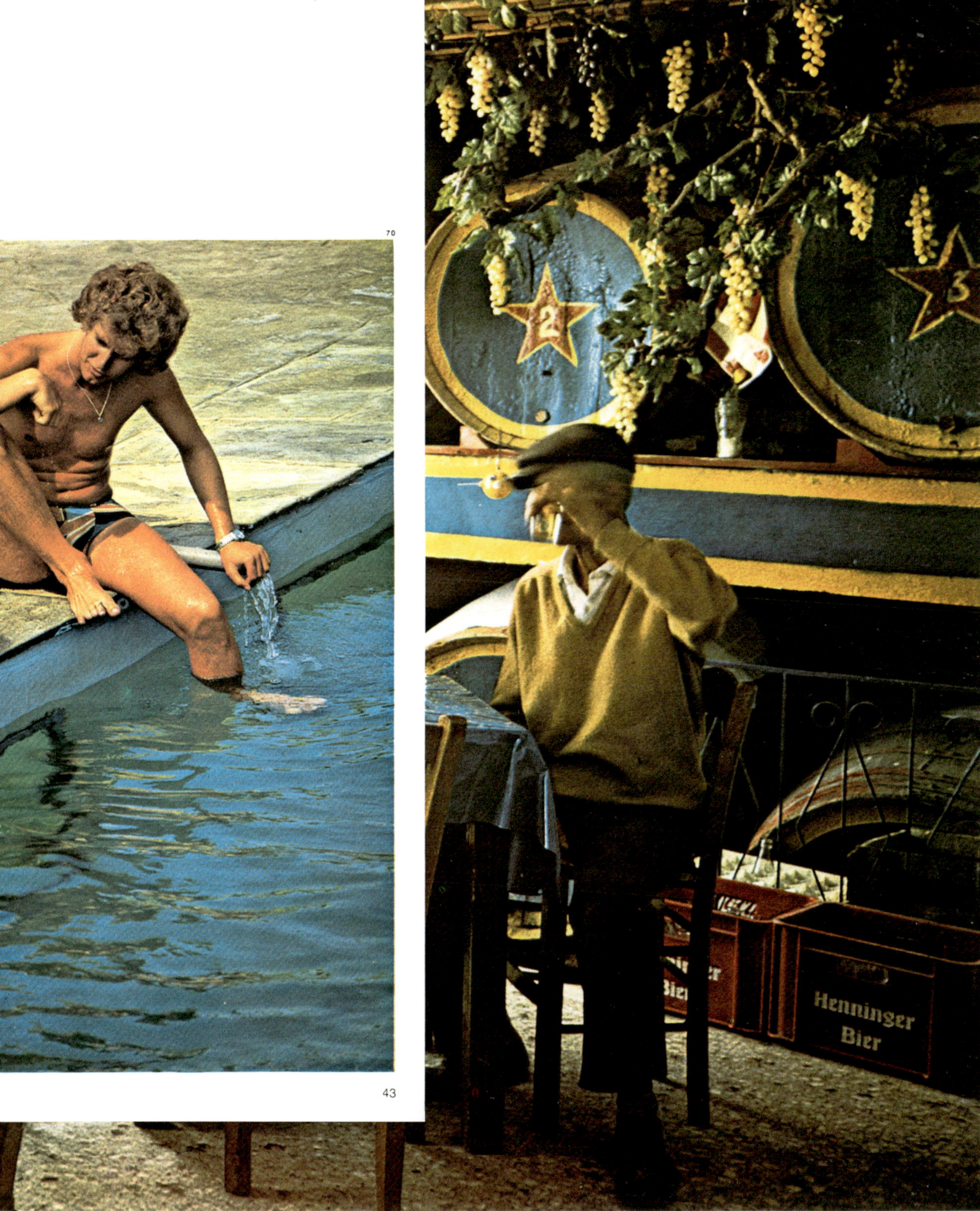

Henninger
Bier

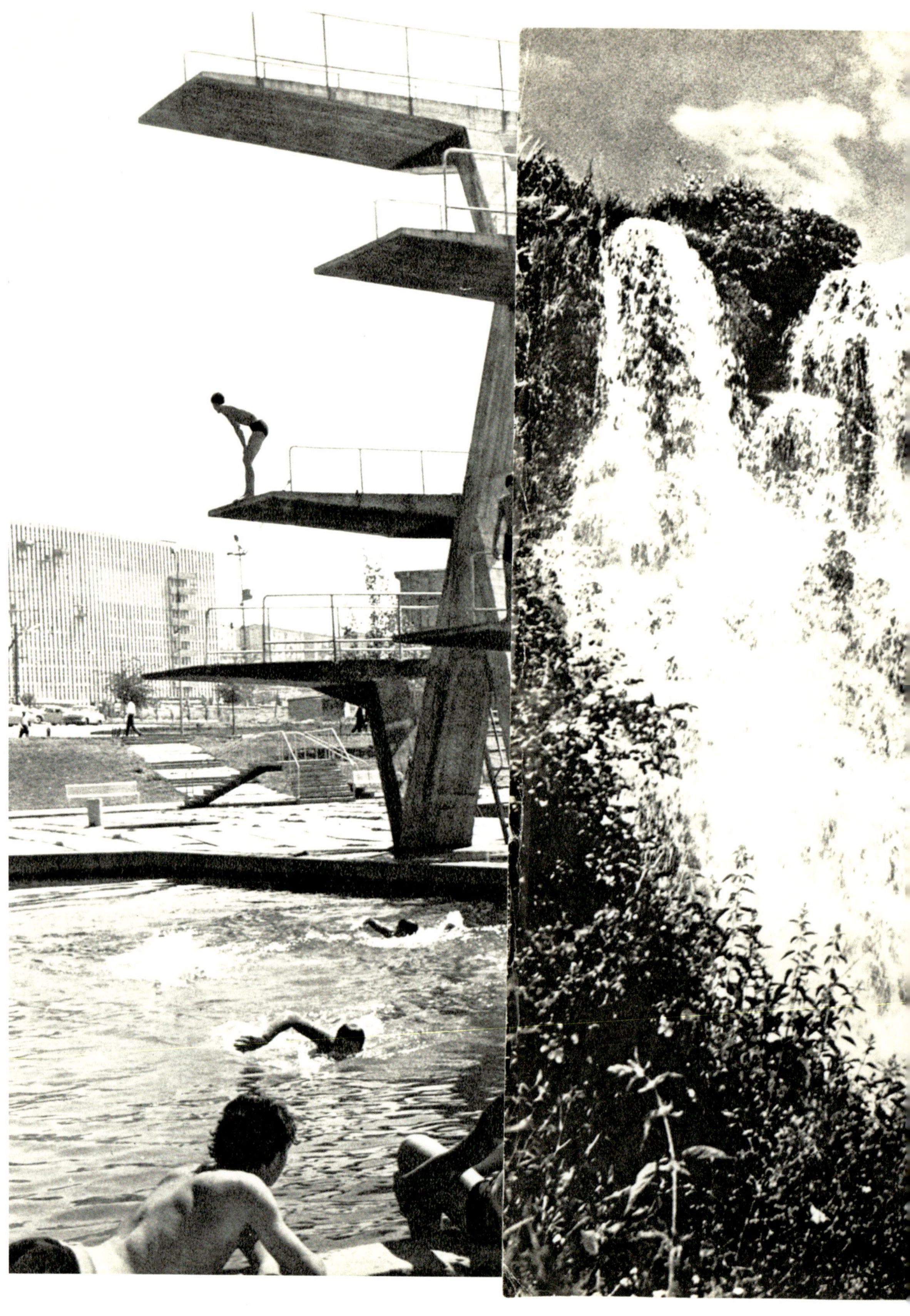

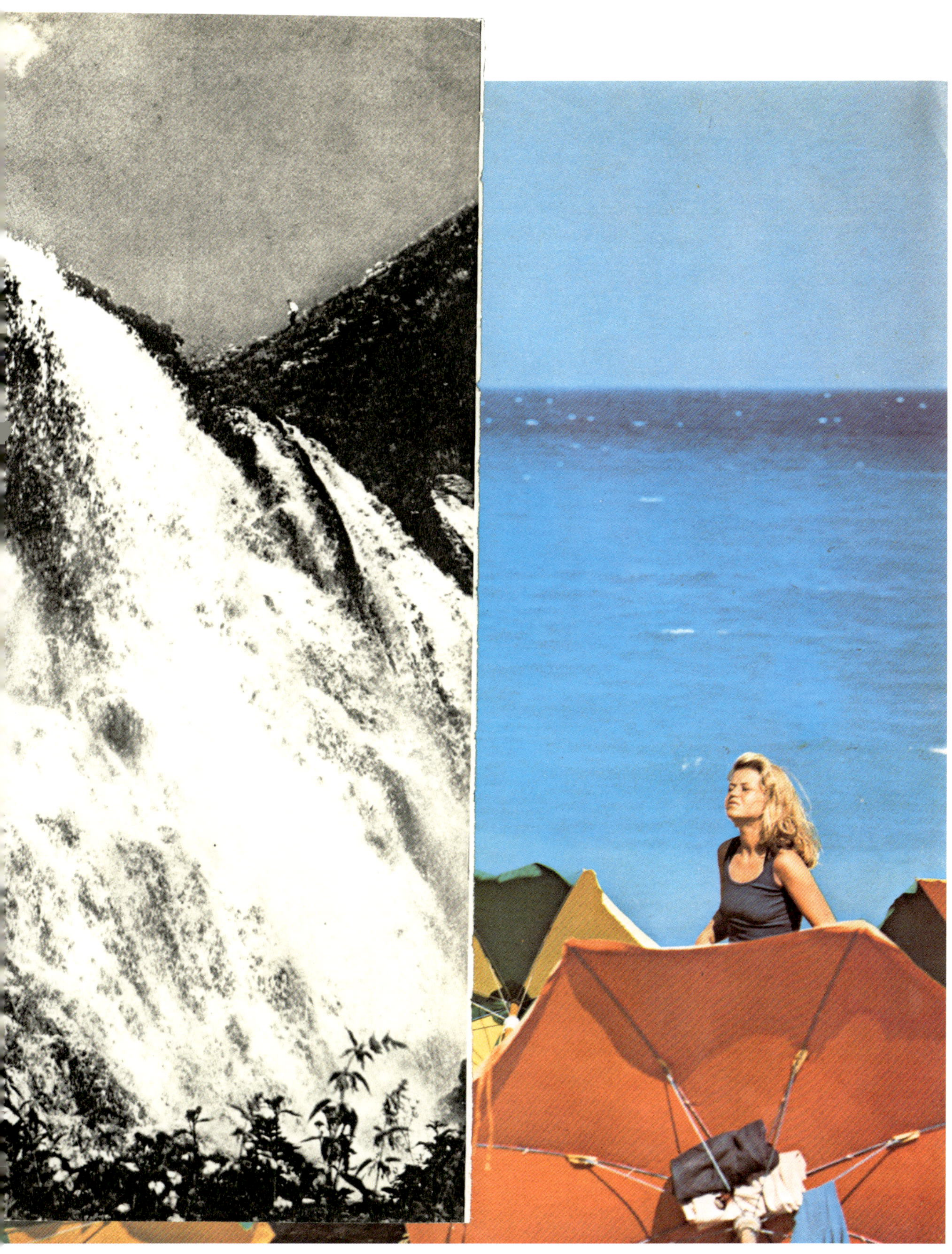

Aikaterini Gegisian, *A Small
Guide to the Invisible Seas*,
Chapter Six, *The Sea of Waves*

Collages on Paper and
Artist's Book, Dimensions
Variable, 2015

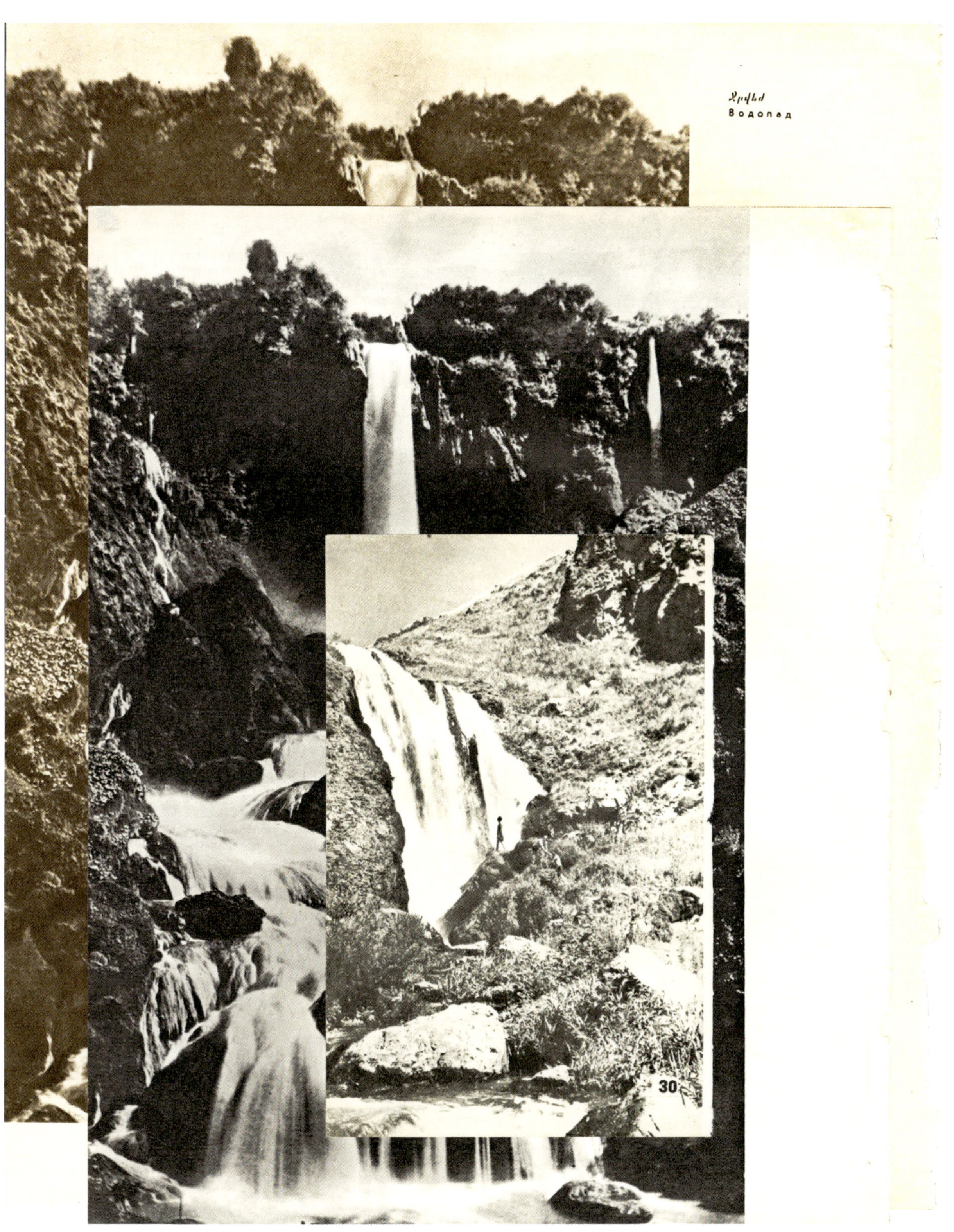

Ջրվեժ
Водопад

Robin Maddock
Nothing We Can't Fix by Running Away

In his project *Nothing We Can't Fix by Running Away*, Robin Maddock attempts to build an egalitarian portrait of English national identity. Drawing from his archive of 20 years of material and new work, Maddock was fully aware of the limits of photography to portray such a complex situation, stating that 'We live in times where the concept of nationhood is in flux and a single mass identity is no longer an option.

I tried to bring disparate aspects of England into close proximity, shaped by the two poles of good and evil – impossible to photograph yet, for me, defining the limits of the country.'

In his project, photographs are complemented by older material from Maddock's archive, found images, collage, and ephemera. When viewed en masse, the project attempts to create an index of what it means and looks like to live in England now.

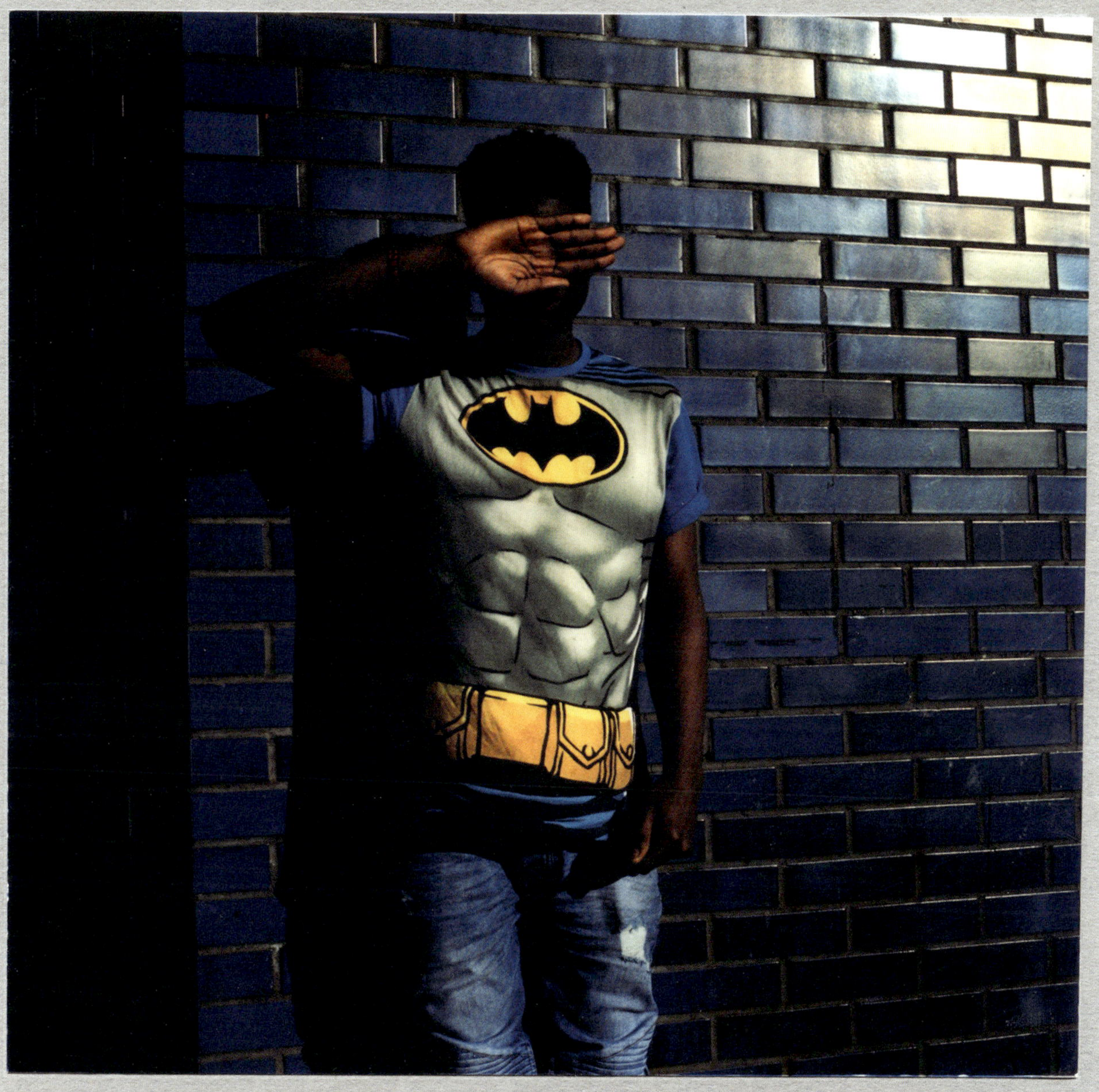

Brexit
Time
England

Robin Maddock

Robin Maddock

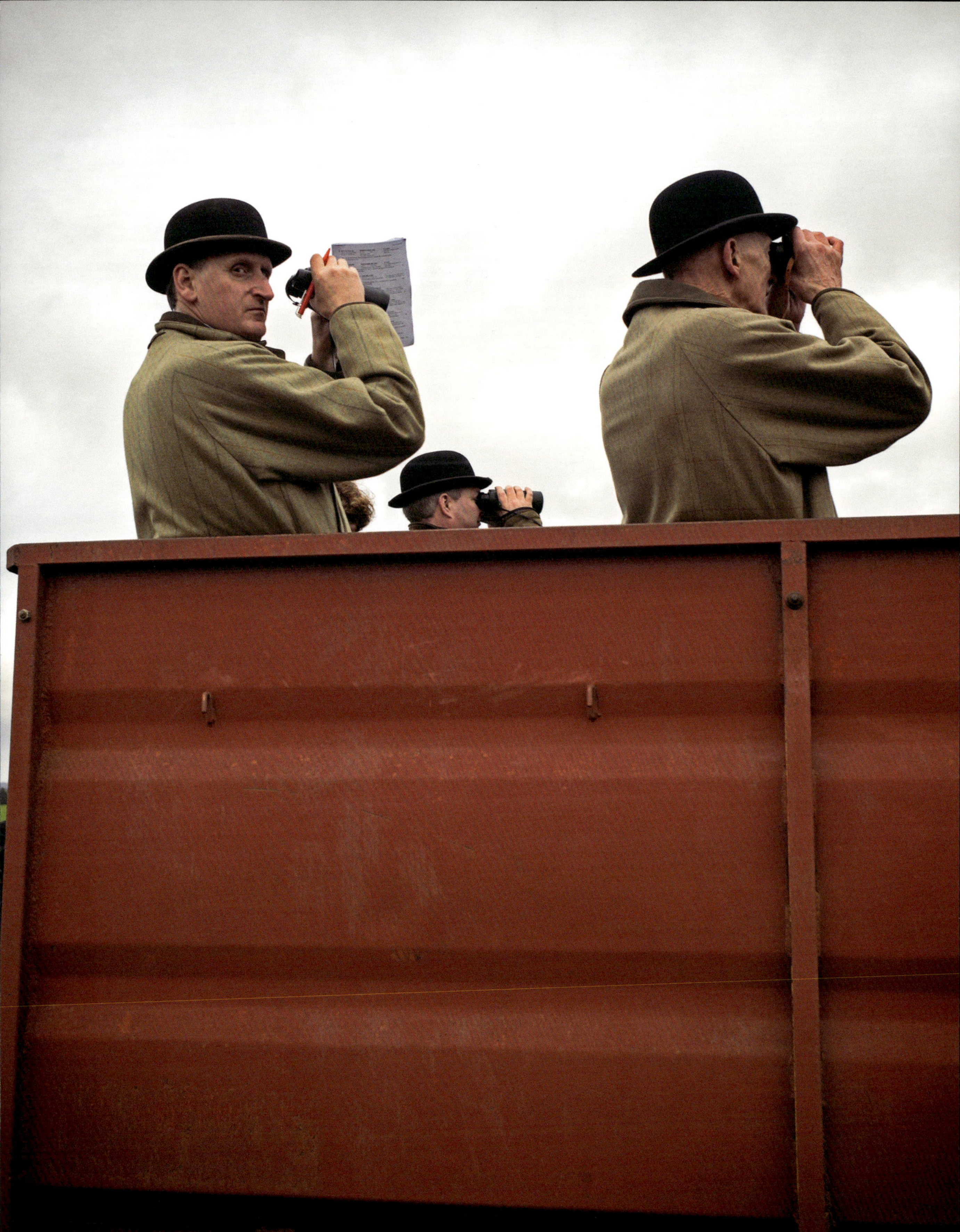

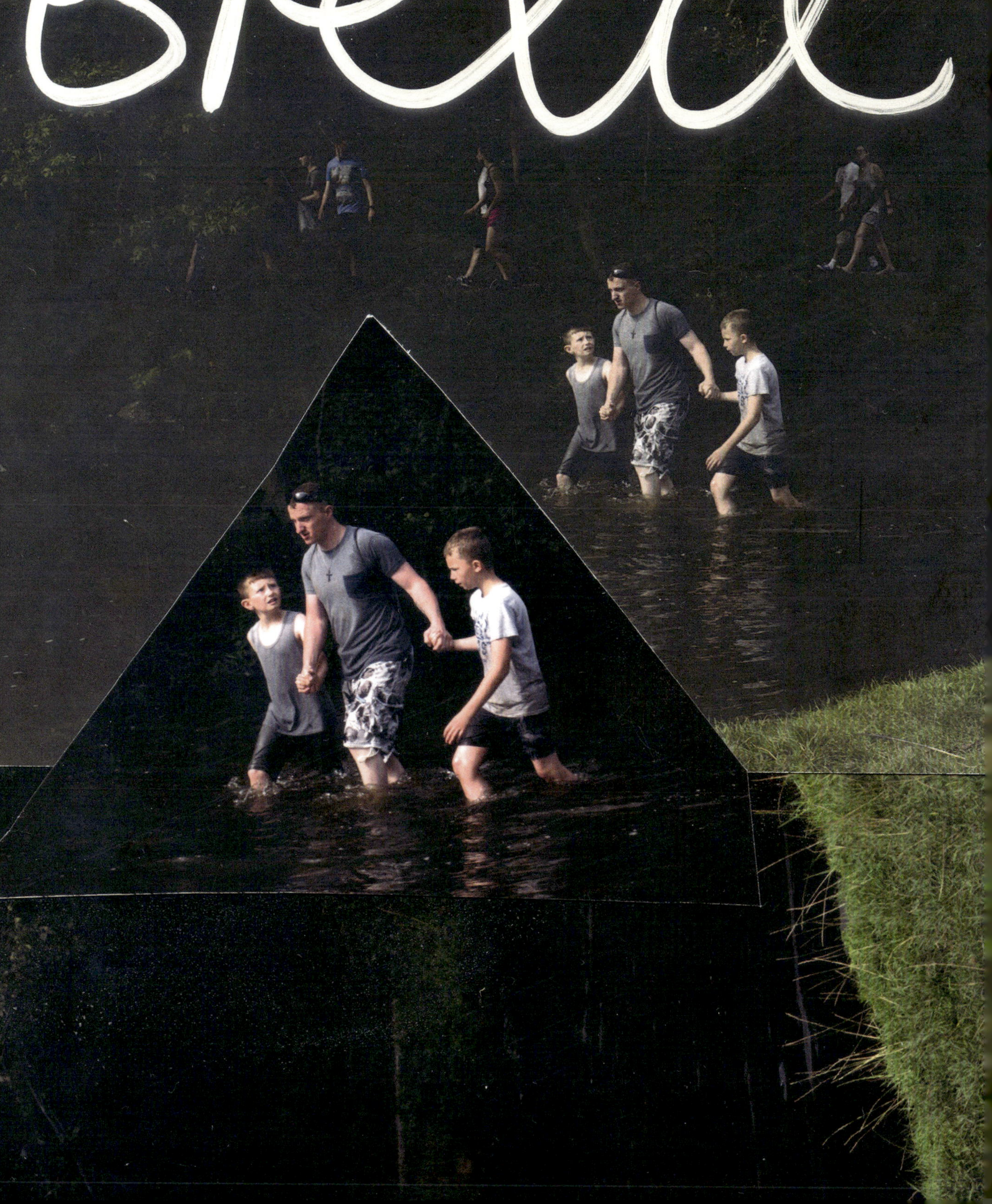

Brexit

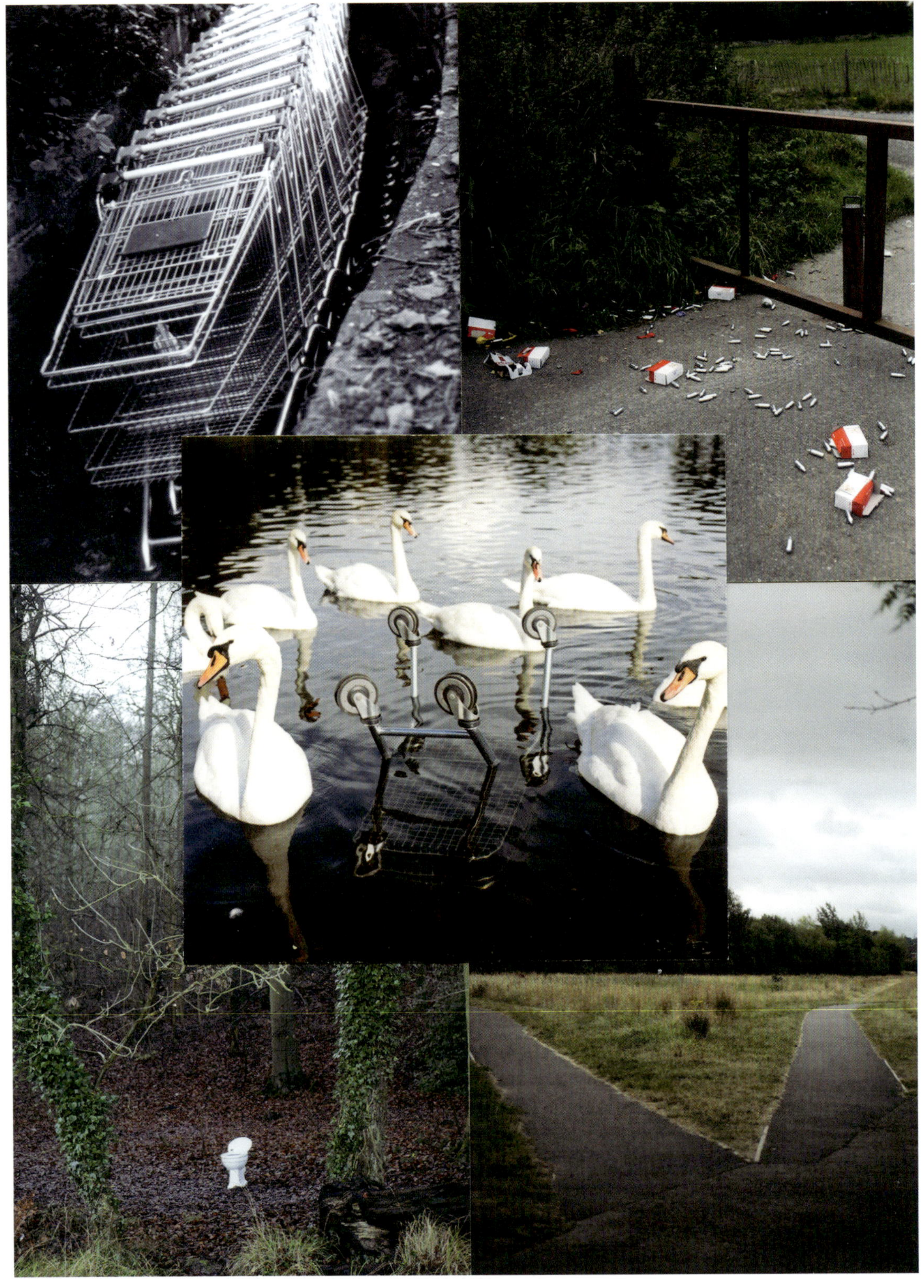

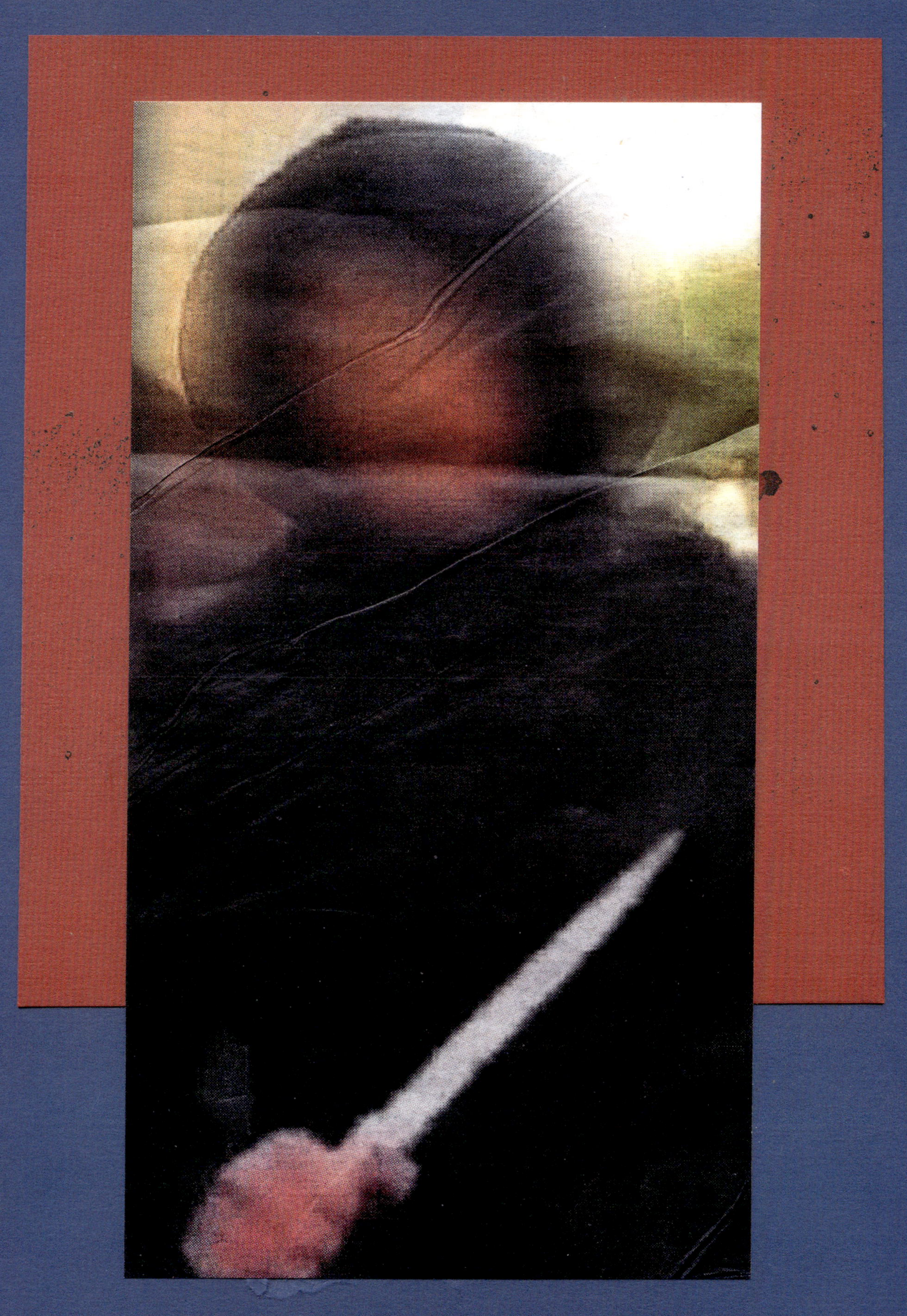

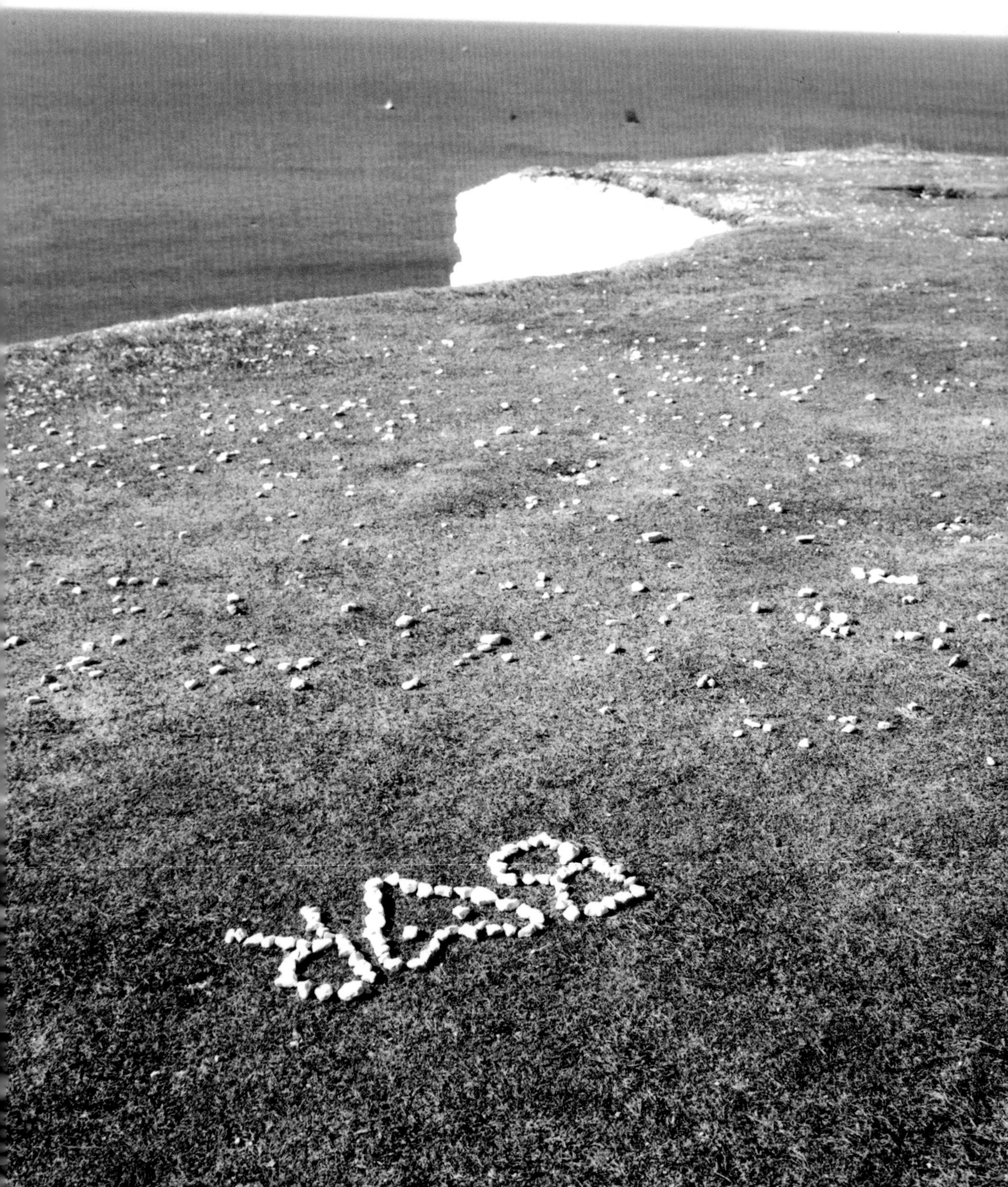

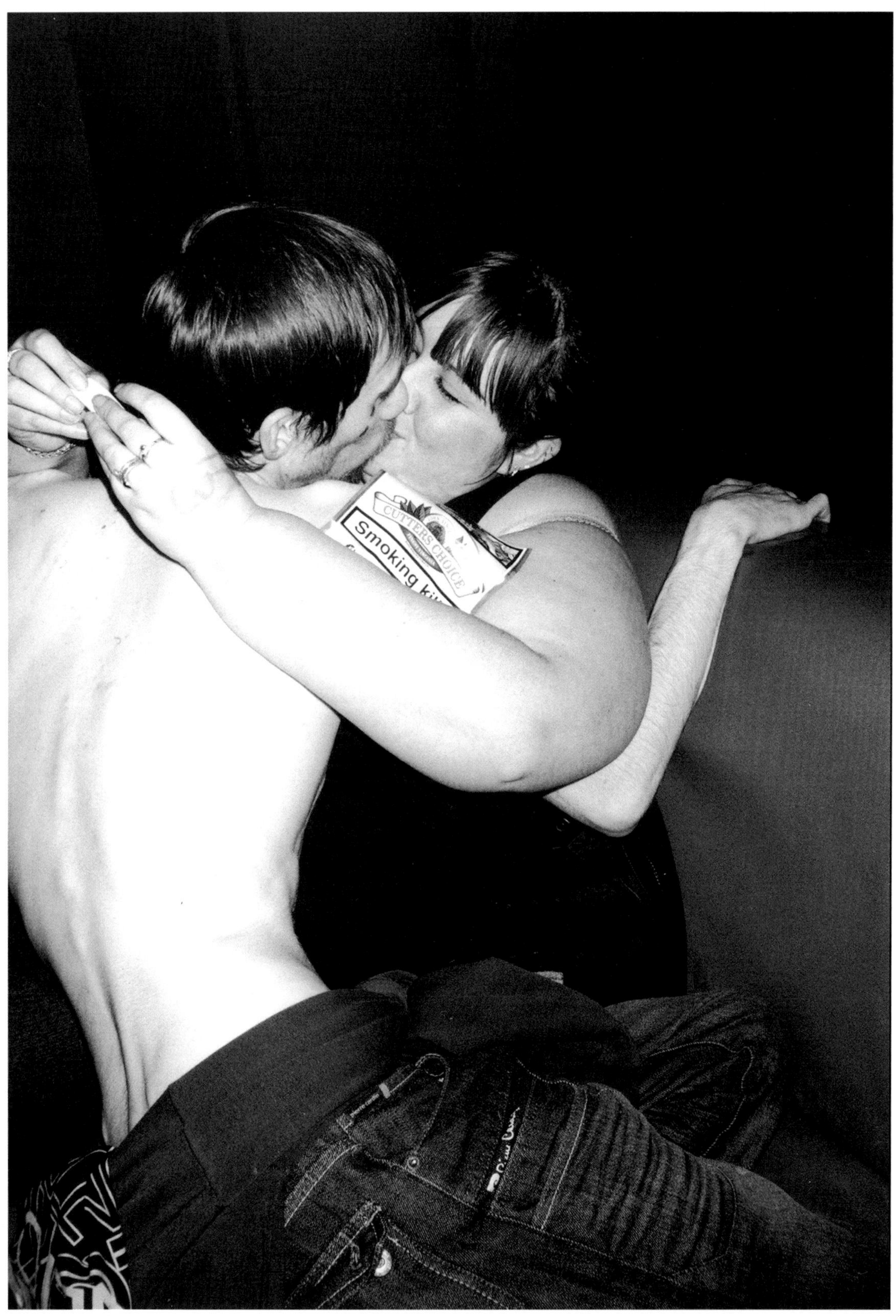

CUTTERS CHOICE
Smoking kills

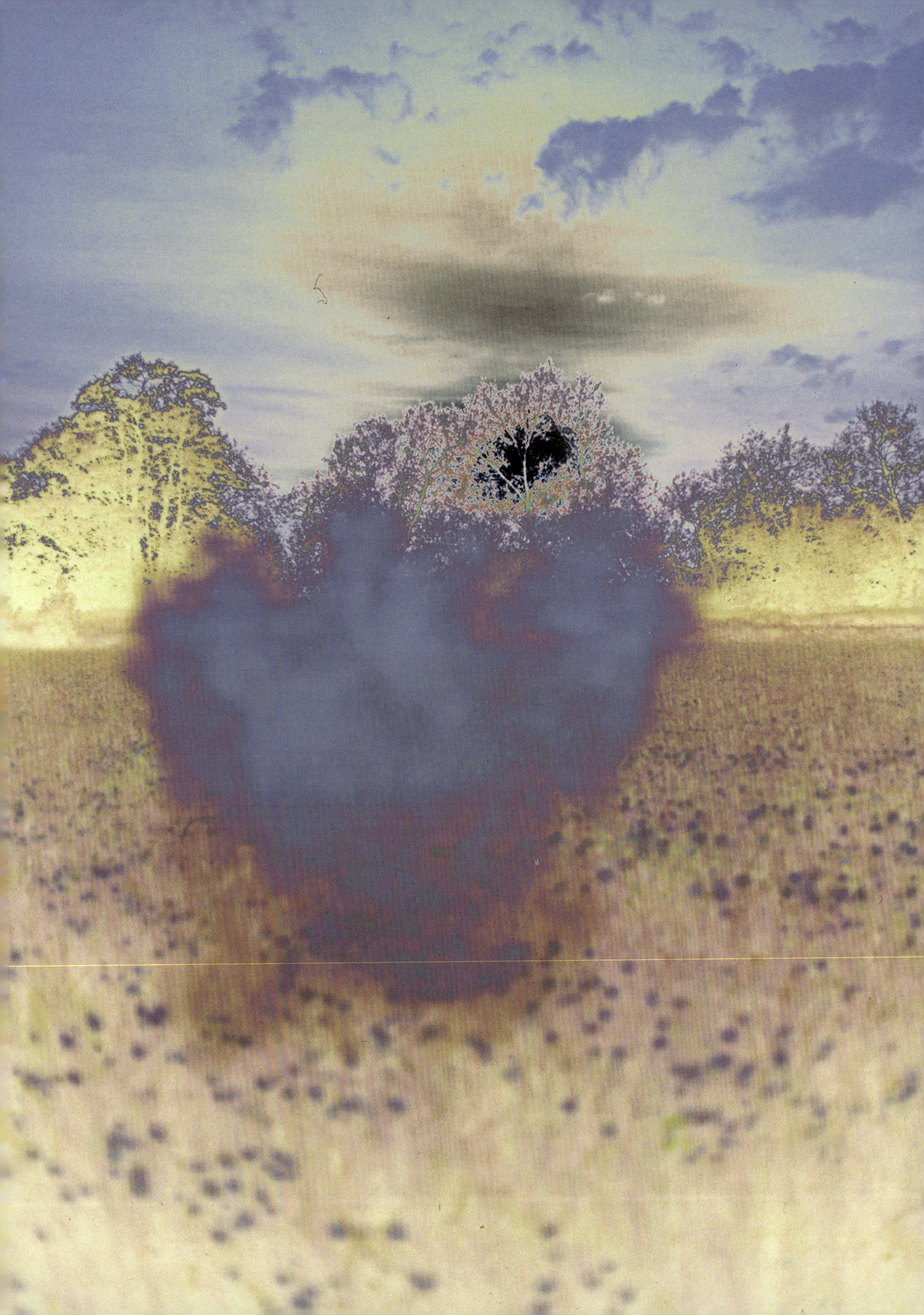

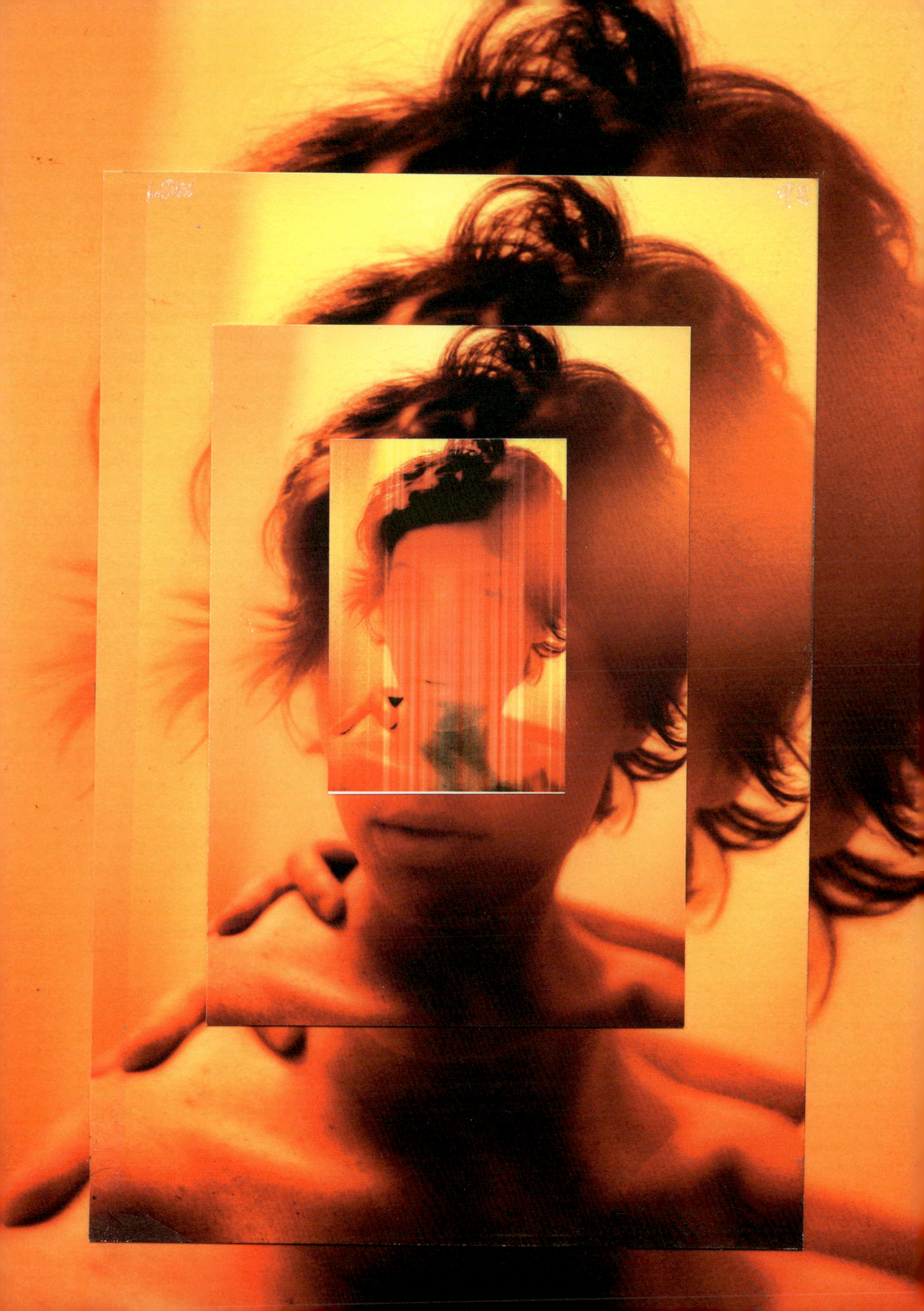

Contributors

Neal Ascherson is a writer in an undefinable genre that fuses history, memoir, politics and meditations on places. He is currently an Honorary Professor at the Institute of Archaeology, University College London. He was previously *The Observer*'s Bonn correspondent and continuous to write mainly for the *London Review of Books*. His books on Poland and his collected essays on the strange Britain to which he returned from Europe in the mid 1980s as well as his non-fiction book *Black Sea* of travel and history were deeply influential.

Tereza Červeňová holds an MA in Photography from the Royal College of Art. She is a Bloomberg New Contemporaries 2017 Alumnus and recipient of the John Kobal New Work Award 2015 and D&AD Yellow Pencil 2014. Červeňová attempts to blur the line between her personal and commissioned work as the centre of both occupies the genre of portraiture. Her work is held in the National Portrait Gallery's permanent collection.

Huw Davies is Professor of Lens Media at the University of Derby and Visiting Professor at HBU/UCLAN in Baoding, China. As a filmmaker, photographer and curator his work has included commissions for many national and international agencies and broadcasters as well as being screened at film festivals in over twenty-five countries.

Anna Fox is a British documentary photographer, known for her highly charged use of flash and colour. Fox is currently a Professor of Photography at the University of Creative Arts, Farnham. She also leads the Fast Forward project *Women In Photography*.

Aikaterini Gegisian is an artist of Greek-Armenian heritage living and working between the UK and Greece. Building on her contribution to the Armenian Pavilion, 56th Venice Biennale (2015 Golden Lion for best national participation), she has developed a series of new commissions exploring the role of images in the construction of national and gendered identities.

Paul Graham is a British artist-photographer, whose work has been described as 'post documentary'. His photography has been exhibited widely, including the Venice Biennale, New York's MoMA, and the Tate, London, alongside of which he has published sixteen monographs and three retrospective books. He lives in NYC.

Eliel Jones is an independent critic, writer and curator based in London, UK. He has previously held positions at Chisenhale Gallery in London, Dallas Museum of Art in Texas, 9th Berlin Biennale for Contemporary Art (with Ei Arakawa) in Berlin, and Frith Street Gallery in London, amongst others. He has written about art, film and choreography for publications including New Museum in New York, South London Gallery in London, and 13th Baltic Triennial in Vilnius, Tallinn and Riga, as well as for art magazines including *Artforum*, *Frieze*, *Mousse*, *Elephant* and *MAP*.

Robin Maddock is a British Photographer and holds an MA in Archaeology from the University of Westminster. His first two photography books, *Our Kids Are Going to Hell* (2009) and *God Forgotten Face* (2011) focus on English society. Maddock's third book *III* (2014) presents playful black and white photographs of American streets.

Shoair Mavlian is director of Photoworks and curated the 8th edition of Brighton Photo Biennial themed *A New Europe* 2018. From 2011–18 she was Assistant Curator, Photography and International Art at Tate Modern, London, where she curated major exhibitions *Shape of Light: 100 Years of Photography and Abstract Art* (2018), *The Radical Eye: Modernist Photography from the Sir Elton John Collection* (2016), and *Conflict, Time, Photography* (2014) among others. Recent publications include *Ursula Schulz-Dornburg: The Land in Between* (Mack 2018) and *Catherine Wagner: Place, History and the Archive* (Damiani 2018).

Ronan Mckenzie is a London based photographer, publisher and curator, whose work celebrates diverse bodies and often explores blackness. Mckenzie has her own publication *HARD EARS,* a contemporary cultural diary and a thoughtful curation of fashion, art and comment by new and established minds, and is currently working on a number of still and moving image projects.

Bernice Mulenga is a multidisciplinary artist, designer and writer prioritising analog processes, based in London. Their work *#friendsonfilm* centres their community and the experiences of Black people in the UK, where they are also part of several collectives including Pxssy Palace, ABOE and BBZ.

Joanna Piotrowska was born in Poland and based in London. She works across film, photography and performance. She studied Photography at the Royal College of Art in London and Academy of Fine Arts in Kraków. Recent exhibitions include: *Antarctica. An Exhibition on Alienation*, Kunsthalle Wien, Austria; *Superstition*, Museum Marres, Maastricht, Netherlands; New York; 10th Berlin Biennale, Germany; *Being: New Photography* at MoMA, New York.

Jamila Prowse is an independent curator, writer and editor. She is the founder of *Typical Girls Magazine*, an in print annual publication which seeks to widen the representation of self-identifying women in the media. Jamila is predominantly interested in widening accessibility to the public arts in an impactful and meaningful way, as well as developing new dialogues around identity through her work. She will be working with artist Ronan McKenzie to bring *Untitled (Dance Piece)* to 1.1 Digital in Basel in March 2019.

Urs Stahel was formerly the founder, director and curator of Fotomuseum Winterthur (1993–2013). He is now a freelance writer, curator, lecturer and consultant. Curator of MAST – Manifattura di Arti, Sperimentazione e Tecnologia in Bologna, consultant to the MAST collection of industrial

photography and to the Art collection of Vontobel, visiting fellow of the University of the Arts London, president of Spectrum – photography in Switzerland. He lives and works in Zurich.

Harley Weir is a British photographer known for creating intimate images in both her personal work and her editorial and fashion commissions. Harley Weir graduated in 2010 from Central Saint Martins College, London, with a degree in Fine Arts, where she largely taught herself photography and experimented with film and collage.

Janine Wiedel is an American documentary photographer and visual anthropologist based in London. Throughout her career she has undertaken many long-term projects covering issues of social concern, documenting communities and subcultures struggling against the changes taking place in mainstream society.

Allison K. Young is the Andrew W. Mellon Foundation Fellow for Contemporary Art at the New Orleans Museum of Art, where her projects have included *Lina Iris Viktor: A Haven. A Hell. A Dream Deferred*, and *Changing Course: Reflections on New Orleans Histories*. She received her Ph.D. in Art History at New York University in 2017. Her writing has appeared in several exhibition catalogues as well as numerous critical and academic platforms including *Art Journal*, *Artforum*, *Apollo International*, *Wallpaper** and *ART AFRICA Magazine*.

Photoworks Annual
Issue 25

Published by Photoworks
154–155 Edward Street, Brighton,
BN2 0JG, England, UK
+44(0)1273 643908
info@photoworks.org.uk
photoworks.org.uk

Photoworks is a company limited by guarantee,
no. 3043169 and a registered charity, no. 1053208

Photoworks Annual, Issue 25:
Commissioning & Managing Editors:
Julia Bunnemann & Shoair Mavlian
Assistant: **Lucie Rachel**
Copy Editor: **Odhran O'Donoghue**
Translation: **Anthony DePasquale**
Art Direction & Design: **Kelly Barrow**
Printed by Pureprint, Uckfield, UK
Printed in the United Kingdom, 2019
Printed on Symbol Freelife Gloss and GalerieArt Matt

UK and European Distribution:
Antenne Books: antennebooks.com

© **Photoworks 2019**. All rights reserved
ISSN: 1742-1659
ISBN: 978-1-903796-55-9

Images:
Front cover: *Tomky, Borský Svätý Jur*, Slovakia
August, 2016, Tereza Červeňová
Inside front cover: *Crossbones Garden*, London
8th June, 2017, Tereza Červeňová
Inside back cover: *Basement Chronicles*, 2018,
Bernice Mulenga
Back cover: *Yoyo's Dip*, 2018, Bernice Mulenga

Image Credits:
© Paul Graham. Courtesy Pace MacGill Gallery,
New York. p.7, 14–39
© Anna Fox. Courtesy James Hyman Gallery,
London. p.51–58
© Ffotogallery, Cardiff, 2010. p.58
© Janine Wiedel. Courtesy the artist. p.61–69
© Huw Davies. Courtesy the artist. p.71–78
© Émeric Lhuisset. Courtesy the artist. p.84, 174
© Hrair Sarkissian. Courtesy the artist. p.85
© Harley Weir. Courtesy the artist. p.81, 87–97
© Tereza Červeňová. Courtesy the artist. Front
cover, inside front cover, p.99–108
© Ronan Mckenzie. Courtesy the artist. p.114–117
© Bernice Mulenga. Courtesy the artist. Inside back
cover, back cover, p.118–129
© Joanna Piotrowska. Courtesy of Southard Reid.
p.134–139
© Aikaterini Gegisian. Courtesy the artist. p.144–159
© Robin Maddock. Courtesy the artist. p.161–169

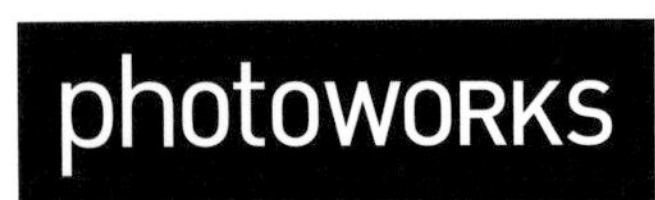
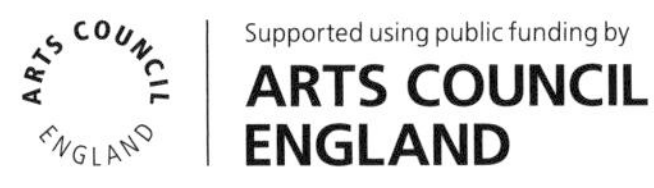

Photoworks

About Photoworks

Photoworks is a platform for contemporary photography. We don't have a permanent home, instead we curate photography in unexpected places or collaborate with museums and galleries across the UK and around the world. We don't collect photography, we help produce it by supporting artists to make and exhibit new work. Our learning and engagement programmes are aimed to break down barriers and invite everyone to participate – regardless of their background or ability. Photoworks is a registered charity and National Portfolio Organisation supported by Arts Council England. Much of what we do is free to access and enjoy.

Photography+

Discover more photography and writing with our online magazine Photography+. Published on our website five times a year, each issue of Photography+ explores the medium's relationship to a single theme. The first issue, # 1 Europe, takes the same theme as this issue of *Photoworks Annual.*

Supporting Photoworks

For a limited time, donations to Photoworks will be matched pound for pound by Arts Council England's Catalyst: Evolve scheme. To discuss making a donation, becoming a Photoworks Patron, or bespoke corporate sponsorship opportunities, please contact Deputy Director Anne Rupert anne@photoworks.org.uk / +44 (0)1273 643908.

Become a Photoworks Member

To support our programme, receive 10% discount in our online shop and enjoy the next issue of *Photoworks Annual* sent directly to your door, you can become a Photoworks Member from just £25 yearly.

Photoworks Team
Shoair Mavlian, Director
Anne Rupert, Deputy Director
Julia Bunnemann, Curator
Claire Wearn, Project Manager
Juliette Buss, Learning & Engagement Curator
Chloe Hoare, Learning & Engagement Coordinator
Ally Lethbridge, Digital Coordinator
Helen Wade, Sales & Marketing Manager
Zoltan Borovics, Office Administrator
Lucie Rachel, Artistic Programme Volunteer

Find out more at photoworks.org.uk

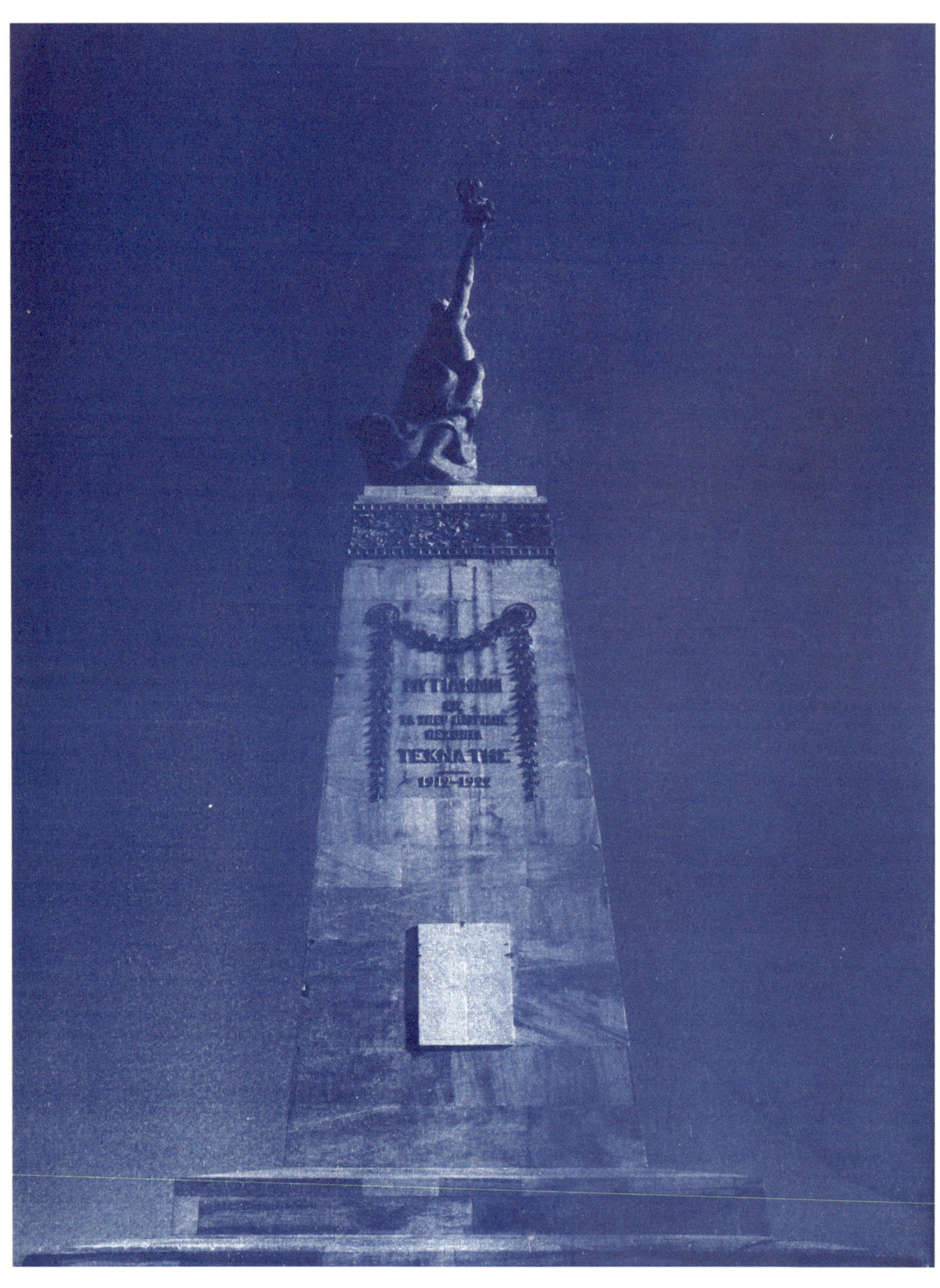

Émeric Lhuisset, *L'Autre Rive*, Iraq,
Turkey, Greece, Germany, France,
Denmark, Syria, 2011–17

174